D0949996

TANGLED UP IN BLUE

ALSO BY ROSA BROOKS

How Everything Became War and the Military Became Everything:
Tales from the Pentagon

TANGLED UP
IN BLUE

Policing the
American City

ROSA BROOKS

PENGUIN PRESS
NEW YORK
2021

PENGUIN PRESS
An imprint of Penguin Random House LLC
penguinrandomhouse.com

LIBRARY OF CONGRESS CATALOGING-IN-PUBLICATION DATA

Names: Brooks, Rosa, author.
Title: Tangled up in blue : policing the American city / Rosa Brooks.
Description: New York: Penguin Press, 2021. |
Includes bibliographical references. |
Identifiers: LCCN 2020032022 (print) | LCCN 2020032023 (ebook) |
ISBN 9780525557852 (hardcover) | ISBN 9780525557869 (ebook)
Subjects: LCSH: Police—Washington (D.C.) |
Law enforcement—Washington (D.C.) |
Criminal justice, Administration of—Washington (D.C.)
Classification: LCC HV8148.D55 B76 2021 (print) |
LCC HV8148.D55 (ebook) | DDC 363.209753—dc23
LC record available at https://lccn.loc.gov/2020032022
LC ebook record available at https://lccn.loc.gov/2020032023

Printed in the United States of America
1   3   5   7   9   10   8   6   4   2

Designed by Amanda Dewey

This book is a work of memoir that chronicles the author's experience
with the DC Metropolitan Police Department. The names and identifying
characteristics of most people mentioned in the book have been changed
in order to protect their privacy. In some instances, events and time periods
have been rearranged and/or compressed in service of the narrative and
to protect individual identities. Dialogue was checked against recordings
when possible. Where recordings were not available, dialogue has been
reconstructed based on the author's notes and memory.

For my mother, Barbara Ehrenreich,
whose courage and relentless curiosity
never cease to inspire me,

and

For the men and women
of the
DC Metropolitan Police Department,
who do what we ask them to do.

We always did feel the same
We just saw it from a different point of view—
Tangled up in blue.

—Bob Dylan

Contents

PART THREE. The Street

PART ONE

Because It Was There

Everyone You Meet

*Assault with a Dangerous Weapon (knife)—Complainant advised
that Suspect came knocking on his door looking for his girlfriend
to fight her. Complainant stated that when he did not let Suspect
in she pulled out a knife and stated "I'll cut you." At which time
Suspect cut Complainant on the right side of his chest. Causing
a severe laceration. Complainant [was] transported to [the]
hospital for treatment. Suspect would not advise [police] what
happened she just stated "yall didn't help me I hate the police."*

—MPD Joint Strategic and Tactical
Analysis Command Center, Daily Report

Everyone you meet here would be happy to kill you," Murphy told me.
His eyes were scanning out the window as he drove, and he was
punching keys on the patrol car's mobile computer with his right hand
while he maneuvered the steering wheel with his left. Cop multitasking.
"That's what you have to remember. These people hate you. They would
dance around your dead body."

It was my first night as a patrol officer, and Murphy was showing me the
ropes. We were driving down Martin Luther King Jr. Avenue in Washington, DC's Seventh Police District. Sandwiched between the Anacostia River
to the west and the Maryland state line to the east, "7D" is the poorest,
saddest, most crime-ridden part of the nation's capital. Gunshots are a common sound, and 7D regularly produces the lion's share of DC homicides.

Still. "Everyone? You think even the little old ladies here want to kill me?" I asked.

Murphy gave me a tight smile. "All right, *almost* everyone. But you have to watch out for some of these old ladies. I'm telling you, people here are different from you and me. You and me, we don't *want* to get in trouble or get hurt or go to jail. Like, it would be a big deal to us. These people? They're so used to it, they just don't care."

We drove past a group of men with hoodies drawn up over their heads, hands in pockets. Murphy gave them a long, hard look, but their expressions remained scrupulously blank as our patrol car cruised by.

"See that guy?" Murphy asked, pointing to a gaunt man in a dirty Redskins sweatshirt. "That guy, I must have picked him up five times for one thing or another. You know, stupid shit. He hits his girlfriend. He steals a candy bar from the 7-Eleven. He's fighting with some other asshole. He's selling K2 in front of the fucking middle school. Then he gets fucking *shot*, like, a month ago. I'm first on the scene, he's lying there bleeding and I'm saying to him, 'Man, who did this to you? Help me get him.' And he's like, 'Oh, I think it must have just been an accident.' He's lying there bleeding, but he wouldn't fucking tell me anything. He almost died. Now he's back at the same corner with the same assholes. You want to explain that to me?"

He shook his head. "These fucking people."

In my forties, with two children, a spouse, a dog, a mortgage, and a full-time job as a tenured law professor, I decided to become a cop.

I could give you any number of plausible-sounding reasons for this. I'm an academic with a long-standing interest in law's troubled relationship with violence and thought that learning about policing firsthand would lead to new scholarly insights. I had just finished writing a book about the changing role of the US military, and believed that becoming a police officer would allow me to better understand the blurring lines between war fighting and policing. I was dismayed by the statistics on police shootings and by the racial disparities in the criminal justice system, and wanted the insider experience that would enable me to become a credible and effective advocate for change. I was a onetime anthropology student, and considered participant observation the best way to understand cultures that might otherwise appear alien and incomprehensible.

All these were perfectly worthy and legitimate reasons for embarking on an otherwise unusual experiment, and they make decent retroactive justifications. But I had other, less noble impulses as well. I was restless, and not quite ready to subside into tenured comfort. I wanted something different and challenging, something nothing at all like a faculty meeting. I had probably read too much crime fiction.

I wasn't completely mad. I didn't quit my day job. Instead, I applied to become a reserve police officer with the Washington, DC, Metropolitan Police Department (MPD).

Many cities have unarmed volunteer auxiliary police, but the District of Columbia is one of the few major US cities in which unpaid reserve officers operate as sworn, armed police officers with full arrest powers. As a reserve police officer in Washington, DC, I would go through the same police academy training as the city's thirty-eight hundred full-time career officers, take the same oath, wear the same uniform and badge, carry the same gun, and patrol the same streets—but as a volunteer, I would be required to offer the city only twenty-four hours of patrolling each month.

Twenty-four hours a month didn't seem like much. Nonetheless, no one I knew thought this was a good idea.

"You're insane," my husband told me. When I applied to the Metropolitan Police Reserve Corps, Joe was in the process of winding down his own career as a US Army Special Forces officer. After more than two decades in the military, he said he was sure of just two things: he never wanted to wear a uniform again, and he never wanted to have to call anyone "sir" again. My sudden interest in policing, a profession that required both the wearing of uniforms and the acceptance of a paramilitary command structure, struck him as inexplicable.

My mother was similarly unenthusiastic. A writer and left-wing activist best known for her own forays into immersion journalism, her memories of being tear-gassed by police at 1960s anti-war marches remained fresh. "The police are the enemy," she informed me. "They are not on our side."

She wasn't the only one who felt that way. Then as now, police violence was constantly in the news. When I applied to the DC police reserve corps in 2015, students at Georgetown Law, where I taught courses on international law, human rights, and constitutional law, were coming to class wearing T-shirts that read "Stop Police Terror."

"The police are killing black people," one of my African American faculty colleagues told me. "I can't even talk about it right now. I just can't."

My father listened as I stumbled through my convoluted justifications, then shook his head.

"Well, you sure do come up with interesting ideas."

I Don't Even Live Here

Homicide (gun): MPD received a radio assignment for an unconscious person at [redacted]. Upon officers' arrival, Victim 1 and Victim 2 were located inside the aforementioned location in an unconscious and unresponsive state suffering from apparent gunshot wounds to their heads. [Medics] responded to the location. Death was apparent and no further action was taken.

—MPD Joint Strategic and Tactical Analysis
Command Center, Daily Report*

No one tried to kill me during my first patrol shift. For that matter, no one tried to kill anyone that night—at least not on any of my calls. Statistics say that somewhere in the dark streets of the nation's capital, someone was hurting someone else, but they weren't doing it in front of me.

Instead, Murphy and I were dispatched to a series of what seemed like fairly minor problems. There were teenage boys standing on the sidewalk, "talking shit" to girls who walked by; Murphy told them to take a hike. They complained: "Aw, shit, man, the fucking *po*-lice, why you gotta come mess with us for no reason? What the *fuck*, man!" But eventually, they took a hike.

We responded to a call for a disturbance in an apartment block: an elderly resident, fed up with the smell of marijuana in the communal stairwell, decided to use pepper spray as an air freshener, which did not endear him to his neighbors. Murphy suggested that everyone stay out of the stairwell for a while, and urged the guy with the pepper spray to invest in a can of Febreze instead.

Later, we were sent to keep the peace while an inebriated man with blood all over his shirtfront removed his possessions from the home of his equally inebriated about-to-be-ex-girlfriend, who helped the process along by throwing most of his clothes out the window. Both parties declined to explain or even acknowledge the blood, but every few minutes, the two would lunge at each other, and we would drag them apart, Murphy yanking on the boyfriend's arm, me yanking on the girlfriend's arm, hauling them off in opposite directions.

"Come on, come on," we told them, over and over. "You hit each other, you both end up in jail for the night; it's not worth it!"

Judging from the cursing and spitting, both thought it might very well be worth it, but we stayed between them, and they had to be satisfied with snarls and the occasional string of insults. Eventually, the disgruntled boyfriend and three trash bags full of his clothing were picked up by a plump young woman in a battered Nissan. After a few valedictory cries of "Fucking skank!" and "I see you again, you be sorry!" the Nissan squealed away, the girlfriend slammed her door on us, and the evening grew peaceful once more.

By my second or third patrol shift, after a few calls for minor disturbances followed by several hours of radio silence, I was feeling relaxed enough to break a taboo.

"It's really quiet tonight," I told Murphy.

"Don't *say* that!" He was dismayed. "Never say that!"

Sure enough, the radio soon erupted into staticky clamor. "All units, priority, all units . . . Multiple shots fired, Code One." Code 1 meant "Get there fast." Murphy had the lights and siren on even before the dispatcher finished giving the address, and we tore down the busy streets. I flinched as we narrowly avoided a head-on collision. We screamed up to the scene along with every other police car in 7D.

By the time Murphy and I jumped out of the car, another officer was already stringing yellow crime scene tape across the road. Unlike us, she seemed to be in no rush.

"So what's happening?" Murphy asked the officer with the tape.

She gestured casually over her shoulder. "Couple guys with gunshot wounds."

We ducked under the tape and headed toward the center of the action. A man lay on the street in a spreading pool of blood, an ambulance pulling up alongside him. Another man, his arm bloody, was pacing up and down, muttering angrily; an officer was trying to coax him into letting the medics take a look at him, but he just kept pacing and tossing his head back and forth, as if trying to shake off a bothersome insect. On the sidewalk, a young woman sat with her back against a tree, staring at us blankly. She was covered with blood too.

"Hey," someone said. It was another patrol officer. "I just talked to the detectives and they want someone to take a witness over to the station. You guys free to help with that?"

The witness, it turned out, was the blood-covered woman, and the blood wasn't hers; it all belonged to the guy lying in the street.

She seemed shell-shocked as we loaded her gently into the back seat of the scout car. "I don't even live here, you know?" she kept saying. "Trey and me, we was just hanging out, and suddenly, there's blood all over. I didn't hear no gunshots. Just, blood all over, all of a sudden. I don't even live here." In the close confines of the car, the faint smell of marijuana wafting off her clothes vied with the iron odor of blood.

Back at 7D, we led our witness into the detectives' room and sat her down on a bench. Blood still dripped from her pants leg, and Murphy brought her some paper towels. I dug around in my pockets for some disinfectant wipes and offered them to her. She made a feeble effort to clean her legs, but there was too much blood. She needed a washing machine, not a paper towel and some wet wipes. After a few moments she gave up and sat with her eyes closed, her head leaned back against the wall.

"Should I offer her some coffee, or a Coke, or something?" I whispered to Murphy. I wasn't sure of the protocol for handling witnesses to violent crimes. Was she a victim? A suspect? Both?

"Nah," he said. "Let the detectives decide."

The detective, an impatient young white guy with a soft chin and male pattern baldness, showed up a few minutes later, muttering to himself about being pulled away from his other work to deal with the shooting. He didn't offer the witness anything, either.

"Thanks for bringing her over," he told us. "We're short tonight. You wanna watch the interview, feel free; you can watch on the monitor over there."

He ushered the witness into a small interview room, and Murphy and I settled ourselves in to watch.

The interview didn't last long.

"Okay," the detective said, "You're not a suspect. You understand? I just want to find out what happened, okay, then you can go."

"I don't even live here," the young woman informed him. "Like I said, we was just hanging out, and then there's blood all over. I don't have any idea how it happened."

I nodded. I still thought someone should offer her a soda.

"Bullshit!" declared the detective, slamming his fist down on the table. The witness and I both jumped.

"You know that's bullshit. You know exactly who did this."

"No, I don't," the witness said sulkily. She glared at him.

"Yes you do," the detective insisted. "And if you don't feel like telling me the truth, you can just leave."

"Fine," said the witness. She picked up her bloodstained purse and stood up, and that was that. Murphy and I drove her back to her car. She didn't say another word.

A little later, we were sent off to the hospital to guard one of the shooting victims, just in case the shooter decided to return and finish the job. A doctor was in with him, and all we could hear from our station in the hallway was an occasional inquisitive murmur from the doctor, and the shooting victim's intermittent yelps.

"Ow! Fuck! Ow!"

"He'll live," the doctor said when he came out. "He has about seven holes in his leg and his butt, though."

Still later, another detective appeared to interview the victim, who refused to say anything to him beyond "Shit, man, my fucking ass hurts, okay?"

"You believe this shit?" the detective asked us.

That sounded like a rhetorical question, so I didn't answer. I looked at Murphy.

He gave a lopsided smile. "You can't make this shit up."

I first heard of Washington, DC's police reserve corps program in the summer of 2011. At the time, I was working at the Pentagon. I had taken a two-year public service leave from my teaching position at Georgetown Law to work for the Under Secretary of Defense for Policy, and I was due back at Georgetown for the start of the fall 2011 semester. I was wrapping things up at the Pentagon when I received an email from the human resources department instructing me to attend a day of mandatory orientation for new senior executive officials.

"But I'm not new," I told the HR staffer who sent the email. "I've been here for more than two years. In fact, I'm leaving in just a few weeks. I don't need an orientation."

"Right," he said, "but you didn't attend this required training when you *were* new, so now the system won't let us check you out, because you never finished checking in. We can't process your exit paperwork until you attend this orientation session."

Ungraciously, I agreed to put the orientation session on my calendar, and the following week, I joined fifty or sixty other grouchy civil servants in an auditorium at the Old Executive Office Building, next to the White House.

We sat through sessions on leadership skills and HR rules, then after a boxed lunch (a stale sandwich, chips, a bruised apple) we shifted to a session on diversity in the federal workplace. The speaker was an animated woman in her sixties. "Listen, everyone has biases," she announced. "And sometimes those biases create no-win situations for people. Ask yourself if you have any biases. You don't think so? Well, I'm telling you, we all do. Okay, here's an example. Think for a minute about the ways we typically react to a senior executive woman with a high-powered, demanding job. Okay? If she's single, everyone figures she couldn't get a man—or she's a lesbian. She's married? She must be neglecting her husband in favor of her career. She's divorced? She probably drove her poor husband away. She's a widow? She probably killed him!"

Polite laughter.

This was better than hearing about HR rules, but I was making a mental list of everything I had to do before leaving the Pentagon, and listening with only half an ear. When I tuned back in, the speaker was telling another story.

"So, stereotypes can be misleading," she was saying. "Look at me. I'm a reserve police officer. I'm the oldest person who ever went through the DC police academy, and no one ever thinks I could possibly be a cop, right? Talk about implicit bias! I'm a sixty-year-old lady with white hair. People think I should be knitting. But let me tell you, putting them in cuffs dispels their stereotypes *really* fast."

She began to tease out the implications of this story for managers in the executive branch workplace, but I had again stopped listening. I was thinking: She's a *police officer*? A reserve police officer? You can *do* that? What does that even mean?

When I got home, I googled "reserve police officer DC" and clicked my way through the Metropolitan Police Department's website. Sure enough, there it was:

> We are looking for dedicated, community-oriented individuals to serve alongside MPD career officers in our mission to serve and protect the citizens and visitors of Washington, DC. MPD invites you to explore the opportunities offered by the Reserve Corps and consider applying for this truly unique volunteer experience. Reserve Police Officers receive world-class training which mirrors that of a career officer and emerge as sworn, armed Police Reserve Officers that work in our Patrol Services or specialized patrol functions.

Apparently, anyone could do this. A sixty-year-old lady with white hair who looked like she should be knitting could do this.

Could *I* do this?

All of a sudden, I wanted to. There was no good reason for me to want to, but I did.

But reading on, I learned that all Metropolitan Police Reserve Corps applicants had to complete police academy training, two nights a week and every Saturday for six to ten months, plus two weeks of full-time firearms training and a week of full-time emergency vehicle skills training.

My heart sank.

Well, I thought, that's that. I can't do this.

At the time, my two daughters were seven and nine years old, and I was a single parent. I couldn't be away from home two nights a week and every Saturday for six to ten months.

Which was fine, I reminded myself, because it made no sense anyway. I was busy. I already had a job. Also, I doubted I could justify such a mad scheme to my colleagues, friends, and family members, most of whom considered the police part of a harsh, unjust, racially biased criminal justice system. I didn't disagree: the US criminal justice system *is* harsh, unjust, and biased, and the police are assuredly part of that system.

At least initially, there was no real need for me to sort through any of my own contradictory impulses about policing, since joining the DC police reserve corps was logistically impossible. But every now and then I thought about it.

I thought about it whenever I felt restless, whenever another birthday came and went, and as my two girls moved from childhood into adolescence.

I thought about it when I remarried in 2012 and my husband deployed to the Middle East, off to prove himself in America's endless murky wars. There I was, safe on the sidelines, keeping the home fires burning like millions of women before me, in a thousand other wars. It wasn't a comfortable role. I thought about it again when Joe came back home.

I thought about it whenever policing was in the news, and between 2011, when I first learned about the reserve corps, and 2015, when I applied to join the DC police, policing was in the news more and more. The stories were rarely positive. Immediately after the September 11 terrorist attacks in 2001, when fifty police officers lost their lives in the collapse of the Twin Towers, there was a burst of media enthusiasm for police and other first responders. A decade later, however, that enthusiasm had mostly faded, replaced by a steady drumbeat of stories about police abuses. There were stories about cruel cops, corrupt cops, racist cops, and incompetent cops. And there were stories about excessive force and the staggering number of Americans killed by police each year. In July 2014, Eric Garner died after being placed in a chokehold by New York City police. In August 2014, eighteen-year-old Michael Brown was shot and killed by a police officer in Ferguson, Missouri, sparking a nationwide outcry. In November 2014, twelve-year-old Tamir Rice was shot and killed by a Cleveland cop who mistook Tamir's toy gun for a real one. In April 2015, Freddie Gray died while being transported to jail by Baltimore police.

American police killed at least 1,146 people in 2015. Inadequate record keeping made it hard to know the numbers for sure, but there was no doubt that those killed by the police were disproportionately young, male, and black, and many were unarmed at the time of their fatal encounters with the police. All over the country, there were investigations and protests. The protests were not as large, sustained, or ubiquitous as those that followed the killing of George Floyd in 2020, but the sense of crisis was the same. American policing was broken. No one knew if it could be repaired.

If I had simply announced that I was planning to write a book about policing, my sudden determination to become a cop would probably have encountered less resistance from my family and friends. As a form of scholarly inquiry, "participant observation" is a long-established sociological and anthropological research method. Outside the ivory tower, reporters call it "immersion journalism." My mother, Barbara Ehrenreich, spent months in low-wage jobs while researching her 2001 book, *Nickel and Dimed*; for instance, working variously as a maid, a Walmart stocker, and a waitress at a chain diner. My brother Ben, also a journalist, spent months living in a tiny West Bank village, preparing to write a book about Palestine. If I had said, "I'm going undercover as a reserve officer so I can expose the brutality and corruption of the police," my family and friends might have worried about my safety, but they wouldn't have worried about my sanity.

But I didn't tell anyone I planned to write a book about policing, because initially the idea didn't occur to me. I just . . . wanted to see what being a police officer was *like* at such a fraught moment. Were police officers troubled by the violence of their profession? How did they view the prospects for change? In 1924, asked why he wanted to summit Mount Everest, British climber George Mallory famously replied, "Because it's there." I joined the DC Metropolitan Police Department Reserve Corps because it was there. It was there, and I was curious.

This is perhaps not the best analogy, as Mallory disappeared during his third attempt to climb Everest. His body was discovered only in 1999, and to this day, no one knows if he succeeded in reaching Everest's summit. My journey into the world of policing was not nearly as grueling as Mallory's journey up Mount Everest, and I did eventually reach my own summit: in June 2018, after six months at the DC Metropolitan Police Academy and another eighteen months of field training and patrol, I passed my certification ride, got through a certification review panel, and was officially designated a "Level One Reserve Police Officer" by the DC Metropolitan Police Department, fully qualified to carry out all police functions on my own.

It was only in 2017, midway through my field training, that I begin to think seriously about writing a book. Colleagues and friends kept asking me if I planned to write about my experiences as a police officer, and after a while it seemed easier to just say yes. Yes, of course I would write about policing, I said. Yes, of course, that was why I had done this crazy police thing. Yes, of course, it was all part of a plan.

For a while, I thought I might write a scholarly book about law and policy, focusing on the problems that plague modern policing and leavened by only occasional anecdotes drawn from my own experiences. But after some time, I abandoned that idea. My scholarly expertise lies mostly elsewhere, for one thing, and for another, plenty of other people—including several of my Georgetown colleagues—have already published thoughtful, well-researched books and articles on policing and the American criminal justice system. In the end, I decided I was unlikely to add much to current debates by writing another book analyzing police shootings or examining the role of racial discrimination in the criminal justice system. But what I could do—what I was perhaps uniquely positioned to do—was offer some stories drawn from my own messy, complicated experiences.

This book contains those stories. Because none of my DC Metropolitan Police Department colleagues and none of the people I encountered while patrolling knew I would be writing a book about my experiences (and I couldn't have told them, since for most of the time period covered by this book, I didn't know it myself), I have changed all names, except those of officials and those whose involvement in events is already public. In many cases I have changed other details as well (including physical descriptions, biographical details, and chronology) to protect the privacy of the people I have written about. I have also removed all personally identifying information from the excerpts from MPD crime reports that are quoted in this book. Excerpts from these reports and other MPD documents are otherwise given verbatim, aside from light editing for clarity (e.g., spelling out acronyms and abbreviations).

As a recruit officer going through the DC Metropolitan Police Academy, I took detailed notes in academy classes, with particular attention to comments that surprised or dismayed me. After graduation, as a rookie patrol officer, I took notes on calls in my official patrol notebook and jotted down my own "unofficial" reactions and observations on my iPhone. As I was writing this book, I also checked my own recollection of events against video footage from my body-worn camera when possible. When I could not obtain videos, I have relied on my notes and my memory, and in those cases events and dialogue are reconstructed to the best of my recollection.

Throughout this book, I have tried my best to show, not tell—to give an honest account of what I saw and what I did. Readers can decide for themselves what to make of it all. And I want to be clear that my experiences are just *my* experiences; I can make no claims about their universality or even their representativeness. This book is about what it was like for me, a particular individual with a particular set of prior experiences and assumptions, to serve as a part-time patrol officer in Washington, DC, with most of my time spent in the very poorest sections of the city. I don't know what it's like to be a police officer in a different city, or a rural area, or a wealthy area. I don't know what it's like to be a detective, or a vice cop, or a harbor patrol officer, or a staff officer assigned to police headquarters. And, of course, my experiences were inevitably filtered through my own identity: white, female, over-educated, brought up on the political left. Can readers generalize from my experiences? I have no idea.

But I hope that the stories I tell here are useful nonetheless. Attitudes toward police in our divided nation are as polarized as our political discourse: to some Americans, police officers are brutal, racist bullies; to others, they're courageous, undervalued heroes. I hope the stories I offer in this book will complicate matters rather than simplify them, and will give pause both to those who think police can do no wrong and to those who think they can do no right.

Police officers have an impossible job: we expect them to be warriors, disciplinarians, protectors, mediators, social workers, educators, medics, and mentors all at once, and we blame them for enforcing laws they didn't make in a social context they have little power to alter. The abuses and systemic problems that plague policing are very real, and readers will see them reflected in these pages, particularly in the flashes of cynicism and casual contempt I sometimes saw in officers with whom I worked. But the compassion, courage, and creativity I saw are real too.

Animals

*Felony Threats (Hate/Bias Crime): Complainant reports that
while inside the location Suspect became irate about inconsistent
paychecks and proceed to yell "You all are a bunch of South East
Ghetto Animals, and South East n*ggers and Southeast b*tches."
Suspect . . . then stated to the Complainant "I will gun you
down, I will destroy you."*

*—MPD Joint Strategic and Tactical Analysis
Command Center, Daily Report*

The unconscious guy didn't look unconscious. He looked dead.

He lay on the sidewalk, his legs on the grass and his torso on the concrete, one arm down by his side and the other extended, palm up, fingers curled. His mouth was open, his lips were gray, and his eyes had rolled up into his head, only the whites still showing. His chest didn't seem to be moving.

The radio call was for a "man down," so a dead guy wasn't completely unexpected. Still, I went and crouched down by his shoulder. With all the gear on my belt and vest, a graceful crouch wasn't possible, and I barely avoided pitching over on top of him.

"Hey. Buddy. You okay?"

No response. I gave his shoulder a cautious nudge. Still nothing.

I tried again, nudging harder this time. "Hey there. You all right?"

To my amazement, his eyes rolled back from his head, his mouth twitched, and he muttered, "Hey, you know, hey, what's going on?"

An ambulance had arrived, and one of the medics ambled over. "Hey, man. You hurt? Did you fall?"

The guy pushed himself up on his elbow. "No, man, no, I jus', I jus', y'know I jus'—" His speech was slurred.

"What'd you take, man?" asked the medic. "What're you on?"

"I din, I jus'—" His eyes flickered closed.

"Listen, it's okay, man, we're not trying to jam you up, we're just trying to help, okay? We just wanna know what you took so's we can make sure you're okay."

The guy didn't answer, just blinked and looked around groggily.

The medic tried again. "Listen, man. What's your name?"

Nothing, just a blank look.

"Buddy," said the medic. "You know what day it is?"

A light went on inside the dull brown eyes. "Hey, yeah, man, it's like, I think it's like . . . it's . . . Sunday, right, man? Sunday."

"You know who the president is?" The medic was running through the standard mental status checklist.

The guy paused, looking puzzled and, for the first time, a little alarmed. "Is *Donald Trump* the president?"

"Sorry, man, yeah."

"Shee-*it*." He closed his eyes again, this time with some determination.

Since the unconscious guy had looked dead, it didn't at first occur to me that the dead guy we encountered later that night was anything other than unconscious. We were called to a housing project we had already visited three or four times that evening, for one thing or another: noisy youths congregating in the hallway, a report of someone selling drugs in the small strip of grass between buildings, a burglary. Then we got a call about an unconscious man. We left the car skewed across the parking lot and ran to the apartment door, me fumbling to jam my notebook back into my pocket without dropping any of my other equipment.

An elderly woman in a nightgown urged us inside. "My husband isn't moving!" Her voice was high and quavery with panic. "He was just watching football, then he went into the bathroom, and when he didn't come out I got worried. I opened the door and he was just lying there. I can't wake him up."

Sure enough, there he was, an elderly man lying on his back on the bathroom floor. He looked like he had passed out, and his dark brown skin had a grayish cast. I hesitated. I had only been a police officer for a short time, and I wasn't sure what to do. Should I try nudging him in the shoulder too? It had worked with the first guy.

My partner for the night, a young Haitian American called Auguste, was more experienced. He pushed right past us and started CPR. Behind us, sirens wailed: the ambulance was arriving. A team of medics rushed in, and within seconds the bathroom was a hive of activity as they ripped off the old man's shirt and attached defibrillator pads to his chest.

I turned to the wife, small and bewildered in her nightgown. "Let's give them some space, okay? Let's sit down and you can tell me what happened."

I think we were both glad to have something to do. We sat on the over-stuffed living room sofa, surrounded by family photos, inspirational needle-points, and small statues of angels. There were angels everywhere: Statues of angels. Pictures of angels. Needlepoints of angels. Salt and pepper shakers shaped like angels.

I took out my notebook and started asking questions: What's your name, ma'am? Margaret . . . Carter . . . ? What's your husband's name? Jesse, with an *e* at the end. Named for Jesse Owens, no kidding. How about his date of birth?

I scribbled everything down in my patrol notebook: phone number, social security number, medical history. Was her husband taking any medications? Had he had any heart problems? Had he complained about feeling weak or sick or dizzy recently? The medics were still crowded into the bathroom, working on her husband, so when I ran out of relevant questions, I started asking irrelevant ones, just to have something to do.

What had Mr. Carter done for a living? Which football teams did he prefer? Did they have children? Grandchildren? Really, how old were they?

After a while the medics slid Mr. Carter onto a gurney. They had him hooked up to an automatic CPR machine, and his chest rose and fell percussively. I couldn't tell if he was alive or dead. The medics carried him past all the angels and out to the ambulance, then sped off, sirens wailing.

"Is he all right?" asked Mrs. Carter.

"I don't know, ma'am," I said. "But the medics, they're the best in the business, and I know they're doing everything they can."

I had no idea if the medics were really the best in the business. But it seemed like the thing to say.

We followed the ambulance to the hospital, where Mrs. Carter was joined in the ER's waiting room by her grown children and their spouses. It was Sunday evening, and they were all dressed like they'd come straight from church. Auguste and I trailed a team of doctors and nurses to an emergency room bay, where everyone bustled around Mr. Carter's inert form. We stood just outside. I tried not to stare. Auguste paced back and forth, scowling.

After a while, all the doctors and nurses abruptly turned and left, a nurse pulling the curtain partially closed around Mr. Carter's bed. They took the CPR machine away with them and everything got very quiet.

I peered through the gap in the curtains. Mr. Carter had EKG stickers dotting his chest. There were tubes taped to his hands, and tubes sticking out of his nose. His eyes were open, staring sightlessly at the ceiling. He wasn't moving.

"Oh, God," said Auguste. He slumped down to the floor and sat with his head in his hands. He looked like he was going to cry.

I put my hand on his shoulder. "You okay?"

He stared at the floor. "I just . . . I just hate death. You know? I hate it."

"You did everything you could," I told him, meaning it. "You were amazing. I had no idea what to do, but you just rushed in and started CPR. I was so impressed. If anyone could have saved him, it was you."

Auguste shook his head. "It just seems so unfair. There he is, watching football on TV, then suddenly he's dead, and his family's going to be so sad, and we couldn't do anything about it. I just hate it."

I stopped a passing nurse. "Mr. Carter's family is out in the waiting room," I told her. "Is someone speaking to them?"

"Yes, the doctor's about to go talk to them," she assured me.

We sat in the hallway for another half hour, Auguste still hunched over with his face in his palms, Mr. Carter still dead. Doctors, nurses, and orderlies rushed by every few minutes, no one giving Mr. Carter's body a second glance.

I was starting to feel anxious. Weren't we supposed to be out patrolling?

A little more time passed. After a while, I asked, "Should we go?"

"We can't," said Auguste from between his hands. "We have to wait for the detective. They have to send a homicide detective to do an investigation, even though it looks like a natural death. I'll call him and see where's he at."

He pulled himself up and went out into the hall. I waited. When he returned ten minutes later, he said, "The detective's on his way. He wants you to go out to the waiting room to make sure the family doesn't leave before he gets here and can talk to them."

"Sure." I pushed through the emergency room's double doors, preparing myself to offer condolences. Mrs. Carter and her family were huddled together on a sofa in the corner. I went and knelt down beside her, putting my hand on her arm.

"Mrs. Carter, I am so, so sorry about your husband."

Her head snapped up. "Is he all right?"

I was confused. "What?"

"How is he? Is he all right, officer?"

Shit.

I took a deep breath. "Mrs. Carter . . . I'm so very sorry. He didn't make it."

Mrs. Carter let out a wail and crumpled over. Around me, everyone else started to wail too. I was mortified. The family had been sitting here for over an hour while Mr. Carter lay there, dead, a few meters away, and no one on the hospital staff had bothered to tell them.

"I'm so sorry," I said helplessly. "I thought the doctor had been out to speak to you. Mrs. Carter, I'm so, so sorry to break the news to you and your family like this."

But no one was listening: they were too busy weeping and clutching one another. I sat down on a chair and watched everyone cry.

Eventually, the detective arrived, and beckoned me back into the ER and behind the curtain. "So, you're new, yeah? Cool, welcome to beautiful 7D. Your partner says you're the one that's got all the information, huh? Okay, give me the rundown. What happened?"

He pulled on rubber gloves and started poking and prodding Mr. Carter's body, looking, I suppose, for anything that might suggest something other than a simple heart attack: suspicious bruising, or a gunshot wound that had somehow escaped the doctors' attention. I took out my notebook and described how we had arrived on the scene.

"Okay, good, good, okay, you got his social and everything?" the detective asked. He pulled aside the blanket covering Mr. Carter's lower body and distractedly lifted his genitals, glancing underneath. I read out the social security number, and the detective shifted his attention to the soles of Mr. Carter's feet, then gave a satisfied nod. He drew the blanket back over the body. "Great, okay, everything here looks fine. Let me just jot that number down and do a bit of paperwork, then I can go talk to the family. I'm not seeing anything that bothers me here, so this should be quick."

While the detective interviewed the still-weeping family, I waited in the corridor with Auguste and one of the medics who had worked on Mr. Carter in the ambulance. Auguste seemed to have gotten over his despondency, and he and the medic were exchanging animated views about the residents of the Seventh District.

"Animals," declared Auguste. "I come here from Boston. As soon as I can, I'm going back there. You could not fucking pay me to live in 7D."

The medic, a middle-aged black guy, pursed his lips. "I live downtown. I'll tell you, I drive around here and I see these kids on the corners, and they say to me, 'Hey man, what you lookin' at?' And I say to them, 'Dead people. I'm looking at *dead* people.'"

"Dead people?" asked Auguste.

"Yeah, man, I call these kids the walking dead. They're dead, they just don't know it yet. Give 'em a few years and some more smack and some more guns, and they're gonna be riding in my ambulance, in body bags. You see what I'm saying?"

"Fucking animals," Auguste agreed dolefully.

"And they keep having babies!" The medic gave a disgusted shake of his head. "They oughta clip these people, you know? Stop them reproducing, stop 'em making more dead people."

Later that night, we were called back to the same housing project, yet again. Police dispatchers in DC indicate the nature of each call on the patrol car's mobile data terminal using a series of acronyms, most of them opaque to the noninitiated: there was MADO, for "Man Down," DISO for "Disorderly Conduct," PWID for "Possession With Intent To Distribute," FADI for "Family Disturbance," and so on. The acronyms were also used to identify calls on shift run sheets and to label body-worn camera videos, but the only way to learn them was through experience; they weren't taught in the academy, and if there was a master list somewhere, no one I knew had ever seen it. As a new officer, I was constantly having to ask my more experienced colleagues to translate for me.

This call was marked "ITT" on the car's mobile data terminal.

"What's ITT?" I asked Auguste.

"'Investigate The Trouble.' Usually means somebody called 911 and asked for the cops, then hung up without saying anything else."

We could hear The Trouble all the way from the parking lot: two irate female voices.

When we entered the stairwell, a woman could be heard screaming from behind the closed front door of a second-floor apartment. "Get away from here! You know you ain't allowed to be here! You get the fuck away from here right now!"

The object of the invisible woman's rage seemed to be a slender girl who was pounding hard on the apartment door. Tears were streaming down the girl's face.

"Let me in!" she cried. "You gotta let me in! I fucking *live* here!"

I was readying myself to offer a textbook police intervention, something along the lines of "Excuse me, ma'am. Did you call 911? What seems to be the problem?"

But Auguste, once again jumping in while I hesitated, rushed up the stairs.

"You stop that screaming," he ordered the girl. "You *know* you can't be here! I'm sick and tired of you acting this way!"

Then everyone started yelling at once—the screaming woman on the other side of the door, the girl, Auguste.

It took a while, but eventually I pieced together some of what was happening. The invisible woman behind the closed apartment door was the girl's mother; her sixteen-year-old daughter had been ordered by a court into her aunt's custody, but the daughter was refusing to stay at the aunt's house, insisting she wanted to "go home" instead. Her mother wasn't having it. Apparently this was a long-standing issue. I never did figure out the background. Had the mother abused or neglected the daughter and the daughter been sent to live with her aunt for her own protection? Had the daughter assaulted the mother and been on the receiving end of a stay-away order?

Either way, Auguste was unsympathetic. "You want to walk out of here, or you want me to drag you out of here?" he shouted at the girl, who kept screaming and banging her fists against the door. From the other side of the locked door, her mother screamed back. Auguste shouted some more, grabbed the girl by the arm, and started trying to yank her down the stairs. She struggled and spat at him. He reached for his cuffs.

"Whoa, whoa," I said. "Let me try to talk to her."

Auguste glared at me but went off, muttering.

I went up to the girl and touched her arm lightly. She was only a little older than my oldest daughter. "Hey. Could we just walk downstairs and talk about this outside? If we stay here, everyone's going to be screaming and yelling, and that's not going to help anyone. Come on. Let's just go outside and try to figure this out. Okay?"

"But this is where I *live*," the girl said, fresh tears filling her eyes. "My bedroom is there. My things. If you just make her open the door, I can show you. I *live* here."

She was sobbing now, raw and brokenhearted, but after a moment she let me lead her down the stairs and out the door.

Once we were outside, Auguste took over again. "All right! Now go! *Get!* You know you're not allowed here! I see you over here again I'm gonna bring you in and you can spend the night in a cell!"

The girl sniffled for a second, scowled at Auguste, then spun around and took off around the corner, walking as fast as her four-inch heels would allow.

It was one a.m. I looked at Auguste. "Will she be okay? Should we go after her, maybe call Child and Family Services?"

He snorted. "She's fine. Leave her. She'll go to her aunt now. This happens all the time."

I must have looked doubtful, because he added, "You don' know this girl like I do. You feel sorry for her, but I'm telling you, she's trouble. I get so many calls about her. The boys treat her bad and she just lets them. She's wild. She's been barred from here and she's got to leave. Let her go. She's fine."

We got back in the scout car and drove slowly out of the project. The girl, half a block ahead, glanced over her shoulder but didn't slow down. Auguste rolled down his window and stuck his head out as we drove past her slight, lonely figure.

"Good *night*," he shouted in a mocking singsong. "I loooove you, sweetheart. Good niiight!"

Not My World

Victim reports on the listed date and time, that he was walking Southbound . . . by the listed location, when he then saw a male on a bicycle riding very fast going Northbound. . . . He then felt immediately after, that he had been shot. Victim stated that he believes he heard someone say, "We hit the wrong guy."

— *MPD Joint Strategic and Tactical Analysis*
Command Center, Daily Report

This was not my world.

I grew up in a family of left-wing activists. My parents marched for civil rights and against the Vietnam War, and my mother was a self-described socialist feminist before Bernie Sanders and Alexandria Ocasio-Cortez made socialism cool. As a child, I joined my parents on picket lines and at protests. We marched for nuclear disarmament, racial justice, abortion rights, an end to apartheid, and an end to US intervention in Latin America. Later, as a college student, I ran the undergraduate community service organization and taught in a summer program for at-risk high school kids. After a master's degree in anthropology I went on to law school, where, through the school's clinical programs, I represented people too poor to pay for legal representation.

After graduating from law school, I worked as a human rights advocate both in the United States and abroad. When I became a law professor, I taught courses on human rights, international law, and constitutional law, and my academic work was punctuated by two stints in government service: first at the State Department's human rights bureau in the late 1990s, and again from 2009 to 2011 as an Obama administration appointee at the Defense Department, where I established an office on international humanitarian policy. In between government stints, I supplemented my academic career with a sideline in journalism. I spent four years as a weekly opinion columnist for the *Los Angeles Times*, and four more years writing a weekly column for *Foreign Policy*, an online magazine. Between my NGO work, journalism, and my government work, I spent time in trouble spots all over the world: Iraq, Afghanistan, Kosovo, Indonesia, Russia, Kenya, Nigeria, South Africa, Uganda, Sierra Leone, Israel, Palestine.

Becoming a police officer was hardly an obvious next step. In the world I inhabited day to day, surrounded by academics, activists, journalists, and policy experts, most people I knew viewed police officers as, at best, witless cogs in a criminal justice machine that exacerbated racial inequities, and at worst, brutal, racist thugs. When I first started thinking about applying to the DC police reserve corps, I tried to imagine how I would tell my friends and family. I pictured myself walking into the faculty lounge at Georgetown Law and informing my colleagues of my plans. I couldn't imagine what words I could use to explain.

From the beginning, it was my mother's likely reaction that worried me most. I had always struggled with her expectations: I wanted to please her and make her proud, but at the same time, I didn't want her choices and commitments to dictate my own.

That balancing act has never been an easy one. With an outsize intellect and an equally outsize personality, my mother wasn't merely an incidental or part-time activist, combining casual attendance at the occasional rally or protest with a full-time job doing something bourgeois and unrelated. She was, you might say, a professional activist, devoting the whole of her career to organizing for social change. She wrote books about health care reform, feminism, and economic inequality; she served on the boards of groups ranging from the Democratic Socialists of America to the National Organization for the Reform of Marijuana Laws; she founded and, at the age of seventy-nine, still runs a journalism organization called the Economic Hardship Reporting Project.

And she didn't like cops.

In some ways, my mother's negative experiences with police formed a core part of her identity, and by extension, my own. Late in 1969 or early in 1970, for instance, my mother marched at an anti-war protest where she was tear-gassed by police trying to break up the crowd. At the time, she was pregnant with me, her first child. I've heard her tell this story many times, and usually she offers, as a coda, the reminder that I was tear-gassed while still in utero ("Which explains a lot," she always quips, and I always chuckle dutifully).

Political activism was a routine part of my childhood. In one of our photo albums, there's a picture from International Women's Day, 1975: there's my mother, in bell-bottoms, with a Gloria Steinem hairstyle, looking beautiful, passionate, and brave. She's on a raised platform, giving a speech. I'm up on the stage too, just four years old, zipped into a hooded parka, holding her hand. Was I happy to be up there in front of all those people? The photo is too blurry to make out my expression, but judging from my body language—I'm not just holding my mother's hand, but clutching it with both of my own and leaning my head into her forearm—maybe not.

There's another picture in the family album from early 1979. My mother, my stepfather, my little brother, and I were engaged in what passed for recreation in our family: attending a protest. There was a nuclear power plant near where we lived, and we thought it should be decommissioned, or torn down, or not built in the first place—I don't recall. A photo of my eight-year-old self shows me with long braids and a Yankees cap, a button pinned to my jacket depicting a nuclear power plant and the legend "Shut them down!" By then I had apparently decided that center stage was an okay place to be: in the photo, I'm grinning, gap-toothed and reckless, even though it's raining and my clothes look soaked. The grown-ups were planning to get themselves arrested by trespassing on the nuclear plant's property, or chaining themselves to its fence, or doing one of those things people do when they think getting arrested is a useful way to make a political point, and I wanted to get arrested too. My mother refused: in our family, getting arrested by the Man was a privilege reserved for the grown-ups.

As I got older, it sometimes became harder to reconcile my family's political commitments with my own needs. Here's another snapshot, this one just a memory, not an actual photograph. It was 1980, and my family was marching on yet another picket line, trying, largely without success, to persuade members of the public to boycott the Nestlé food company. Nestlé, my mother explained, was killing babies in the third world. Well, not killing, precisely, but selling powdered baby formula to women who lacked access to safe drinking water, leading ultimately to the deaths of their babies.

This was troubling. I was a loyal, obedient child, and I wanted to save the third world babies, but Nestlé made every candy bar that I loved, including my favorite, the $100,000 bar. My mother acknowledged this dilemma, but explained that we must all be willing to make personal sacrifices to live by our principles. So I abstained from $100,000 bars, and all other Nestlé products—no Nestlé Crunch, no Baby Ruth, no Nestlé Quik chocolate or strawberry milk powder with the picture of a rabbit drinking through a straw.

But the longer I abstained, the more I dreamed of that gooey caramel, crispy rice, and rich, sweet chocolate. Scott's Five and Dime sold Nestlé $100,000 bars for twenty-five cents each, and I had a quarter burning a hole in my pocket. My mouth watered whenever I thought about it.

Finally, the temptation became too much. I was in Scott's with my mother and one of her feminist friends from New York City, and they were momentarily distracted by the copies of *Playboy* and *Hustler* peeking discreetly out from the forbidden top shelves of the magazine racks. My mother's friend decided to shock the small-minded, small-town customers by picking up one of these magazines and leafing through it ostentatiously, offering a high-decibel commentary on the female orgasm and its inexplicable absence from mainstream pornography. I was mortified, and I imagine my mother was as well (despite the activism and the public speeches, she has always been a deeply private person), but it worked briefly to my advantage, as the eyes of everyone in the small shop were drawn to the two crazy feminists by the magazine rack.

I seized my chance. I slipped over to the counter, grabbed a $100,000 bar from the shelf, thrust a quarter at the clerk, and ran.

I ran. I ran as if I had stolen the chocolate bar instead of spending a quarter from my own allowance on it. I raced out the door, around the corner, and into the alley behind the row of shops, where, huddling behind a dumpster, I ripped off the bright red wrapper and stuffed the candy into my mouth, gorging, almost choking on chocolate, caramel, crispy rice, defiance, and shame.

After an eternity, but much too soon, there was nothing left. I hid the telltale scarlet wrapper under some other trash and skulked back into Scott's, guilt seeping from every pore.

No one had noticed my absence.

I tell these stories so it will be clear: when I say that I feared my mother wouldn't approve of my decision to become a reserve police officer, I don't just mean that I expected her to be skeptical or concerned. I mean: I knew she would loathe the idea.

To my mother, police officers weren't heroes, crimes solvers, or protectors of the vulnerable and lost. They were the German paramilitary officers who murdered Rosa Luxemburg in 1919, smashing in her head with a rifle butt, then shooting her and dumping her body in Berlin's Landwehr Canal. They were the Alabama cops who arrested Rosa Parks in 1955 when she refused to sit in the back of the Montgomery bus. (That's right—who else would I be named for? I got a twofer.) They were Bull Connor in 1963, ordering his men to use fire hoses and dogs against African American civil rights pro-testers in Birmingham, Alabama. They were Chicago cops in 1968, using their clubs on protesters at the Democratic National Convention. They were the sadists who used cattle prods to coerce confessions from suspects in Chicago, sodomized Abner Louima with a broomstick at Brooklyn's 70th Precinct station house, and beat Rodney King until he lay bloody and un-conscious by the side of a Los Angeles road.

Because I'm my mother's daughter, her stories fill my head as well. I knew all about the cops who used tear gas, clubs, and fire hoses against people like my mother and my two namesakes. But these were not the only stories I knew. Back in the mists of time, there was a great-great-great-grandfather, James McLaughlin, who worked as a police officer in Dillon, Montana, in the late nineteenth century. He died of syphilitic paralysis, which is not to his credit, but he must have done something right, because his daughter, Mamie McLaughlin Howes, features prominently in many of my mother's family stories. (Mamie is usually invoked to explain the family's break from organized religion: enraged by the local Catholic priest's refusal to administer last rites to her dying father without payment of an exorbitant fee, Mamie, attended by a priest on her own deathbed just a few years later, summoned up her last strength and, in a final act of defiance, flung the crucifix across the room.)

There was also my mother's uncle Dave, an officer in the California

Highway Patrol who, when she was a young teen, sometimes let her drive his patrol car. (This was probably not sanctioned by California Highway Patrol regulations.) When I was a girl, we visited Uncle Dave, by then long-retired and running a gift shop in Barstow, California, and it was obvious that my mother adored him. She made no effort to take him to task for his years policing California's highways, and whenever she saw me watching *CHiPs*, a hit television show throughout my childhood, she reminded me that Uncle Dave had been a highway patrolman just like Ponch and Jon.

And there were cops everywhere in our blue-collar town. In the early 1970s, a short-term college teaching job, followed by divorce from my father, left my Montana-born mother temporarily marooned in the small Long Island town of Syosset. When their marriage broke up, my father sensibly retreated to Manhattan, but something—maybe inertia, maybe a budding romance with the young steelworker who later became my stepfather, maybe sheer stubborn perversity—kept my mother in Syosset, where she carved out a defiantly bohemian niche for herself on the wrong side of the tracks.

In Syosset, you can still find Gatsbyesque mansions in the part of town stretching toward Oyster Bay and the old Gold Coast of Long Island's North Shore. On our side of the tracks, ramshackle Victorians quickly gave way to the cookie-cutter Levittown houses of the respectable white working class. Our house, a modest white ranch, was just a few hundred yards from the railroad line, and most nights I fell asleep to the sound of train whistles and the clickety-clack of wheels on the metal tracks.

While my brother and I attended protests and circulated petitions, our classmates went to Sunday school and played in Little League games. Our parents were socialists, while theirs were Archie Bunker–style Republicans. Our parents had PhDs, while most of our friends' parents hadn't gone to college, and most held blue-collar jobs. My best friend Laura's father was a fireman; Caroline's dad ran a construction company; Audrey's dad co-owned the local Irish bar. Gwen, Billy, and Pat's fathers were all cops, as was Pete's big brother Jimmy.

We didn't belong. But I liked those fathers and big brothers—so solid, so respectable. These were fathers and brothers who took you fishing, set off fireworks at Fourth of July picnics, took you to the ball game—so different from my own family of radicals and bookish oddballs, where picket lines and boycotts counted as family fun, and displays of patriotism were met with immediate denunciations of militarism, imperialism, and patriarchy. Whenever I could, I attached myself to these large, comforting men, insinuating myself into their family gatherings. Laura's family took me along to the local Catholic church on Sundays (I kept mum about great-great-grandmother Mamie). Caroline's dad took us out on his boat. Pete's brother Jimmy persuaded the other local cops to look the other way when, in our early teens, we were all caught drinking beer and smoking weed on the beach. The weed had been spirited away from my mother and step-father's stash, but I kept mum about this, too.

And I liked detective novels and cop shows—*CHiPs* and *Columbo* and *Barney Miller*. I liked the suspense, the adrenaline, and the clarity. No matter how complex the plot or how devious the perpetrator, these stories mostly boiled down to the same basic formula: there were bad guys, there were flawed but dedicated police, the police investigated, and—generally after a car chase or two—the bad guys were brought to justice. Simple, stirring, and satisfying. There was violence, yes, but it was always in the service of justice and the greater good.

The Abyss

Officers Injured/Use of Force: Officers attempted to affect a stop on a fleeing suspect. The suspect brandished a handgun and fired at the officers multiple times striking the officers. In response to the aggression from the suspect, Officer [redacted] fired his service pistol and the suspect was struck. Both officers were transported to an area hospital for treatment of gunshot wounds to the body. The suspect was transported to an area hospital where he succumbed to his wounds.

—MPD Joint Strategic and Tactical Analysis
Command Center, Daily Report

I have always been fascinated by violence: why people are drawn to it, and how they make sense of it—justifying it, glorifying it, condemning it, or trying to constrain and control it. At various points in my career, I have studied and written about South African police culture during the transition from apartheid, concentration camps in Bosnia, blood feuds in Kosovo, capital punishment and immigration detention in the United States, Ugandan and Sierra Leonean rebels, corporal punishment in Kenyan schools, Taliban and Iraqi insurgents, al-Qaeda and ISIS terrorists, and US wars and counterterrorism drone strikes—trying, in each case, to understand how it is that people come to believe the things they believe about violence. My more recent book, *How Everything Became War and the Military Became Everything*, looked at the ways in which post-9/11 America came to view so many problems through the lens of war, and how that has transformed and distorted our laws and institutions.

By any measure, policing in the United States is a breathtakingly violent enterprise. American police kill more people each month than police in most developed countries kill in several decades. For instance, during the first twenty-four days of 2015—the year I applied to the MPD Reserve Corps—police in the United States killed more people than police in England and Wales killed in the previous twenty-four years. Adjusting for population size, American cops kill people sixty-four times as often as police in the UK.

Ask how the United States became a country where police kill more than a thousand citizens each year, so many of them young black men, and you'll get two standard but quite different answers. The first, offered most frequently on the political left, is that American policing is fundamentally violent and racist—American police officers kill so many young black men because police are the agents of a brutal state that does not value black lives. For America's first two centuries, black people were enslaved by white Americans; for a century after slavery ended, black citizens were denied access to wealth and political power by overtly discriminatory laws; in the decades since *Brown v. Board of Education* and the Civil Rights Act of 1964, racially biased policing practices and mass incarceration have replaced older forms of discrimination and brutality to become "the new Jim Crow," as legal scholar Michelle Alexander puts it. American policing is violent because violence has always been a key means through which the country's white majority defends its unearned privileges against the encroachment of minorities.

The second answer, offered most frequently on the political right and understandably preferred by many police officers, casts police in the roles of heroes and victims, not villains or racist thugs. In this version of the story, the problem is not the violence of police, but the violence of American society more broadly. America charges its police officers with the difficult, dangerous task of preventing and responding to violent crime—of which the gun-saturated United States has far more than its share—and in the United States, young black males commit a disproportionate number of violent crimes. The reasons for this are complex, but certainly not the fault of the police, and the relatively high rate of criminality among young black men brings them into more frequent contact with police officers than other demographic groups. The disproportionate number of young black men killed during encounters with police reflects this unfortunate statistical reality and nothing more, and although there are always a few bad apples who make other cops look bad, it is not fair to blame police officers for simply doing their dangerous, poorly paid, underappreciated jobs.

These two competing stories about policing don't exhaust the possibilities, of course, and well before I decided to become a police officer, my instinct was that the true causes of US police violence are far more complicated than either of these narratives acknowledges.

Violence is a puzzle. We all say we oppose violence and want to reduce it, but no human society gets by without it. Violence, or the credible threat of violence, lies behind the laws and institutions of even the most seemingly placid society. In some societies, the state's violence is right out there in the open; in others, it's well hidden. But as the legal scholar Robert Cover argued in a now-classic 1986 article, "Violence and the Word," we should not be fooled by surface decorum. In criminal trials, for instance, the defendant "sits, usually quietly, as if engaged in a civil discourse. If convicted, the defendant customarily walks—escorted—to prolonged confinement, usually without significant disturbance to the civil appearance of the event." Yet, wrote Cover, "It is, of course, grotesque to assume that the civil facade is 'voluntary' except in the sense that it represents the defendant's autonomous recognition of the overwhelming array of violence ranged against him, and of the hopelessness of resistance or outcry." If most prisoners walk into prison, it is because "they know they will be dragged or beaten into prison if they do not walk."

We tell ourselves that a central project of law and political institutions is the reduction of violence, but this is mostly a fairly tale. Law and politics play a role in structuring violence, but rarely "reduce" it. In every human society, soldiers, police officers, "criminals," and ordinary people all create their own stories about violence, stories that explain—to their own satisfaction, at least—why some violence is acceptable and some is not. It would not be too extreme to say that much of human "civilization" revolves around the problem of violence: not how to reduce it, but how to channel and control it, how to make sense of it and assign it moral meaning.

It's always easy to condemn the violence of others; we label the violence we don't like as savage, unthinking, immoral. To Murphy and Auguste, struggling to make sense of the crime and dysfunction they see as they patrol in DC's Seventh District, the residents of Southeast DC become "these fucking people" and "fucking animals." To those protesting police shootings, the police themselves are brutes and animals: robo-cops, killers, crackers, pigs.

It's the same the world over. Virtually no one conceives of their own behavior in such derogatory, dehumanizing terms. Instead, we construct stories—whole systems of meaning, often accompanied by elaborate legal and institutional structures—to explain and justify our own biases and behavior.

And humans can justify almost anything to themselves, no matter how horrific. In his 1992 book, *Ordinary Men: Reserve Police Battalion 101 and the Final Solution in Poland*, the historian Christopher Browning writes about the German police officers ordered to hunt down fleeing Jewish families in the forests of Poland in 1942. They didn't see themselves as war criminals; for the most part, they persuaded themselves that they were doing painful, difficult, but necessary work for the sake of their comrades and friends. It wasn't that hard for them to convince themselves—after all, everything they did was "legal" under Nazi laws, and they operated within an institutional architecture that praised and rewarded those who killed Jews, and often punished those who didn't.

The Germans who participated in the Holocaust weren't unusual. Look at any of the worst horrors humans have inflicted on one another—the Holocaust; the Soviet gulag; genocide and ethnic cleansing in Cambodia, Rwanda, Bosnia. In each case, it took only a few short years for thousands of ordinary, "decent" people to join in the abuses and the killing—and most did so in the full belief that their actions were justified, patriotic, even praiseworthy.

Even those whose acts of violence aren't sanctioned by the state readily persuade themselves of their own righteousness. In the late 1990s, I was sent to Uganda by Human Rights Watch to investigate reports of atrocities carried out by a rebel group calling itself the Lord's Resistance Army (LRA). In terms of numbers, the LRA had nothing on the Nazis or the Rwandan *genocidaires*—the LRA's victims numbered in the thousands, not the millions. But in terms of sheer brutality, the LRA gave the Nazis a run for their money. Like many rebel armies, the LRA looted, raped, murdered, and press-ganged others into serving their cause. But unlike most rebel groups, the LRA focused particularly on children. To replenish their ranks, LRA units abducted children from villages throughout northern Uganda to serve as servants, concubines, and soldiers. Since the children rarely served willingly, the LRA developed gruesome rituals to separate their child captives from their past lives. Often, they would force their young conscripts to slaughter others, including their own family members, telling them that they could choose: they could kill, or they could die. I met children who had been forced to beat and hack their own friends and siblings to death.

To this day, nothing I have ever seen or encountered comes close to the sheer horror of LRA activities in northern Uganda. But despite their seemingly gratuitous cruelty, even the toughest LRA fighters worked hard to convince themselves that their brutality was justified. Those they killed were possessed by evil spirits, they sometimes claimed, so killing them was in fact a kindness; alternatively, they argued that the killing they carried out or ordered was necessary to set an example. "We [only kill people] because they are misbehaving," a vexed LRA commander told a young captive who had the courage to challenge the group's actions. "Jesus did not ask his disciples to come with him, he just told them, 'Follow me.' But today Ugandans do not follow the Holy Spirit, so they must be forced. . . . You don't know what we are doing. . . . One day . . . you will see we are God's people."

When I told my mother about my plan to join the DC police reserve corps, I tried to say some of this. We were in the car, heading out from Alexandria, Virginia, where we both lived, for a quiet family weekend on Maryland's Eastern Shore.

"I just don't understand this police officer idea at all," my mother said. "Police use violence to suppress dissent. They oppress poor people. They oppress minorities. That is not an incidental aspect of what they do. It's at the *center* of what they do. Why would you want to join them?"

I was defensive. "I'm not 'joining' them. I'm trying to learn about them. If we want to understand why police officers do what they do, we need to understand how they see the world."

"So go interview some cops. You don't need to *become* a cop."

"But maybe I do," I insisted.

The kids and the dog were in the back seat, the dog snoring and the girls plugged into their earphones, oblivious to our tense exchange.

Violence, I argued, can be understood only through a nuanced attention to the narratives people create to justify and explain their behavior. If I became a police officer—a part-time police officer, yes, but a police officer all the same—I could, maybe, begin to understand how the world looks through the eyes of those with badges and guns, and how so much that seems baffling or wrong from the outside has come to seem acceptable, even necessary, to those on the inside.

I don't remember how the argument proceeded, except that at some stage my mother quoted Nietzsche on gazing into the abyss, at which point she was interrupted by one of the girls asking for a bathroom break. I pulled into the first gas station we passed, and took the dog for a walk while my mother and the girls went in search of restrooms and snacks. I was upset, but after walking for a while I calmed down.

When the drive resumed, neither of us returned to Nietzsche and the abyss.

"It's so quiet and peaceful here," my mother said, looking out the window at the meadows and, in the distance, the afternoon sun glinting off the water of the Chesapeake Bay.

"You know," I said, "one the neighbors I met out here told me that the guy who lives three houses down is a retired DC homicide detective."

My mother didn't respond.

I Am Pleased to Inform You

Reserve Corps members shall . . . Conduct themselves in a professional manner as governed by applicable Federal and District of Columbia laws and regulations . . . [and] While on Department duty, be held to the same duty obligations as career sworn members, including the duty to make arrests for crimes committed in their presence, the duty to take appropriate police action when required, and the duty to comply with all laws, regulations, Department directives, and lawfully issued orders.

— MPD General Order OMA 101-03

In the summer of 2015, despite the near unanimous opposition of my family and friends, I submitted an "expression of interest" through a form on the Metropolitan Police Department's website, averring that I was a US citizen, was at least twenty-one years old, had completed sixty semester-hour credits at an accredited postsecondary educational institution, and was in possession of a valid driver's license.

My form vanished into cyberspace, but a few weeks later, I received an email inviting me to attend a reserve corps information session at the police academy.

If your image of how police academies look was formed by the 1984 movie, you've got the wrong image. In *Police Academy*, the eponymous academy looks like a small liberal arts college, complete with landscaped grounds and a green, manicured central quad. In real life, no such luck, at least not in budget-strapped Washington, DC.

The DC Metropolitan Police Academy is tucked away in Southeast DC—in what I later learned was part of the Seventh District—off a small road no one would ever take if they weren't a city employee. You drive past the fire department's training center, full of burned-out buildings and vehicles the firefighters use for practice, then past a lot full of parked city buses, then you get to a locked gate.

The gate is chain-link metal, ten feet high—just in case anyone's trying to break into the police academy, though it's a little hard to see why someone would. The gate opens, slowly, with the swipe of a magnetic card, if you possess the right kind of card. If you don't, you push the call button and hope someone decides to answer. (This is Washington, DC, a city President John F. Kennedy famously described as combining "southern efficiency and northern charm," so maybe they'll answer and maybe they won't.)

When the gate opens, you drive into a scruffy parking lot. The asphalt is pocked with ruts and potholes, and the scraggly grass on the edge of the lot is choked with weeds. To the left is the headquarters of MPD's K-9 unit, and sometimes a few large, silent German shepherds follow you with their eyes as you drive into the lot. (Slowly. You really don't want to speed in here.) You back into a space so you can park facing out, because cops always park facing out; it's supposed to make a quick getaway easier, though no one ever manages a quick getaway from the Metropolitan Police Academy. It's a sticky sort of place.

Off in the far corner of the academy is the Tactical Training Center, a vast, hangar-like structure containing a mock town where officers can practice clearing rooms, approaching dangerous suspects, and dealing with school shooters. There's a small "gas house" where recruits can learn what it's like to be tear-gassed and practice putting on their gas masks. Up some cracked concrete steps, there's a big brick building that houses classrooms, offices, a cafeteria, a gym, a pool, and the firing range. Behind that, a smaller annex building holds more classrooms and an auditorium.

Inside the main building, the smell of food from the cafeteria mingles with smoke and gun oil drifting up from the underground firing range and chlorine from the pool.

Over time, I grew to hate that building. It was a place of push-ups and punishment runs, shouted orders and the sour sweat of two hundred frightened recruits. I was just a part-timer, immune from the worst of it, but even so, I'd feel my stomach muscles tighten as I drove through the academy gate, and clench tighter as I walked up the buckling concrete steps. But on that first evening, as I followed the emailed directions and went past the main building, past more dying grass and pitted sidewalks to the smaller annex behind it, I was just surprised by the academy's air of neglect. It was evening, and the parking lots were nearly empty. Deer were grazing in the trees next to the Tactical Training Center, and they paused to gaze at me. A sign declared the parking space closest to the building RESERVED FOR CHIEF OF POLICE. Another sign, at the top of the pitted and cracked steps, urged passersby to HOLD ON TO RAILING IN CASE OF WET OR SLIPPERY CONDITIONS.

The door was propped open, and a sign directed me to a room filled with tiered rows of seats, each facing a large computer keyboard and monitor.

"Welcome, welcome . . . Ms. Brooks! So glad you could make it! Take a seat, take a seat."

The genial man at the front of the room didn't look much like a cop; he was too friendly. I couldn't see him very well, though, because the computer monitors facing each seat blocked my line of sight.

"I'm so sorry about this room; it's the only one we could get. I'm so sorry!" This guy was much too nice to be a cop.

Scattered around the room were a handful of other potential reserve corps applicants. None of them said anything to me, and after that night, I never saw most of them again.

The too-nice-to-be-a-cop guy walked us through a short PowerPoint presentation about the reserve corps. The Metropolitan Police Department was the "lead law enforcement agency for the nation's capital," he informed us enthusiastically, responsible not only for ordinary crime prevention and investigation but also for "the largest number of National Special Security Events of any US city," including mass protests, presidential inaugurations, and frequent visits from foreign heads of state. The MPD Reserve Corps (which strove for "Excellence in Volunteer Policing") provided supplemental manpower both to patrol districts and to specialized police units.

Manpower was the right word: the PowerPoint presentation was full of photos of smiling police officers, all of them male. But despite the dearth of colleagues with two X chromosomes, MPD reserve police officers were, apparently, happy people. In the presentation, they smilingly directed traffic, rode mountain bikes, practiced defensive tactics, spoke into their radios, and posed with President Obama. Maybe they smiled as they arrested people too, but there was no way to know, as the presentation didn't show anyone being arrested.

The PowerPoint was as sleek and professional as the academy grounds were seedy. Later, I learned that Mr. Too-Nice-to-Be-a-Cop was a reserve officer, but in his day job he worked in the Marine Corps' public affairs office. The Marine Corps is very, very good at making PowerPoints.

"That was a good PowerPoint," I told him on my way out.

He beamed. "Thank you! Ms. Brooks, I'm *so* glad you were able to come. I really enjoy meeting people who are interested in the reserve corps. You can contact me *any*time if you have questions."

I did have questions. First, was I really doing this? But I could hardly pose that question to the nice recruiting officer.

The reserve corps application process was a lot of work for something I wasn't sure I really wanted, or ought to want. I filled out lengthy forms, listing every address and job I'd ever had and every school I'd ever attended. I provided MPD with my birth certificate, my driving record, and my credit report. I was fingerprinted and weighed, and submitted to a vision test, a hearing test, a physical exam, an EKG, and a body fat analysis.

A police psychologist administered a lengthy battery of psychological tests designed, presumably, to weed out the more blatant sociopaths and sadists from the applicant pool. I was skeptical about the efficacy of the tests—all but the dimmest sadists surely knew not to give an affirmative answer to questions such as "I enjoy watching other people suffer."

I was hooked up to a polygraph and grilled about my past, and successfully ran a short obstacle course in the police academy gym, racing up and down stairs, dragging a heavy dummy along a mat, crawling under tables, clambering over a chain-link fence, and dry-firing a pistol.

None of this was hard, exactly, but there were a lot of steps. The reserve corps application process took months, with periods of complete silence from the MPD recruiting office alternating with sudden imperious demands: Report to the Police and Fire Clinic at 0800 tomorrow for a physical; schedule a home visit ASAP; provide copies of all medical records by next week.

Finally, on Christmas Eve 2015, I received an email from a sender identified only as "D.C. Metropolitan Police Department." The body of the message was brusque: "Dear Rosa Brooks: Attached to this email is a letter from D.C. Metropolitan Police Department regarding your application for employment. Please open the attached letter and review it immediately."

I felt a jolt of anxiety. Perhaps, I thought, I had somehow messed up during the application process. I had too much body fat. I had failed the polygraph. The psychologist who interviewed me had seen through my bland insistence that I "just wanted to serve my community." Looking at my résumé, he had discerned that I was really an activist, an academic, a journalist: the Enemy. I would be dropped from the applicant pool. Not that it mattered, I reminded myself, since I wasn't going to do this anyway, was I?

When I finally opened the attachment, I saw that I had gotten it all wrong.

> *Congratulations! I am pleased to inform you that you have been selected for the position of Reserve Police Officer effective April 12, 2016 with the Metropolitan Police Department.*
>
> *Beginning in 1951, Reserve Corps members have served the Department and the District of Columbia by performing law enforcement, crime prevention, crime detection, community policing and other specialized functions. The Reserve Corps plays an integral part in the Department's endeavor to provide high quality police service . . .*
>
> *Reserve Corps training classes occur every Tuesday and Thursday evening from 6:30 PM until 10:30 PM in addition to Saturdays from 8:00 AM until 4:30 PM (excluding the 1st Saturday of each month). The training will last approximately 50 weeks with occasional breaks for major holidays. You may be required to take firearms training during standard business hours (80 hours) and vehicle skills (40 hours).*
>
> *You are to report to the Metropolitan Police Academy (MPA) on Tuesday, April 12, 2016 at 6:30 PM to begin your training.*

Dirt in My Eye

ADW (Knife): On the listed date, between the listed times,
Complainant reports being stuck in traffic . . . While in traffic,
Complainant reports allowing pedestrians to cross in front of his
vehicle and while doing so the driver of a silver colored vehicle
became upset that he was allowing [a] person to cross in front of
him. Complainant then states as he was allowing the pedestrians
to cross Suspect began to blow his horn at him. Suspect then
exited the vehicle and approached him with a knife in his hand.
Suspect and Complainant began to argue and Suspect stated to
Complainant: "You gotta respect me mutha fucka!!"

—MPD Joint Strategic and Tactical Analysis
Command Center, Daily Report

What was I trying to prove?

I could offer up my usual rationalizations: my interest in police reform, my previous writing on violence and the law, and so on. The trouble is, as my mother argued, none of this required me to *become* a police officer. I could have just read books and articles about policing. I could have interviewed cops, done police ride-alongs as an interested community member, or asked for permission to observe academy classes.

Maybe I was just bored. I lived in a pleasant, leafy Virginia suburb; I took my kids to school each morning in a Honda minivan; I walked the dog and drove to the office each day. I missed the excitement and variety of my earlier work for human rights groups, the State Department, and the

Defense Department. Driving to work in my minivan was painless; I could listen to the radio or put on an audiobook. But it was nothing like traveling by helicopter over the green jungles of Sierra Leone or the arid mountains of Afghanistan.

Or maybe I just missed being young, and some subterranean part of my brain decided it was time for a midlife crisis. But I didn't swap my minivan for a sports car or have a wild affair. Instead, I became a part-time police officer.

So maybe it was all to do with my childhood and the muddled, conflicted messages about authority, gender, and class I absorbed from the adults around me, my mother most of all.

A s a little girl in the 1970s, I was what people used to call a tomboy. In our blue-collar Long Island neighborhood, there were no other girls on my street, only boys. After school each day, we ran around in a loose pack, climbing trees, wrestling, tossing balls, and trading tattered baseball cards.

When I was six or seven, I had a crush on a boy named Johnny, the sixth grader who served as de facto leader of our little wolf pack. I didn't like his three rambunctious younger brothers, Tony, Nicky, and Victor, who often complained about letting a "stupid girl" into their games. But when Johnny gave them a stern look, they fell into line.

My own younger brother, Benjy, was, in my opinion, as unsatisfactory as Johnny's brothers, though for different reasons. Benjy was small, blue-eyed, blond, and much admired by adults. In contrast to my drab brown locks—imprisoned each day in untidy braids after a tearful struggle with my mother and a hairbrush—his hair was soft, silky, and so flaxen that my mother declared it "too beautiful" to cut. As a result, he was occasionally mistaken for a girl in his early years. In fact, my brother seemed to me to possess many of the same girlish qualities so scorned by Tony, Nicky, and

Victor: he cried easily, and could neither throw nor catch a baseball; when a ball headed in his direction, he covered his head and ducked.

True, Benjy was only three or four, but at the time I did not view this as a mitigating factor, and I couldn't understand why our mother fussed over him so much. If she had made anything clear to me, it was that feminine qualities were to be despised. She spoke scathingly of her own mother's rigid commitment to feminine propriety, and explained that girls and women had for millennia been forced into the most trivial pursuits, such as playing with dolls, cooking, cleaning, and prancing about in skirts and impractical heels. Meanwhile, boys and men got to do all the fun stuff: baseball, camping, boxing, winning wars, running the world. My generation, she told me, must resist such sexism.

I was fully on board with this program—no one was going to get me into a skirt and heels. (Benjy, in contrast, was fond of playing dress-up, and often appeared in my mother's clothes and shoes.) When I was eight—it must have been shortly after that anti-nukes protest—I cut my braids off and jammed a Yankees cap over my newly shorn hair, hoping people might mistake me for a boy. One day, when several little girls from the next street over appeared and invited me to play, I cautiously agreed, but when it transpired that they wanted to play house with Barbie dolls, I refused to accept any role other than that of the family dog. I growled and nipped at the Barbies. After that, the girls stayed on their own street.

When I was nine, we moved to a different, larger house. It was only a block away from our old house, but it might have been on another planet. If my old street had been a world of boys, this new street was a world of girls. By now, Johnny was already lost to me: vanished into adolescence, no longer interested in tree climbing or games of cops and robbers. When we moved, I left Tony, Nicky, and Victor behind as well, along with Richie, Michael, Billy, and the rest of the gang.

Instead, our new street offered Laura, Caroline, Sandra, and Audrey, the very girls whose attentions I had previously spurned. At first, sullen and distraught, I refused to join their after-school games. But after a few lonely post-move weeks, I succumbed to the lure of a game of hide-and-seek, and a truce was drawn. I would play with the girls, as long as I was not required to *act* like a girl, and they would play with me, as long as I stopped growling at their Barbies.

Then I met Gabriel, the new boy in our fourth-grade class. He was Johnny all over again, only better, because he was my own age. We crawled through drainage tunnels in the park together, and found a way to shinny up onto our elementary school's roof, where we built small, illicit fires and roasted marshmallows.

When Gabriel confessed that he had a crush on Laura, it didn't take me long to figure things out. By then, Laura, whose house was directly across the street from mine, had become my other best friend. She was as pretty and blond as my little brother, and she had two older sisters. She could climb trees and tell heart-chilling ghost stories, but thanks to her sisters, she also knew all the arcane secrets of girlhood: how to shave your legs, how to wear a barrette, how to smile coquettishly. (Once, I overheard two female teachers note, with disapproval, that Laura was "a fast one, just like her sisters.") Gabriel, entranced, still wanted to talk about baseball with me, but now he also wanted to talk about Laura. Did I think she liked him back? Did I think she might want to be his girlfriend?

By the end of fifth grade, Laura and Gabriel were holding hands during the slow song at the roller rink on Saturdays, and I had admitted defeat. I grew my hair back out, and asked Laura to teach me how to put on eye makeup.

Learning how to be a girl took time. Laura lent me some of her skirts, and Caroline and Sandra explained barrettes to me. Laura's oldest sister taught me how to shave my legs, while her middle sister offered tips on flirtation methods.

"Fast" or not, the proximity of Laura's older sisters was a stroke of good luck, as my mother resolutely ignored the fact that I was approaching puberty. She never mentioned it, and, taking her cue, I kept silent as well. When I noticed that my once-flat chest was becoming less flat, I wore heavy sweatshirts and walked hunched over. When that became insufficient, I surreptitiously spirited away a few of my mother's bras from her dresser drawer. When I got my period, I kept silent about it for six months, sneaking feminine hygiene pads from under her bathroom sink. Finally, struck almost dumb with mortification, I blurted out my secret, staring at the ground.

"I'm so proud!" my mother declared, giving me a hug. But she didn't mention it again after that, and she never asked if I needed pads or tampons, leaving me to buy them myself or tuck them discreetly under the groceries in our supermarket shopping cart. She never bought me a bra, or suggested we shop for one—I was in college the first time I wore a bra that hadn't been purloined from her dresser drawer.

In the spring of 2016, shortly before I started classes at the police academy, I was arguing constantly with my mother about joining the reserve corps. One night, I had a dream in which I was furiously angry at her. In the dream, I knew that my anger had something to do with my brother (who, despite his early aversion to wrestling and baseball, grew up to be thoroughly heterosexual and devote himself to such aggressively manly activities as war journalism). In the dream, I was weeping and almost shouting at my mother, something I have almost never done in real life. "I even cut my hair off so I would look more like *him!*" I shouted in the dream.

I woke up at this point, thinking: Oh. Well. Of *course*.

Most of the time, I chalk this up to normal sibling paranoia. If I grew up with the distinct sense that our mother admired the masculine and viewed the feminine as contemptible, my brother tells me he grew up with an equally strong conviction that she viewed masculinity as toxic and dangerous. Both of us are probably right.

Our mother's own romantic choices certainly suggest some ambivalence. She married and then divorced our father, an academic from a middle-class family of urban intellectuals. Her second husband, my stepfather, Gary, could hardly have been more of a contrast: he was a working-class bruiser, an autodidact with a wicked sense of humor. A union organizer, Gary could quote Marx and Adorno, but his day-to-day conversation leaned heavily on the phrase "motherfucking fucker," and his organizing tactics were often of the creative, not exactly legal variety: when a company initiated employee lockouts, for instance, he enlisted my brother and me to help him apply Krazy Glue to the locks on the plant doors in the middle of the night. ("They want a fucking lockout? We'll give them a fucking lockout.")

If I loved my father for his thoughtfulness, empathy, and calm, I loved my stepfather for his determination not to "take any fucking shit" from those "motherfucking rat bastards." My father was not the kind of man who got into physical fights; my stepfather's response to threat and insult was to get right in the other guy's face.

As for my mother: well, she divorced my father and married my stepfather.

All this is to say that as a child, I internalized some notions about gender that were, as my brother Ben put it in a recent conversation, "pretty messed up." My mother's silence about such matters as puberty and menstruation suggested that the details of being female were either so trivial as to be beneath notice, or so shameful they could never be acknowledged. Sexism was bad and patriarchy was bad, I deduced, but so were femininity and passivity. Wars were unquestionably bad, at least when they took place in Southeast Asia, but toughness and aggression were clearly admired.

During my tomboy stage, I was a fighter. My stepfather taught me to yank an opponent's thumb or arm backward until he cried for mercy (police, I later learned, call these "control holds"). I gained other skills from the series of short-term boarders who took up residence in our basement guest room. There was a Dutch guy who taught me yo-yo tricks, wrestling holds, and a few karate moves, and a Greek Cypriot, fresh out of the Army, who used my brother's toy rifle to demonstrate how to bayonet an enemy to death. I practiced over and over, stabbing sofa cushions with an angry roar.

For several weeks when I was in fourth or fifth grade, Gabriel and I lay in wait after school every day for a boy called Jason. Each afternoon, Jason would walk down the school driveway, backpack over his shoulder, and each afternoon, Gabriel and I would jump on him as soon as he left the school grounds, knock him down, and toss him around a bit. Looking back, the best I can say about this is that we did not really hurt Jason, and I don't think he was particularly traumatized by being knocked down every afternoon; he seemed to regard the whole thing with good-humored tolerance, as if it was just our way of being friendly. Maybe it was.

I got into only one real fight during my childhood, and it started because of my brother. I was nine, and though at age seven Benjy no longer had shoulder-length hair (and was only a year or two away from insisting that he be called "Ben" instead of Benjy), he was still much too pretty, and a magnet for bullies. Waiting for the school bus one morning, a boy called Mark began to taunt him.

Mark was a nasty kid, the kind who poked injured kittens with a sharp stick. I had seen it. It wasn't long before the word *faggot* was used to describe Benjy's demeanor.

I told Mark to lay off. He ignored me.

I told him to lay off, or *else*.

At this, he sneered, "What are you going to do to stop me?" and gave Benjy's shoulder a little shove.

I threw myself at him, and soon we were in an all-out fight. At first, I had the better of it. Although Mark was taller and heavier, surprise was on my side, and I managed to knock him flat. I sat on him triumphantly, not sure what to do next.

To my amazement, he started to cry, first a little bit, then loudly.

"I have dirt in my eye!" he wailed.

Good, I thought savagely. I hope it hurts.

My triumph didn't last. Mark recovered, shoving me off and landing a hard punch to my jaw, and it was my turn to cry. Turning, I hightailed it down the street toward home.

I pushed through our front door and into the kitchen, where I found my mother sitting on her favorite kitchen stool, smoking a cigarette. My face hurt, and I launched into a series of tearful explanations (Mark hit me! He started it, he was being a bully, he hurt me, it wasn't fair!), but she wasn't listening. She rose, pointed at the door, and said, in her most dangerous voice, "*Get* back out there, and get on that school bus."

I was stunned. I'm not sure what I was expecting—that she would stride vengefully down the street, seize Mark by the scruff of his neck, and haul him back to his parents for a good thrashing? I assumed, at least, that she would offer sympathy: hugs, an ice pack, maybe an assurance that after my ordeal, it would be better to just stay home from school and rest up.

But I went back out, and got on the school bus. I sat alone in the front row, head down, trying to hide my tears.

Writing this book, it occurred to me, for the first time, to wonder what had become of Mark, so I started googling. He hadn't left much of an internet footprint; the first and only reference Google could find was a 2013 obituary. Mark had grown up to become an officer in the New York City Police Department, then died at age forty-two. The obituary didn't give the cause of death, and I could find no other trace of him in any news databases, so it's safe to assume his death wasn't in the line of duty. (An illness, maybe? An overdose? Suicide? An accident?) Other than that, the internet offered no further clues. Mark the bully became a cop, had two children, and died, leaving behind only a four-sentence obituary in a local newspaper.

No one comes to adulthood as a blank slate, and for me, it's probably fair to say that issues relating to authority, violence, and gender are all tangled up together. It added up to a heavy dose of ambivalence. So much, in fact, that I spent the months following my acceptance into the reserve corps training program telling myself I didn't plan to go through with it.

If I decided to show up at the police academy, I told myself, I'd be showing up just to see what it was like. I could go for a few weeks to satisfy my curiosity, then leave. And even if I decided to complete the academy training, I didn't have to go out and be a cop when I finished. This was a volunteer position. I could always go through the academy, then say, "Thank you, that was interesting, good-bye."

But things take on their own momentum. I had put so much energy into the reserve corps application process that it seemed silly not to go through the police academy training course. After that, I decided to start patrol duty—because of the sunk costs, because I was curious, and because everyone around me either condemned or laughed at the idea, which cemented a perverse determination to go through with it.

My mother still made frequent cracks about "fascists" and "racist pigs." It was hurtful and exasperating, but I didn't want to keep arguing with her, so I tried to push my uncertainties and ambivalence to the back of my mind. I was going to become a reserve police officer, and that was that. "I understand you don't like this," I finally told my mother, "but it's what I'm doing, and I don't have to justify it to you."

But yes, I had a lot to prove. I wanted to prove that I wasn't weak, or scared, or just a "stupid girl," as Tony, Nicky, and Victor had charged all those years ago. I still burned with shame when I remembered running away from that fight at the school bus stop. I wanted to prove that I could learn to do push-ups, fight, handcuff people, and shoot a gun—that I could survive insults, challenges, threats, a face full of pepper spray, and whatever else anyone wanted to throw at me.

PART TWO

The Academy

Model Recruit

*The Metropolitan Police Department is an organization which
functions optimally in accordance with certain rules and
regulations that govern the demeanor and performance of its
recruit and lateral officers.*

> —*Reserve Recruit Officer Training Handbook,*
> *DC Metropolitan Police Department*

On April 12, 2016, I reported to the DC Metropolitan Police Academy as instructed, along with fifteen other would-be police officers in Reserve Recruit Class 2016-01. There was Wentz, a former NYPD cop, now in "consulting." He was in his late twenties or early thirties, smart and cocky; even on day one, he exuded a slight aura of "Do I seriously have to go through this shit?" There was Woodson, a former enlisted marine from Texas, now also in "consulting." (In the DC area, that's usually a euphemism for contractors doing classified work for the Defense Department or an intelligence agency.) There was Ramos, a young Cuban American army sergeant still on active duty, and Rodriguez, a Mexican American lawyer from California who had worked for a civil rights group; he looked like he thought he might have walked into the wrong room. I suspect I looked like that too.

There was Turner, a black guy about my age, also in consulting, and Smith, a quiet, self-contained coast guard lieutenant. She was the only other woman in the class. There was Gregson, a florid fiftysomething white guy in an expensive suit who introduced himself as "the CEO of a major international health care company." There was Brandt, an air force colonel. There was Lowrey, a middle-aged NASA engineer. He was friendly, lumbering, and slow-spoken, and it became immediately clear that he was destined to become the butt of a thousand rocket scientist jokes. ("What the fuck, Lowrey, it doesn't take a fucking rocket scientist to know that when I say I want you to do those push-ups now, I mean, I want them *now*. Oh wait, I forgot, you *are* a fucking rocket scientist! So you should have no fucking problem with this!")

All these people had first names too, but it was apparent that no one was planning to use them. I became Brooks, or Recruit Officer Brooks, though later, as a small form of rebellion, I occasionally introduced myself as Rosa and referred to my classmates by their first names.

The youngest reserve recruits were in their early twenties; the oldest, in their early fifties. We were not otherwise a terribly diverse group: two African Americans, three Latinos, and the rest of us all white. Just two women. Twelve of my classmates were current or former military, and three or four had prior law enforcement experience in other jurisdictions.

Our first day at the academy was fairly painless. We arrived in civilian clothes and spent a few minutes introducing ourselves before the instructors launched into a discussion of what we could expect during our time there. We were told to purchase gray T-shirts and gray shorts for our physical training classes. Given our abbreviated evening sessions at the academy, we would do group PT only on Saturdays, but would be expected to train on our own during the rest of the week. We would be issued recruit officer uniforms, which would be mandatory attire in all subsequent classes, but should purchase our own boots (black, at least six inches high), a "garrison belt," and four black leather belt keepers, whatever those were, each to be adorned with two brass snaps.

We were to refer to all instructors and academy staff as sir or ma'am, or by their title and surname, and were required to greet them if they passed us in the hallways or entered the classroom; we were to raise our hands and wait to be recognized prior to speaking in class; we were to rise from our seats whenever an instructor or other official entered the room, and remain standing until told to sit. We were not permitted to step onto the rectangular rug bearing the MPD seal in the annex lobby—it lay below photos of MPD officers who had died in the line of duty, and as new recruits, we were unworthy to set foot on it. Instead, we were to walk carefully around the edges. We would be expected to be present and on time for all classes; tardiness or unexcused absences would be cause for dismissal.

We would take numerous exams, and would have to achieve a score of 70 percent or higher on each exam, as well as on each substantive subtopic being tested. Good note-taking skills would be required for success; to that end, we should always come to class with notebooks and pens, but we were to use only pens containing black ink, blue ink being prohibited by MPD.

We were informed that along with the career recruit class that had also just started at the academy, we were the first group to have the benefit of the academy's new curriculum, which would be scenario-based and, we were assured, a great improvement over the old curriculum. (There was no textbook and, at first, no handouts or assigned readings; the new curriculum, it transpired, was being prepared week by week. None of our instructors had seen the lesson plans before, and occasionally our class went too fast and ran out of curriculum, causing temporary training lulls.)

Our first lesson covered the history of policing, from which I gleaned the following:

First there was the Code of Hammurabi (PowerPoint slide: Babylonian stele showing Hammurabi handing a scroll to a minion). "If a man destroys the eye of another man, they shall destroy his eye. If one breaks a man's bone, they shall break his bone." Moral: people have had laws for a long time. But Hammurabi forgot to assign anyone to enforce the law, an oversight corrected by Augustus Caesar, who created the Praetorian Guard (PowerPoint slide: Roman holding spear). Later, the emperor Justinian re-formed Roman law and established the right to a fair trial.

Unfortunately, Rome fell. But then King Alfred reigned, and did something important but not specified in the lesson (PowerPoint slide: King Alfred). Later, each English shire had a chief called a reeve, and the shire reeves collected taxes, which is why today we have people called sheriffs. Then there was King Charles, who made use of the Court of the Star Chamber, which no one liked, so he was beheaded by Oliver Cromwell. Charles II, reflecting on his father's fate, signed the Habeas Corpus Act, requiring law enforcement officials to persuade a judge of the validity of arrests and launching the modern era of law (PowerPoint slide: Charles II on throne).

By this time, England had colonies in North America. The colonies imported English law to the New World, then fought the Revolutionary War and became independent. Then as now, it was dangerous to be a police officer. In 1791, New York sheriff Cornelius Hogeboom became the first law enforcement officer in the new American republic to be killed in the line of duty; while serving a "'writ of ejectment' to move squatters off a parcel of land . . . he was ambushed, shot, and killed by a group of men disguised as Indians" (PowerPoint slide: gravestone of Cornelius Hogeboom).

This was one of the more tendentious oversimplifications in a lesson full of tendentious oversimplifications. In 1791, upstate New York was essentially the Wild West, and land ownership in the region was frequently ambiguous and constantly disputed. Legal and political skirmishing over control of land on what was then the frontier of the expanding young nation continued for decades, and in many cases turned violent. Much of the time, the interests of wealthy gentry were pitted against those of small farmers. It was in this context that Sheriff Cornelius Hogeboom met his end in the town of Hillsdale.

After the death of wealthy landowner John Van Rensselaer, Rensselaer's son-in-law Philip Schuyler sought Sheriff Hogeboom's help in evicting some farmers who had settled on land that Schuyler considered part of his wife's rightful inheritance. Schuyler went to court and obtained a writ of ejection ordering farmer John Arnold to leave his land, but when Sheriff Hogeboom arrived to oversee the ejection and the forced sale of John Arnold's personal property, the sheriff and his party were set upon by seventeen men "painted and in Indian dress," some with their faces "blacked."

The *Albany Gazette* reported on subsequent events: the "companions of the sheriff desired him to spur his horse or they would all be shot; to which [Hogeboom] replied that he was vested with the law, and they should never find him a coward." At this, one of the supposed Indians "leveled his piece, and lodged a ball in the heart of the sheriff; upon which [Hogeboom] said, 'Brother, I am a dead man!' fell from his horse, and expired." The farmer John Arnold and several others were subsequently arrested and tried for Hogeboom's murder, but to the great consternation of the landowning elites, local juries acquitted them all.

Thus the first law enforcement death in the United States—like so many that came later—involved complex elements of race and arose out of conflict between the haves and the have-nots.

None of this made it into the Metropolitan Police Academy's history of policing. Instead, Reserve Recruit Class 2016-01 moved briskly from Sheriff Hogeboom's death to Sir Robert Peel and his London "bobbies" (Power-Point slide: a portrait of a London police officer, circa 1850), and thence to the reforms of Chief August Vollmer by way of Tammany Hall. The police corruption endemic in the era of machine politics was replaced with professionalism, and police call boxes were replaced with portable radios.

In the 1960s, the civil rights movement began, Martin Luther King Jr. was shot, and there were riots in numerous American cities. Subsequently, police departments diversified. Rodney King was beaten. The Justice

Department investigated many police departments. Reforms ensued. Later, the 9/11 attacks "provided a clear example of what modern policing can be at its best," and placed terror prevention "at the forefront of modern policing, especially here in the nation's capital."

Our instructor concluded "The History of Policing" by speed reading out loud from the end of his lesson plan: "We have covered almost four thousand years of history over the course of this lesson. As we've seen, police work has been constantly changing and evolving and will continue to do so over the course of your careers."

Winded, he looked up at us with palpable relief. "Any questions?"

No one had questions; the whirlwind tour of four thousand years of law enforcement history had left all sixteen members of Reserve Recruit Class 2016-01 numb and bewildered. I was still wondering how King Alfred fit into the picture.

In any case, I had pledged to myself that I was going to keep my mouth shut. My goal, I had decided, was to be as invisible as possible. I was not going to act like a law professor, a journalist, or an ACLU member. I was not going to act like a smart-ass. Insofar as possible, I was determined to act like a model recruit: I would be respectful, obedient, and dull. I would strive to perform solidly on all exams, while eschewing academic excellence.

Good grades always came easily to me, but by the end of elementary school I had figured out that no one likes kids with straight A's. By the time I started high school in 1985, I had learned to throw in a few egregiously awful grades to balance out the excessively high ones, and to add a small amount of bad behavior to my generally straitlaced existence. I was never much of a drinker, but I raided my parents' liquor cabinet and marijuana stash so I could show up at the occasional high school party with an illicit offering. From time to time, I skipped school, just to show I wasn't a goody-goody. At some point, protective coloration became habit: by 1987, I had become what DC law calls a "habitual truant," ultimately missing more than half the school days during my final year of high school. I'd sleep until noon or one, sometimes making it to school at three for sports or drama practice, but mostly I just stayed home all day, sleeping or reading. School officials left puzzled phone messages on our answering machine. After a while their tone became stern, then angry, warning that I was jeopardizing my chances of graduating. I deleted the messages.

In hindsight, I was depressed. Things at home were falling apart. My mother and stepfather's marriage had grown tense and angry, and my mother was struggling with back pain that sometimes kept her in bed for days at a time. My stepfather worked long hours as a union organizer; at home, he paced around, muttering curses, or planted himself in front of the television with a sheaf of papers on his lap. My brother, Ben, now fourteen, joined him most evenings in front of the TV, where together they formed an impenetrable male wall of silence, responding to my occasional interjections with indifferent grunts. My mother's public speaking career had taken off and she was away from home more and more. When she wasn't traveling or confined to bed with back pain, she buried herself in her writing, disappearing all day into her office in the basement. She didn't wake me in the mornings to tell me to go to school, and if we happened to encounter each other in the kitchen early in the afternoon, she taking a quick lunch break and I eating a late breakfast, she always seemed surprised to discover that I was still home.

This was the eighties, before the term "helicopter parent" was coined, and no one was talking about adolescent anxiety and depression. No one asked me if something was wrong, and it didn't occur to me to tell anyone how miserable I was, or to ask my mother or brother or stepfather if they were miserable too. None of us had the right vocabulary for such a conversation. We could all talk with wit and eloquence about politics, history, or philosophy when the occasion seemed to demand it, but we didn't know how to talk to one another.

My erratic grades and the increasingly menacing calls from school officials upset my father, who warned me about the importance of self-discipline. My mother took the opposite line: when school officials finally called a meeting to discuss my diminishing odds of graduating, she nearly sabotaged my father's campaign to persuade the school that my chronic absences stemmed from some sort of debilitating but undiagnosable ailment by tartly informing the principal that *her* daughter had "*better* things to do than waste time at your school." But I had already gotten an acceptance letter from Harvard, and in the end—after some well-timed musings from my father about what the local media might say if a Harvard-bound student with an obscure but challenging health problem was kicked out for poor attendance—the principal decided it was simpler to delete the "no credit" notations from my transcript and wave me off to Cambridge.

My mother and stepfather drove me to college a few months later. Strolling through Harvard Yard in a shiny satin Teamsters jacket, my mother kept up a stream of commentary on the pretentiousness, corruption, and general worthlessness of elite Ivy League institutions. She insisted that we all visit the office of the Harvard Union of Clerical and Technical Workers, which was then locked in a bitter struggle with the university over unionization, and assured the union's president, Kris Rondeau, that her daughter was eager to support the workers' struggle. I was resentful and embarrassed. But a few days after my mother and Gary left, I found my way back to the union office and asked how I could help.

Freed from the miasma of depression and anger hanging over our home,

I pulled out of my funk, but I still struggled to balance being my mother's daughter with becoming my own separate self. How do you rebel against a rebel? I marched with union workers, demanded that the university divest from apartheid South Africa, and picketed Harvard's all-male finals clubs. But when it came to romance, I ignored the earnest campus activists and went off instead with prep school boys, self-declared future investment bankers, and ROTC cadets. I wanted their acceptance and admiration; I wanted to tell them to go fuck themselves.

Unsurprisingly, few of these relationships lasted long. But this was okay, I told myself. I was infiltrating.

You could say I was struggling to find myself, though this has always struck me as a strange formulation—not only because the notion of the "self" is an odd construct, but because when we say "I want to find myself," usually we mean exactly the opposite: we really want to escape from our muddled, unsatisfying selves and become some other, better kind of self. The kind of self who goes to art galleries and listens to classical music, or does push-ups and tracks down serial killers. The kind of self who knows how to have honest conversations with the people they love.

In 1988, during my sophomore year in college, I stumbled onto a new ambition: I wanted to go to medical school. If I became a doctor, I thought, I could help people in direct, immediate, and uncomplicated ways, with no need for picket lines or internecine quarrels about socialist-feminist theory. Relieved to have come up with a postcollege plan, I enrolled in pre-med courses and called my mother to share the news.

"So, I figured out what I want to do after college. I want to go to medical school and become a doctor."

Long silence.

Finally: "A doctor?"

I was unnerved, but repeated, "Yes, a doctor."

More silence.

Then: "Anyone can be a doctor."

"Right. So, I could be a doctor."

"But doctors are dumb."

I had forgotten that my mother, who had a PhD in cellular biology, had started her writing career with several books on the flaws and follies of the American medical profession. There was *The American Health Empire: Power, Profits and Politics*, which she coauthored with my father, John Ehrenreich, and published in 1971, along with several feminist critiques of the medical profession, including *Complaints and Disorders: The Sexual Politics of Sickness*, published in 1973, and *For Her Own Good: Two Centuries of the Experts' Advice to Women*, published in 1978, both coauthored with my godmother Deirdre English. All in all, my mother didn't think much of doctors.

"Doctors are dumb? So, I'd be a smart doctor," I countered.

I could feel my mother's consternation through the phone line. "But— Rosa, you need to do something *special*. You could write brilliant novels. Or lead great movements for social change."

I don't remember how the call ended, but I do remember my sense of pained frustration. I yearned for my mother's approval, and at some other time, I might have been flattered that she thought so highly of my potential. But right then, I just felt burdened. What if I didn't *want* to do something special? What if I couldn't? What if I just wanted to be ordinary, like the blue-collar parents of my childhood friends?

Still, I dropped the pre-med courses.

I wanted to be an ordinary police recruit too. Or at least as ordinary as possible, given my gender, age, and day job. As one of only two women in my academy class, I couldn't exactly blend in with the crowd, but I promised myself that I could, and would, keep quiet about the lacunae and inadequacies of the recruit instructional materials. I didn't yet know much about the Metropolitan Police Academy or my classmates, but I was fairly sure that launching into a disquisition on the history of policing and class conflict in the early American republic would not lead to being voted most likely to succeed. So I nodded attentively at the end of the history lecture and wrote "KING ALFRED" in my notebook.

During our next session, we were issued khaki recruit uniforms. I hadn't worn a uniform since my brief membership in the Brownies as a seven-year-old (a membership terminated a few weeks later for nonpayment of dues, which I justified by arguing, to my mother's delight, that I preferred to try to integrate the Cub Scouts, anyway). I found I didn't much care for the recruit uniform. In fact, it bore a passing resemblance to my long-ago Brownie uniform, being similarly mud-hued and shapeless. The uniforms were supposedly unisex, which meant, in practice, designed for male bodies. Pants that fit around the hips pooled at my ankles and gapped at my waist; shirts that fit around the waist were too tight at the bust.

"We had a guy in a reserve class here a few years ago," one of the instructors observed as we paraded out of the gym locker room in our ill-fitting khakis. "When he realized he was going to have to actually wear a uniform, he up and quit. Can you believe that?"

Yes, I could. But in my new role as model recruit, I refrained from comment.

Although we worked our way through the same curriculum as the career recruits who filled the academy's classrooms during the day, the majority of our instructors were reserve officers themselves, rather than full-time academy staff. While many had been reserve officers for years or even decades, they had day jobs as lawyers, engineers, web designers, and, of course, "consultants," and with a handful of exceptions, they had little interest in the hazing and paramilitary discipline that pervaded the police academy experience for career recruits. We wore the same uniform as the career recruits, but did far fewer push-ups, and received only a desultory introduction to drill and formation.

"It's pointless," our instructor declared. "And you don't have to be good at it, because it's completely irrelevant to anything you will ever do as a police officer, but you need to learn it just well enough to avoid embarrassing the reserve corps during your graduation ceremony, because you're going to have to march alongside the career recruits." I positioned myself between two former marines and parroted everything they did. I was always half a beat behind, but the instructor declared my marching marginally acceptable, and we moved on.

Exams at the academy were challenging only insofar as the questions often appeared to have been written by people determined to win a prize for "most bizarre multiple choice questions." Occasionally, I suspected the exam writers of having a little fun at our expense:

> Q. *The city's emergency shelter for women who are victims of domestic violence is called:*
>
> A. My Brother's House
> B. My Sister's Place
> C. The Abusers' Place
> D. The White House

We learned to write police reports. At first, I was scolded for offering too much dialogue and detail. "This isn't *War and Peace*," the instructor admonished. "The more you write, the more likely you are to say something that gets you into trouble. Less is more." Initially, I also failed to master the passive voice. With practice, however, I developed what I considered a not-insignificant talent for the language of police bureaucratese:

On the above-listed date and time, the aforementioned officers were dispatched to the listed location to investigate a report
of a robbery. Arriving on scene, officers were informed by Complainant that his wallet had been stolen by a person unknown to
him, but described by Complainant as a male of dark complex-
ion but unknown height and build, wearing jeans and a dark-
colored hoodie. Complainant stated to officers that his wallet
was grabbed by Suspect from his jacket pocket, after which
Suspect fled on foot in an eastward direction. The area was
canvassed by officers but Suspect was not located.

We progressed through the new curriculum, covering, in rapid succes-
sion, topics ranging from ethics to the nature of the Metropolitan Police
Department's command structure and rules concerning the wearing of
uniforms. "Ironing a recruit BDU uniform is something a recruit officer
must know. . . . A recruit's uniform is required to be neatly pressed each
day they report to work. Additionally, the presence of being able to have
sharp creases [sic] is a key detail of a professional appearance."

Further:

Brilliantly shined boots are a hallmark of police uniforms.
They indicate devotion to duty and attention to the smallest
detail. Each polished boot represents hours of patient work.
During your time at the academy you are required to maintain boots that are polished to a luster on the toe and heel.
"Polished to a luster" means the toe and heel are shined so that
they will reflect light. In the most exceptional cases boots can
be shined so that a person's reflection may be seen in the
finish.

This was accompanied by instructions on boot polishing. ("The basic steps are: Create a workspace. Prepare the boot. Apply the base coat. Apply the polish coat. Shine. Finish.") Brass polishing received similar attention:

> When preparing to wear the new brass buckle of either the garrison belt or the Sam Browne, it must be shined to a luster. When new the buckle will have a clear coating that protects the finish during shipping. Recruits are required to remove this protective finish by placing the belt buckle in boiling water for a minimum of 10 minutes. **Be careful after the buckle is boiled. It must be allowed to cool to room temperature before it is touched.**

The ethics lesson was slightly less detailed than the guidance on the proper wearing of uniforms. After a brief foray into "sources of ethical standards," we were advised that "Making good ethical decisions requires a trained sensitivity to ethical issues and a practiced method for exploring the ethical aspects of a decision and weighing the considerations that should impact our choice of a course of action. Having a method for ethical decision making is absolutely essential. When practiced regularly, the method becomes so familiar that we work through it automatically without consulting the specific steps."

The method, as detailed in the PowerPoint slides displayed on the screen, was simple:

Make a Decision and Test it.

- Considering all these approaches, which option best addresses the situation?

- If I told someone I respect—or told a television audience [think CNN]—which option I have chosen, what would they say?

Act and Reflect:

- How can my decision be implemented with the greatest care and attention to the concerns of all stakeholders?
- How did my decision turn out and what have I learned from this specific situation?

The instructor summed it up: "Basically, don't do shit that will look bad on the news. Because if you do, you are roadkill."

Everyone laughed.

"No," he said, "I'm not kidding. You do something stupid, do not think for one moment that the department is going to stand by you. You make the department look bad, you will be hung out to dry."

We learned about prohibited weapons (machine guns, blackjacks, sandbags, slungshots, sand clubs, knuckles, and sawed-off shotguns) and were provided with instruction on the proper use of leg irons and flex cuffs. We studied lists of Schedule I Controlled Substances, were instructed on the appearances and odors of various drugs, and memorized "the nine MPD forms that allow sworn members to properly process and safeguard property." There was the Property Bag, the Property Tag, the Property Record, the Property Continuation Report, the Property Released on Scene form, the Property Release form, the Property Ownership/Classification card, the Property Receipt, and the Property Book. The Property Book, however:

[Is] not a form but an actual book located in each station. Officers are required to input information regarding any and all property taken into the custody of the department onto a page of the Property Book (PD82). This should be all of the same information from the Property Bag, or Property Tag. The Property Book Page and Book Number should then be recorded onto the Property Bag and Property Tag. The left side of the property book [*sic*] is for the recording officer when the officer comes into possession of the property. The right side of the property book [*sic*] is for station personnel and is used when returning property to the owner. Any corrections made to the Property Book must be made in red ink.

The Real Lesson

Situational awareness is vitally important. It is not unheard of for officers to receive a call for a seemingly innocuous incident, and because of the nature of the call let down their guard, only to discover too late the call was a set-up for an ambush in which they are injured or killed.

—*Metropolitan Police Academy Recruit Instructional Aid, "Basic Investigative Incident Reports"*

The chief lesson learned at the academy was this: Anyone can kill you at any time.

This topic wasn't listed on the formal lesson plan, but it was implicit in the stories the instructors told and the videos the recruits obsessively watched both in class and during break time. Week after week, we watched footage of cops getting attacked, injured, or killed. The world, it seemed, was a dangerous place for police officers; they were perpetually being stabbed, shot, punched, kicked, run over, drowned, poisoned by fentanyl, and bitten by savage dogs.

The instructors referred to these as "officer safety" videos. When we had breaks, or "got ahead of the curriculum" and had nothing else to do, which happened a lot, we huddled around iPads and laptops and watched more videos. Like kids bonding over their favorite YouTube clips, recruits sat around in the lunchroom and swapped suggestions of cops-in-trouble videos to watch.

"Oh, shit, man, you gotta see this one—this one guy, in Oklahoma or someplace, he gets, like, electrocuted. He goes to help this girl when a tree falls on her car, and there's, like, a downed power line, and he just gets . . . *fried.* Yeah, just google 'cop electrocuted,' it should come up. . . . That's it! Yeah, that one. . . . Aw, fuck, look at that. . . . The guy had no fucking chance. *Fuck.*"

There were, we learned, a thousand ways for cops to be hurt or killed. On our screens, unwitting police officers conducted traffic stops, only to be gunned down by meth-heads previously invisible behind illegally tinted rear windows. Officers rushed heedlessly toward disabled trucks and inhaled fatal levels of anhydrous ammonia. They stopped to assist stranded motorists and were struck by passing cars. They responded to domestic violence calls and were hit over the head by poker-wielding husbands. They were pushed off bridges by fleeing felons and drowned in raging river currents. They were overpowered by combative suspects who grabbed their service weapons and shot them in the head. They were beaten to death by crazed PCP addicts who kept right on pummeling them despite being repeatedly Tasered. They were poisoned, strangled, and pushed off the roofs of tall buildings.

The dead cops were all heroes. But, it was quietly intimated, they were also failures. Mostly, we were told, they died because they *weren't prepared.*

They let down their guard. They neglected to take appropriate tactical precautions. They decided their ballistic vest was hot and uncomfortable, so they left it home when they went on patrol, and *suffered the consequences when they were shot six times in the chest!* They sat in their cars, too busy scrolling through personal text messages on their phones to notice the deranged drug addict lurching toward them—*until it was too late and he shot them in the head!* They interviewed domestic violence suspects in their kitchens, forgetting that kitchens are full of weapons—*until the suspect grabbed a butcher knife from a drawer and stabbed them in the heart!* They told the meek-looking elderly driver to go ahead and retrieve his registration and insurance, figuring he was harmless—*until he shot them in the neck with the gun he pulled from the glove compartment!*

"There's no such thing as a routine call," the instructors told us. Even the most seemingly quotidian and benign situations could turn lethal in an instant. You had to approach every situation "tactically," which meant you had to always be thinking about the numerous ways in which you could be killed, and act in a manner calibrated to keep you from becoming a dead hero.

"Your top priority is scene safety," the instructors said.

This meant, among other things:

- Maintain situational awareness at all times.
- Turn off your lights and sirens when you're a few blocks away from your destination—don't give the bad guys advance warning of your arrival.
- Don't park directly in front of the address you're going to. Park down the street or on the next block.
- Back into parking spaces so you can get out fast if you have to.
- Peer into windows before you ring the bell or knock on the door—and stand off to the side after you knock, so you'll be out of the line of fire if someone comes out shooting or swinging.
- Make sure you know who's supposed to be in the house or the apartment before you walk in, so you won't be taken by surprise.
- Try to determine the locations of all the exits and entrances before you walk in.
- Never walk into an unknown situation with your notebook or flashlight in your strong hand—you need to be able to draw your weapon instantly if necessary.

- Always control the situation. Never let victims, witnesses, or suspects take control. *You* decide where they sit and stand and who you interview first.
- Always find out how many people are in the house and assess their threat level before you get pulled into a conversation or start a detailed interview.
- Don't let suspects wander around opening doors and drawers and reaching into bags and pockets.
- Don't interview potential suspects in the kitchen; kitchens contain too many potential weapons.
- Don't let potential suspects sit on sofas or in soft chairs; weapons are easily concealed between and behind cushions.
- Don't look at a potential suspect's eyes. Always watch their hands instead. ("Their eyes can't hurt you. Their hands will.")
- Never let anyone stand behind you.
- Keep all potential threats more than twenty feet away from you. At twenty feet, a knife-wielding suspect could run at you and stab you faster than you could draw, aim, and fire your weapon.
- Never waltz right up to the driver's window during a vehicle stop—you have no cover. Instead, stand just behind the driver, where you're protected by the car's B-pillar.
- Shine your patrol car's spotlights directly into the mirrors of cars when you conduct nighttime traffic stops, so the occupants will have trouble seeing you against the glare. If the driver complains, too bad. You need to be the one controlling the situation.

"A good day is a day you go home safe," the instructors told us.

Accordingly, Saturdays at the academy were devoted to physical training and defensive tactics. Our PT instructor was Sergeant Flanagan, a short, well-muscled Irishman in his fifties. I liked Flanagan, despite the fact that he immediately announced that we should come in each Saturday wearing white T-shirts with our surnames written in black marker on the back, rendering obsolete all the gray T-shirts we had previously been told to acquire.

We lined up in the gym, facing him, all in our new white T-shirts.

"Okay, the first thing you're going to learn is how you stand. Set your feet about shoulder-width apart, with your dominant leg back a little bit. Your toes on your dominant foot should be pointing right toward me, but the toes on the other foot are going to be angled away from me by about forty-five degrees. Knees loose; don't lock the knees. Now you're going to clasp your hands in front of you, a little bit above waist level. No, Lowrey, what are you doing? Aren't you supposed to be some kind of rocket scientist? Don't weave your fingers together like you're doing 'Here is the church, here is the steeple.' Just keep your hands loose!

"Okay, if you're right-handed, keep your hands a little to the right of where your belt buckle would be if you were wearing a belt. If you're left-handed, keep your hands a little to the left. If you don't know if you're right-handed or left-handed, I can't help you."

Sergeant Flanagan looked us over. Several of us were having trouble getting our feet at the correct angles and placing our hands at the correct height, and he had to walk around and reposition us. Finally, he got us all to stand in more or less the same posture.

"This is what we call the 'interview stance.' This is how you're going to stand when you're talking to someone. Okay. Why do we stand this way?"

Wentz, who was somehow managing to maintain the interview stance while simultaneously creating the impression of a guy sitting with his feet propped up on a coffee table and a beer in his hand, was the only one to volunteer an answer.

"Because this way you're ready to do whatever you need to do. You're in a stable position. If you're facing someone and you're flat-footed, they can push you over." Wentz stifled a yawn.

Flanagan gave him a hard look. "Right. What else?"

"Um, since your dominant foot is at a bit of an angle, it's easier to turn and run if you have to?" offered Lowrey.

"No! No. Lowrey, you're a cop. For Christ's sake! You are *not* going to turn and run away."

Lowrey looked crestfallen.

Wentz saved him by jumping in again. "This stance keeps your weapon angled away from the person you're interviewing, so he can't easily make a grab for it, and it keeps your strong hand near your weapon, so you can access it quickly if you need to."

"Yes!" Flanagan said. "The goal is to position yourself so you can adapt quickly if things go bad. This is also why you're *not* going to lace your fingers together, Lowrey."

Lowrey carefully unlaced his fingers.

"You don't want your fingers all tangled up," Flanagan explained. "You want to be ready to grab your tools if you have to, and you want your hands where you can move them up fast to protect your face if someone takes a swing at you. Okay. This is the interview stance. Everyone got that? Good. Now we're going to learn the combat stance.

"The dominant foot moves back. You're going to lean forward, weight balanced on both feet, and you're going to blade your body some more. When your body is bladed, you're not such a nice, fat, juicy target for the bad guy in front of you. Right? And then, you're going to bring your hands up to protect your face.

"No, not your belly button, Gregson, your face! Your head! Because your head is where you keep your brain, *if* you happen to have one."

Gregson's ruddy face got redder, but he moved his hands up.

"Your head is your computer, Gregson. You have to protect it from harm.

Somebody tries to punch it, you want your arms up where you can block the punch, and hit back if you have to.

"Got it? Okay, everyone get into the combat stance."

We all shuffled into position and raised our hands.

"Now here's what we're going to say when we're in the combat stance. We're going say, *'Back down!'* Come on. Say it!"

There was a muted chorus of "Back down!" but no one put much enthusiasm into it. It felt silly to order the empty air in front of us to back down.

"No! No!" Flanagan wasn't happy.

"You need to use your command voice here, people. Not 'Please, sir, kindly back down, if you would.' You're a police officer! Say it like you mean it. *'Back down!'"*

"*Back down!*" we shouted.

"Better. Much better. Okay, let's put it together now. We're going to practice going from our interview stance to our combat stance, and every time we go into the combat stance, I want to hear you shout, 'Back down!' nice and loud and firm.

"Okay, let's go. Interview stance!"

We moved to the interview stance.

"Combat stance!"

We rushed into our combat stances, shouting, "Back down!" Lowrey, next to me, got his feet mixed up and almost fell over.

"You've got to work on that left foot/right foot thing, Lowrey."

Lowrey offered Flanagan a sheepish smile and untangled himself. I patted him on the shoulder.

This seemed like a silly game. In real life, I couldn't imagine myself shouting "Back down!" at someone. Maybe "Stop!" or "Don't move!" or even "Hey, cut that shit out!" But not "Back down!"

We repeated the exercise for the next few minutes, until Sergeant

Flanagan declared himself provisionally satisfied with our combat stances and our command voices.

As spring turned to summer, Reserve Recruit Class 2016-01 progressed from relearning how to walk ("You are never, ever going to turn your back on a suspect! You need to move away from a suspect, you're going to take a step *sideways* and back, never straight back, or you'll lose your balance and fall on your ass!") to learning to fight and use "control holds" and "pain compliance" measures. We practiced on punching bags, rubber dummies, and one another, learning kicks, palm strikes, and elbow strikes. We learned how to break someone's finger grip and how to twist an arm back painfully to force a bad guy into compliance.

Chokeholds were forbidden by MPD. Too many people placed in a chokehold ended up dead. "Like Eric Garner, in New York. So no chokeholds. Prohibited, verboten," said Flanagan.

Wentz, the former NYPD cop, broke in. "That's idiotic. Properly used, chokeholds are perfectly safe. It's just a training issue. People just don't understand how to use them. Eric Garner didn't die because he was put in a chokehold. He died because of positional asphyxia."

Flanagan was unmoved. "Technically, yes. But what everybody and their cousin saw on TV was Eric Garner being choked. We'll talk about positional asphyxia in a minute, but for now, just remember, no chokeholds. The policy is what the policy is."

"Better to be judged by twelve than carried by six," countered Wentz.

Flanagan was getting impatient. "Look, Wentz, you find yourself in an actual life-or-death situation and you have to grab someone around the neck to keep him from killing you? I'm not going to tell you not to do that. If it's life or death, you do what you have to do. But the department's policy is, no chokeholds. So here in MPD, we don't use chokeholds just because someone's a pain in the ass and resists cuffing. No chokeholds. Okay?"

We moved on to discuss positional asphyxia. Restraining a subject by putting your knee or foot on his back while he lay facedown was also prohibited by department policy, because being prone for an extended period, particularly with weight on the back, could kill someone, especially if the subject happened to have a weak heart or other medical issues.

"You're struggling with a suspect, it's a fight, you end up on top of him and his face is in the dirt? It happens."

I thought about Mark and the fight at the school bus stop.

"But you don't stay in that position," Flanagan went on. "You get the guy under control and you get off him, fast, because the longer he's facedown, the more risk there is." (Four years later, George Floyd's death became an infamous and tragic case in point).

Wentz looked like he was about to argue.

"It's the same as chokeholds," said Flanagan. "Policy says no. You need to understand that. But if it's life or death? If you're all alone, and you can't get the cuffs onto his wrists, and the guy weighs three hundred pounds, and the second you shift your weight off his back he's going to throttle you? Well, you have a right to go home at the end of the day."

Wentz nodded, satisfied by this concession.

"Just be aware," Flanagan added, "you're still going to have to explain why you violated department policy."

This tension was articulated over and over, in the academy and, later, out on the streets. Cops had two messages drilled into them.

On the one hand: You were in constant danger. Any situation, no matter how seemingly low risk, could turn deadly in an instant, and you had to always be ready to do whatever it took to protect yourself.

On the other hand: You had to abide by MPD policies, because if you deviated from them in a way that made the department look bad, you would be hung out to dry. The department would not give you the benefit of the doubt. You'd be suspended, fired, or prosecuted in a millisecond.

Even for us reserve recruits, this created a constant gnawing feeling of vulnerability. Soon, we'd be sent out to the streets, where, according to our instructors, we would find ourselves trapped between a hostile public, full of people eager to hurt or kill us, and a hostile departmental bureaucracy, eager to throw us to the wolves if required by PR considerations.

Every week or two throughout our six months at the academy, we were issued another piece of equipment. It came in dribs and drabs rather than all at once, and in no particular order. Equipment showed up when it showed up. We got our Sam Browne belts, and I finally had a use for the four brass-snapped belt keepers I had been ordered to acquire. We received leather magazine pouches and hard plastic holsters to attach to our duty belts, though we wouldn't receive guns or ammunition until we finished firearms training. One day, radios appeared as well, and we signed forms acknowledging that we had just been handed something very expensive. ("These cost thousands of bucks to replace, and that will be paid from your own pocket if you're the stupid fuck who leaves yours in the McDonald's restroom.") We were issued oleoresin capsicum (OC) spray, the stronger, law enforcement version of self-defense pepper spray, and received our ASP brand telescoping metal batons. We were fitted for ballistic vests, which we were ordered to wear at all times while in uniform.

As time passed, getting dressed for classes at the academy became increasingly challenging. MPD collar pins and name tags had to be positioned correctly, and the leather duty belt—the Sam Browne—was so heavy and stiff, it was difficult to fasten. It often took ten minutes or more to get everything properly attached. The snaps on my belt keepers generally either refused to snap closed or would close but then instantly pop open again.

The radio had microphone wire that had to be threaded through a shoulder epaulette and then clipped to your shirt.

The whole getup was uncomfortable, from the poorly fitting uniform to the heavy belt, now weighed down by metal and plastic objects that poked unpleasantly into my thighs and waist. I soon found myself starting to walk with what I had always thought of as "cop swagger," a rolling gait with legs set a little apart and arms akimbo. Cop swagger, it turned out, had nothing to do with attitude. It was involuntary; as our belts got loaded up with equipment, a normal walk became impossible. You couldn't let your arms fall naturally at your sides; the holster, radio, and baton all got in the way. You had to keep your elbows raised and wider than usual.

The worst thing, for women, was the difficulty in getting out of the duty belt once it was on. I avoided drinking liquids before or during classes, because a full bladder meant wrestling everything off and then on again.

My classmates started showing up with non-issued items. By week six, Gregson, the red-faced health care CEO, looked like he was on a SWAT team: his belt was adorned with pouches for rubber gloves and an extra set of cuffs he had purchased himself, and he had added big Velcro patches that read "POLICE" to the back of his ballistic vest and to the side of his spanking-new black patrol bag. Wentz showed up with black leather gloves that had hard plastic knuckles and a Leatherman multi-tool attached to his belt. Woodson had a black rescue knife with a glass breaker and a seat belt cutter, and Ramos appeared with a clear plastic Secret Service–style earpiece for his radio and a clip-on infrared flashlight for his lapel. Soon, we all started acquiring these little extras. No one ever explained what you were supposed to buy, and it wasn't written down anywhere. Recruits absorbed it through osmosis.

I began to develop opinions on surprising matters. Belt keepers: Leather or nylon? (Nylon.) Snaps or Velcro? (Velcro.) Boot blousers, yea or nay?

(Yea.) Holster: Best worn as issued, or best to purchase extra spacers so the holster is angled slightly away from the hip? (For most women, best with extra spacers; otherwise, the curve of the hip angles the holster too far inward, and extracting the gun becomes awkward.)

I couldn't suppress some enthusiasm for all the gear. When my children were babies, I always had the best-stocked diaper bag. I carried extra diapers, clothes, wipes, toys, snacks, bottles, medicine, picture books, paper, crayons, you name it. Now I had another opportunity to over-prepare.

I loaded up my patrol bag with everything I might need to survive a weeklong siege: protein bars and water bottles, insect repellent and disinfectant wipes, a multi-tool, a rescue knife, permanent markers in three colors, plastic baggies for evidence, a parachute cord bracelet in case I needed rope, a compass (I could not imagine many situations in DC that would require a compass, but it came free with the parachute cord bracelet, so I tucked it into my patrol bag in case I got lost in Rock Creek Park), a magnifying glass (if it was good enough for Sherlock Holmes, it was good enough for me), waterproof matches, a reflective vest for traffic control, a whistle (same), extra radio batteries, extra phone chargers, a small camping towel, sunglasses, a small clip-on flashlight, an MPD baseball cap, a wool MPD beanie, extra nitrile gloves, hand sanitizer, hand warmers, extra socks, a warm fleece, Band-Aids, first aid gear, an extra tourniquet, extra belt keepers, notebooks, pens, radio earpieces, nameplates, collar pins, and business cards. Also a clipboard, and a folder containing MPD forms, maps, a list of fines for various vehicular offenses, and a dozen other reference materials I never had time to consult during patrol shifts.

As long as I could keep my patrol bag with me at all times, I was prepared to survive in the woods, confront an active shooter, or dig myself out after an earthquake. In my heart, I knew I'd never need most of this stuff, but I liked having it.

Most of our gear was issued to us at the academy. Occasionally we were told to report to the department's equipment and supply office to pick something up. This wasn't too onerous, but the one thing we quickly learned to avoid at all costs was a trip to Muscatello's.

Jimmie Muscatello's Washington Uniform Center was the only private vendor contracted to provide uniforms to MPD and other DC city agencies, from Metrobus drivers to school security guards, and it was a small corner of purgatory. Muscatello's always had a line, whether you arrived when they opened at eight a.m., or just before four p.m., when they closed. You couldn't simply pick out the items you needed from racks or shelves; almost everything was hidden in inaccessible storerooms, and at any given time half the customers needed to be measured for clothing that would be tailored to fit. People hoping to buy a single T-shirt or baseball cap still had to wait in line behind those who needed to be measured for a whole new uniform. And the line at Muscatello's was like that at a Cold War–era Soviet grocery. You'd stand in one place for a full hour, watching as various employees, all of whom seemed to be from India or Bangladesh, had leisurely chats with one another or fussed endlessly around a single customer, checking and rechecking his inseam while the other thirty people in the queue muttered and shifted mutinously from foot to foot.

It was like the Hunger Games: if you stuck it out long enough, the weaker contestants would break. Some would rush the counter in a vain effort to gain recognition. Once, I heard an irate Metrobus driver demand to speak to "Mr. Muscatello." This tactic never succeeded, as Mr. Muscatello, had he ever existed, had long since moved to a retirement home or cemetery somewhere far away, and rushing the counter merely caused the staff to avoid eye contact or feign an inability to speak English. More often, the weak would simply give up and make for the exits, cursing about how they had just wasted their whole goddamn lunch break standing in line for nothing. If you were willing to remain standing for two or three full hours, you could usually count on outlasting everyone else in line, and eventually you would be having your inseam measured and remeasured by the staff, who rewarded your perseverance and survival with delighted smiles and enthusiastic approval of your sartorial choices. ("Yes, very fine, very dignified police lady; this midnight blue dress blazer most becoming for police lady, very slimming.")

I usually entertained myself while waiting in line by reading old Yelp and Google reviews of Muscatello's:

"THIS IS THE ABSOLUTE WORST UNIFORM STORE EVER."

"IT'S LIKE SLOW TORTURE."

"CUSTOMER SERVICE IS THE TWILIGHT ZONE."

"GARBAGE!"

"I HAVE VOWED TO LET AS MANY PEOPLE KNOW ABOUT THE HORRIBLE SERVICE I RECEIVED AS POSSIBLE. MUSCATELLO'S SUCKS."

"LONG ASS LINES AND HIGH ASS PRICES. WELL ACTUALLY ALL MY EQUIPMENT IS FREE BUT THEM LONG ASS LINES ARE PAINFULLY ETCHED INTO MEMORY."

"THEY ARE PERFECT IF YOU ARE TRYING TO KILL TIME."

All in all, going to Muscatello's wasn't a rewarding experience, but going home wearing my uniform and all my gear was even worse. My younger daughter was inclined to goof around with the handcuffs and baton, which bothered me—these weren't toys, and policing wasn't a game, and I didn't want her to ever imagine it was. But I didn't want to burden her with the weight of my own ambivalence, so I let her run around handcuffing herself to various household objects.

My older daughter, fourteen at the time, declared my uniform ugly and found it as ridiculous and embarrassing as I had once found my mother's satin Teamsters jacket.

"Other kids' mothers take yoga classes if they want to have a hobby," she complained. "Why do you have to go to police school?"

When I was a kid, *my* mother never took yoga classes, I reminded her. She wrote books and marched on picket lines.

"Well," my daughter said, "Grandma's weird too."

Grandma, pressed into coming over to have dinner with the girls while I was out at "police school," didn't care to have picket lines and police training lumped together as indistinguishable forms of maternal madness. She kept up a running series of sour jokes: "Oh, don't worry, *officer*, you don't need to handcuff me to the sink; I promise I'll stay and help with the dishes, though I was thinking of taking the kids out for ice cream after dinner. But I didn't know how you'd feel about that, and I knew you might hit me with your baton if you didn't like it."

"I'm not going to hit anyone with anything," I snapped, though right then, I was tempted.

10-33

*Under the National Incident Management System (NIMS) many
jurisdictions, including the Metropolitan Police Department, are
transitioning to and using more "plain language" on the police
radio in place of using ten signals for communications. The
following are still being used throughout the Department and
will be practiced here throughout your training:*

    10-1   Unable Copy

    10-4   Acknowledgment used for a two-member unit

    10-99 Acknowledgment used for a one-member unit

    10-8   In-service (ready to handle a call for service)

    10-7   Out-of-service

    10-33 Officer in Trouble

      —MPD Recruit Instructional Aid, "Use of Police Radios"

I didn't like it that my mother looked at me like I was some kind of thug. I *wasn't* a thug. In law school, I had represented indigent people; as a human rights researcher, I had championed victims of political repression, torture, and genocide. And as a rule, I didn't hit people. I hadn't hit anyone in anger since that episode with Mark the bully, thirty-five years earlier.

Nonetheless, in the academy gym, we continued to spend hours learning how to hurt people under Sergeant Flanagan's watchful eye. We learned elbow strikes and palm strikes and the best places to kick someone if you wanted them to fall to the ground. We practiced wrist locks and arm locks—"control holds" designed to cause just enough pain to "induce compliance" in combative subjects. We whacked one another with foam batons, and slammed punching bags and dummies with our expandable metal batons, learning the "weapons strike," the "clearance strike," and the "straight strike." Baton strikes were to be delivered to the arms, torso, and legs, never to the head, neck, spine, sternum, or groin, but we were instructed to "strike as hard as possible as long as the threat continues."

We practiced weapon-retention skills—we'd grab at the red training gun in someone else's holster, and he'd have to try to grab the gun back.

We pointed our training guns at one another. "Bang, bang!" we shouted.

"You guys know what a 10-33 is?" Flanagan asked.

Most of us did not.

"It's radio code for 'Emergency, officer in trouble,'" Wentz informed us.

Flanagan nodded. "That's right. It's the radio code for an emergency. Someone pulls a gun on you, or starts beating you, or you're surrounded by a big scary group of guys on PCP and they start moving closer and telling you they're going to tear you limb from limb, you're going to push that big orange emergency button on your radio and shout, '10-33, 10-33!'

"Pushing that orange button knocks everyone else off the air, so your transmission takes priority. When you say, '10-33,' every officer in your district is going to drop whatever else they're doing and go Code 1 to your location to bail your ass out. So, if your life or the life of another officer is in imminent danger, you get on that radio, hit that orange button, and say, '10-33.' Got it?"

We got it.

"Okay, you're going to say, '10-33,' and then what are you going to say?"

We all looked at one another.

"Um, 'I need help'?" suggested Lowrey.

Flanagan gave him a withering glance. "No, Mr. Rocket Scientist, you are not going to say, 'I need help.' Everyone already knows that, because you just hit your emergency button and said, '10-33.' What *else* are you going to say?"

"My location," said Wentz.

"Yes, *thank* you, Wentz. Lowrey, you are going to tell everyone where the fuck you *are*, because if you do not tell them where you are, no one can find you or help you! Got that?"

Lowrey looked dismayed. "Shouldn't the dispatcher already know that? Isn't there some kind of GPS in the radio?"

Flanagan rolled his eyes. "Are you going to trust your life to some piece of equipment that might or might not work, and a dispatcher who might or might not be doing her nails instead of monitoring the radio? I hope not. You better know exactly where you are, all the time, and you better get on the air and tell everyone.

"So, listen up, everyone. When you hear Lowrey come on the air and shout, '10-33!' you need to move, and move fast. You getting to your colleague fast could be the difference between life and death. Okay? So we're going to practice. Every now and then, when we're in the classroom or doing PT, I'm going to blow my whistle three times and shout, '10-33.' And when I do that, you are going to stop doing whatever it is that you're doing, and you are going to run—not walk, not jog, *run*—to the gatepost at the front of the academy, and touch that post.

"You can walk back, for all I care. But you'd better get there fast, because whoever gets to that post last is going to do it all over again. You need to get used to moving fast the second you hear '10-33.' And I don't want to hear you complain. When the career recruits run 10-33s, they have to run to the post and then run all the way around the whole academy parking lot too."

After that, running 10-33s became a routine part of our training. Flanagan would wait until we were all preoccupied with something else, then blow his whistle, and we'd all scramble up and sprint out to the gatepost.

I wasn't particularly good at any of this, but for the most part, I wasn't bad enough to be a problem child, either. Sergeant Flanagan seemed to approve of me. With their military backgrounds, most of my classmates breezed through the physical training and defensive tactics lessons. Smith, the young coast guard officer and the only other woman in the group, was particularly impressive. She could do one-armed pull-ups, and punched out more push-ups than most of the men. I was nowhere near as fit, but I mostly managed to keep up with the group. Still, as time went on, I grew more and more anxious about the PT test we would all have to take in order to graduate. It consisted of sit-ups, push-ups, a sprint, and a 1.5-mile run.

The passing threshold varied by age and gender, and when we took an early practice test to establish our baseline, I had no trouble getting a passing score on the sit-ups, push-ups, and the sprint. On the 1.5-mile run, however, I struggled, huffing and puffing my way around the track, legs and lungs burning. I was much too slow. I had to get serious about running, or I wouldn't pass when the time came for the real test.

Despite my determination not to complain, I resented the PT test. The 1.5-mile run struck me as particularly pointless. Sprinting made sense—you might have to chase a suspect, or respond to a genuine 10-33. But no suspect was going to lead you on a 1.5-mile run around the city. You'd either catch him or lose him in the first few hundred yards, and losing him was far more likely, since suspects tended to be fit young men in athletic shoes and comfortable clothes, while cops—even the young, fit ones—wore clunky boots and were weighed down by thirty pounds of uncomfortable, clanking equipment. Adding insult to injury, the PT test in the academy was the only one ever required; after graduation, MPD officers were free to grow as fat and slothful as they wanted.

Flanagan was too smart to waste his time questioning bureaucratic dictates. When I complained about the 1.5-mile run, he just shook his head. "Yeah, you'll probably never actually run that far. Me, I don't chase people anymore anyway. I'm too old. I stay in the car and leave the foot chases to the young guys."

Being a middle-aged lady law professor, I suggested tentatively that I too might leave the foot chases to the young guys.

Flanagan shook his head again. "You're missing the point here. The point of this isn't whether you're ever really going to run for a mile and a half on patrol. You're not. No one does that. The point is to make sure you build up some cardiovascular endurance. On average, it takes about three minutes for backup to arrive in an emergency. Maybe three minutes doesn't sound like a lot of time to you, but trust me, when someone's sitting on you and trying to pound your head into the pavement, it's forever. If you're all alone and you get into a fight, you need to be able to hang in there for three minutes without giving up and letting the bad guy win. And running's one way to build up your endurance."

So every other day, I laced up my running shoes and went out to the track at a nearby middle school. I ran and ran. I read dozens of internet articles on how to start running if you were a complete beginner, and did exactly what they advised. At first, I alternated between walking and running, and increased speed and distance only gradually.

Each week, I ran a little farther and a little faster. I started to think I'd pass the 1.5-mile run after all. But although I was getting faster and could now run the whole course without as much panting, I was in more pain with each passing week. Despite all my warm-ups and stretches, each week, more body parts started to hurt. My shins were covered in bruises. My knees swelled up. My hip joints hurt so much I could barely walk.

"This is not good," Flanagan said. He inspected me and eyed a scar on my swollen left knee. "Did you get that knee injured at some point?"

"A long time ago," I admitted. "I messed it up skiing."

Flanagan nodded. "Why don't you take a break from the running, and work on the exercise bike to get in some cardio while the rest of the group runs. See if your knee settles down."

Wentz, who had just had knee surgery himself, was also consigned to the exercise bikes in the academy gym.

"Don't worry about it," he told me as we pedaled side by side. "They're not going to stop us from graduating just because we can't run a mile and a half in whatever time it is."

I wanted to believe him. "You think?"

"Sure. They know this running shit is stupid. In New York we didn't even have to take a PT test at the academy. If running a mile and a half was actually job-related, everyone would have to retake the PT test every year, not just recruits. The truth is, cops don't really need to run. Maybe they'll make us do something else, like bike for the same amount of time to show we can do it without keeling over, but MPD's short on officers. They need us. And look at all the fat slobs out there on patrol. If they really cared about fitness they'd fire their lazy asses."

It was true that Flanagan didn't seem particularly troubled by the fact that neither Wentz nor I was running with the rest of the class. He reserved his wrath for Lowrey, who had a tendency to flop down on his back, panting, halfway through his sit-ups.

"He thinks Lowrey's not trying hard enough," Wentz observed. "Whereas he can see that whether you're running or not, you're willing to bust your butt."

I thought Lowrey was trying his best, and wished Flanagan would go easier on him. Lowrey was a good guy, just a little out of shape. I empathized. I was definitely busting my butt, though. I hurt all over. And I wasn't sure Wentz's view of the PT tests was correct. I had to find a way to run farther and faster without falling apart.

I went to a physical therapist, who analyzed my gait and put me to work with foam rollers and giant rubber bands. But I still hurt. I started getting scared. What if I couldn't do this? After all those fights with my mother, after memorizing all those property forms and weapons offenses and learning to shout, "Back down!" in a command voice, what if I blew it all because I couldn't manage the long-distance run?

Then it was time for firearms training.

The academy's firearms instructors, we were told, refused to work weekends or evenings, so everyone in our reserve recruit class would have to slot in with one of the career recruit classes for two weeks of daytime range training.

At the academy, the day began for the career recruits at six thirty a.m. and ended around three. "You need to arrive here by oh-six-hundred if you want to find a parking space," Flanagan warned. "And after that, you want to go right downstairs to the classroom next to the firing range and you want to *stay* there in that classroom, because the career recruits have drill and formation first thing in the morning. If you're standing around upstairs in a recruit uniform, one of the class officers is going to start screaming at you and try to put you into the formation."

He looked at our alarmed expressions and laughed. "Don't worry. If that happens just explain that you're a reserve recruit, just there for firearms training, and they'll lay off. But trust me, it's going to be a different world. You guys have no idea how easy you have it here, coming in the evenings and working with nice guys like me. Now you're going to see how the other half lives."

What Happens on the Range

*Deadly force [is] any use of force likely to cause death or serious
physical injury. The primary purpose of deadly force is to
neutralize a subject who poses an immediate threat of death
or serious injury to the member or others.*

— MPD General Order 901.07, "Use of Force"

Upstairs, the police academy's main building has sunlit classrooms, offices, a lunchroom, a cafeteria, and a gym. But go down two flights of stairs and you really are in a different world. It's windowless and dank, filled with the acrid smell of copper and lead, spent powder, and gun-cleaning oil.

"What happens on the range stays on the range," Officer Kowalski declared with a jovial smile. He had twenty-five of us in his classroom—twenty career recruits and five reserve recruits—ready to start firearms training, and he was warming up the crowd.

We all chuckled dutifully.

"Hey, did I fucking say something funny?" Kowalski hoisted his belt above his bulging belly and glared around the room. "I did not fucking say something funny."

Everyone instantly stopped chuckling.

"All right, okay," he relented. "Let's just do some introductions here. Name, where you from, what you did before this. If you just fuckin' sat around jerking off, do not tell me. I don't want you to share that. This is not a fucking college campus. This is not a place where we over*share*, snowflakes. Okay, you first, Creatine."

"Creatine" was a meaty-looking kid with a blond crew cut and the physique of a serious bodybuilder. He gave a slow, good-natured shrug. "My name's Graves, I'm from New Jersey, and I used to drive trucks, then I went back to school, and now I'm here."

"So, how many times you work out a day, Creatine?" demanded Kowalski.

"I try to work out three times a day," Graves said modestly.

"Fuck, okay! So on the range I'm gonna be standing behind you when the bullets start flying. Because your fuckin' giant hard muscles can stop bullets, right, Creatine? Ha ha no, dude, I'm just kidding you, man. Don't stop wearing your ballistic vest. But hey, maybe your fuckin' thick skull will stop bullets for real, right? Okay, next?"

Next were twin sisters of Serbian origin, Mirjana and Yasna. Kowalski dubbed them Marta and Sparta, and asked if they'd committed any war crimes lately.

After that was a young black guy from Louisiana, fresh out of the army. "Shit, Louisiana?" said Kowalski. "I used to know a guy from there. His name was, like, Gumbo or something. You people eat that shit there, right? Hey, you happen to know him? Big black dude called Gumbo?"

This went on.

"Anyone else here in the military?"

A young Hispanic guy raised his hand.

"What service?" asked Kowalski.

"Coast guard," answered the recruit.

"No, I mean the *real* military, not the fuckin' puddle pirates. Oh hey, man. Where'd you get that little tattoo on your bicep? Adams Morgan?

Tattoo Delight? Guy called Z? No fuckin' kidding! I got the exact same tattoo, except mine's on my dick, so it's a little bigger."

To the Indian American woman: "Sweetheart, I can't even fuckin' pronounce your name. No, sweetheart, I'm not gonna even try. What is it, like Kumaraswamy or something, or Mulligatawny? Isn't that another fuckin' soup, like gumbo? Listen Mulligatawny, you know how to cook that shit? You gonna cook us some soup?"

To the arson investigator: "Okay. Arson. Hey, Arson, you spend your time setting things on fire when you were a kid?"

I reluctantly copped to having gone to law school, and was dubbed Counselor. I was relieved. I'd gotten off lightly. Privately, I dubbed Kowalski "Lawsuit," as in "this guy is a hostile environment civil rights lawsuit waiting to happen."

Kowalski favored a stream-of-consciousness instructional style that often had little to do with the nominal topic of the class:

"Man, back when crime here was high, in the eighties and nineties, it was fun to be a cop. Now it's just these crappy little crimes. A woman calls us this one time, someone's taken thirty-seven cents out of her ashtray. I couldn't believe it—she wants me to dust for prints like we're on fuckin' CSI. I said, 'Lady, that crackhead is *gone*, your thirty-seven cents is *gone!*' She's still moaning and wailing about it, you know, 'Why you ain't *invest-igatin*',' and shit. I couldn't believe it. Thirty-seven cents! I started to curse her out, but we're not allowed to do that anymore.

"So, you gotta be careful out there. You know, sometimes you can't tell the chicks from the guys. This one time, I'm coming home from the beach, and I get pulled over by this Maryland state trooper, and I've got my badge out and I'm all like, 'Sorry, sir,' when I see that the trooper has a fucking bun. It's a fucking chick! She's a chick, but she's built like a goddamn *tree*. Like, she could fit two of you inside her uniform, Creatine. Anyway, so I switch over to 'Oh, so sorry, ma'am,' because I knew she could crush me if she just leaned against my car, her butt was so big . . .

"Anyway. These days you get these, you know, *trans* people and shit. Maybe she was actually a guy after all. I don't know. I don't want to know. But you gotta be careful out there, because if you're a dude and you're patting down some other dude and suddenly he's all like"—Kowalski went falsetto—" 'Oh, *excuse* me, officer, but I *identify* as *female*,' well guess what? You're fucked, man, and you gotta get on the radio and ask Marta and Sparta to come over and help you finish the fucking frisk, because *trans* people get to choose their fuckin' gender and choose which gender searches them.

"Hey. You guys think I'm fuckin' fat? It's okay, you won't hurt my feelings. I didn't use to be fat. What happened was, I got hurt trying to arrest this dude. You know that Starbucks by Dupont Circle? So this dude was just one of my regular crazy guys, he was always hanging out by the door to Starbucks bothering people and asking for money, and I was always telling him to move on and not be blocking the fucking door to Starbucks, because people need to have free access to their fucking soy skim caramel lattes. But one day he decides he doesn't *want* to move on, and finally I had to put my hands on him. Well, so he's this skinny little black guy, and this is Dupont Circle, right? So you know what *that* means. Hey, where's my little special ed child? Yeah, you, Creatine. So what does that *mean*, Creatine?"

Creatine looked blank.

"Fuck, Creatine, you need to go get a protein shake or something, man, you're fuckin' even dumber than usual. Don't say we don't hire the handicapped. Okay, come on, people, what does Dupont Circle mean? It means there's, like, a thousand rich white people with their fuckin' soy lattes in one hand and their fuckin' iPhones in the other and they're *all recording*. Because I'm struggling with this guy, just trying to get him into cuffs, but he's actually incredibly strong and he's kicking at me like crazy, with, like, steel-toed boots or something, and I feel something in my ankle go 'pop!' and it hurt like you would not believe, I was practically fucking crying.

"By now I'm pissed, and I'm thinking, man, if this was 7D I'd be beating on him. Used to be, you could use a neck restraint in a situation like that, which worked pretty good. But not these days. These days, no neck restraint, no chokehold, no tickee, no laundry, not allowed; you do that, you're gonna be the poster child of stupid, and the department's gonna throw you under the bus. So I am treating this fucking crazy dude like he's made of *glass*, but it doesn't matter, because all these Dupont Circle rich white assholes with their cell phones see is this big white cop roughing up this skinny little black dude, and I realize I just gotta arrest this guy quick and get the fuck out of there before I'm the next YouTube sensation. So, long story short, finally I get the guy cuffed but now my ankle's swelling up like a balloon. He fucking kicked it so hard he fractured it. And then I couldn't work out—not like you, Creatine, which is actually a fuckin' blessing—but anyway that's how I got so fucking fat."

We spent most of our first week of firearms training sitting in the classroom memorizing the parts of a Glock 17, MPD's primary duty weapon, and trying to avoid being singled out by Kowalski. At first we just studied blurry diagrams, labeling them appropriately. There was the extractor, the magazine floor plate, the slide stop lever. We repeated the Four Rules of Safe Firearms Handling in a chorus:

- Treat all firearms as if they are loaded.
- Point the muzzle in a safe direction.
- Keep your finger outside the trigger guard and off the trigger until you are ready to fire.
- Know your target and what is beyond it.

"Okay," said Kowalski. "So I'm just standing here, and suddenly I see Creatine reach to his waistband and it looks like he's starting to pull out a gun. What am I going to do?"

"Shoot him?" suggested Lowrey.

"Fuck no, Rocket Man! I shoot Creatine, and the bullet passes right through his big, empty head, and guess what it does when it comes out the back of his head?"

We all peered behind Creatine.

"It takes out Marta and Sparta, who are sitting right behind Creatine, that's what it does. I eliminated the threat from Creatine, which is good, but guess what? I accidentally also just fucking killed two innocent bystanders, and this is not going to look good on the Use of Force report I'm going to have to file. 'Know your target and what is *beyond* it.' If what is beyond your target is Marta and Sparta, or a busload of crippled orphans on their way to the natural history museum, don't shoot, assholes. Clear?"

Creatine didn't like this. "So, what are you supposed to do? Someone pulls a gun and since you can't shoot him without taking out someone behind him too, you just, what, let him shoot *you*?"

"Creatine, anyone ever explain the concept of taking cover to you? That's what you do. You pull out your gun, you aim it and shout, 'Drop the gun,' or 'Freeze, police!' or whatever other fucking cool-sounding TV thing you feel like saying, and you duck behind the nearest big tree." Kowalski dropped to a crouch behind the desk. "Or just shove your partner out in front of you. That works too. Trust me, you shoot a bunch of crippled orphans by accident, the department will fuck you over so hard you will *wish* you were dead."

On Thursday Kowalski was gone, and for two blessed days we were instructed instead by Officer Garcia, a calm, soft-spoken man who never yelled and who treated everyone with quiet courtesy. And finally, he handed out real guns. We were called up one by one to be issued our duty weapons.

Garcia handed us each a gun with the slide locked back. "These are unloaded and the slide is locked back, but when I hand this to you, I'm still going to be pointing the barrel at the floor, right? Because why?"

"Treat all firearms as if they are loaded," we chorused.

"Yes. Exactly. And you're going to take your weapon, and—still keeping it pointed at the floor—you are going to place it in your holster, slide locked back, and you go sit down. When you sit down again, that gun is going to stay in your holster until I tell you different. You are not going to take it out and play with it. You are not going to touch it at all. Got it?"

"Yes, sir," we chorused.

Garcia wasn't done. "I'm not kidding about this. I see any safety violations, now or on the range, and guess what you're all gonna be doing? You're gonna run a 10-33, going all around the parking lot, every single time I see any safety violation. I see you with your finger on the trigger when it shouldn't be on the trigger? 10-33. I see one of your classmates with his gun holstered and the hood on his holster isn't snapped shut? 10-33. It doesn't matter if it wasn't you. You need to help each other. You see someone else doing something unsafe, it's *your* job to point it out and fix the situation. Anyone screws up, *everyone* runs a 10-33."

When we were all back in our seats, guns holstered with their slides locked back, Garcia said, "Okay. Now you're going to reach slowly for your weapon. You're going to draw it out of the holster, and you're going to place it, slowly and carefully, fingers nowhere near the trigger, on the desk in front of you."

We obeyed. Garcia studied us, nodding. "Let me tell you something. Fully loaded, the Glock 17 weighs about two pounds. And that's the heaviest two pounds you're ever going to carry. Remember that."

For the rest of the day, we practiced field-stripping and reassembling our Glocks. On Friday, we were finally allowed on the range.

By then we had already run several 10-33s. (Sparta dropped her gun on the floor twice, and Creatine accidentally pointed his gun right at Garcia.) Running in full uniform, in the swampy Washington summer heat, was miserable. Most of the recruits were two decades younger than I was, and I generally came panting along at the tail end of the group. I was sweating and shaky, and my knees and hips still hurt, pretty much all the time.

The only person consistently slower than I was was Hardy, a slender black woman in her early fifties. She jogged to the gatepost when 10-33s were called, but didn't even pretend to run after that. She just walked the rest of the way. "I'm *way* too old for this kind of juvenile shit," she told me.

"I hear you."

In addition to my aching joints, I had developed several odd bruises on my right arm. They didn't hurt, but they were deep red ovals. They looked a lot like fingerprints, as if someone with strong hands had grabbed my arm and pressed down hard.

I couldn't figure out where I'd gotten them. Maybe I had been banging my arm against the slide on my gun without noticing? We had to keep the slide locked back when the guns were holstered, and in that position the slide stuck up a bit and jammed uncomfortably into my forearm. I tried to keep my sleeves rolled down as much as I could to hide the bruises, but it was hot, and sometimes I forgot.

As we filed out of the classroom to head to the range, Garcia stopped me. He pushed my sleeve up all the way and inspected my bruises, then looked earnestly into my eyes.

"Are you okay?"

"Oh, yes, thanks," I said.

"No, I mean, are you *okay*?"

It hit me that he was wondering if I was a victim of domestic abuse. "Seriously, Officer Garcia, I have no idea where these bruises came from. It's weird. They don't even hurt. They just look bad."

Garcia looked unconvinced. "Well, you need anything, just let me know. You can always come talk to me, anytime."

"Absolutely! No problem. Thanks. I'm good!" I gave him my model recruit smile, which was hard to produce because my heart was pounding and I felt simultaneously hot, cold, and clammy.

At first, things on the range were fine. Before getting to the academy, I had fired a gun only a handful of times, skeet shooting and firing a .22 at summer camp. Astonishingly, my pistol shots mostly hit the targets, which were big, human-size cardboard torsos. Maybe I'll be good at this, I thought. Given my difficulties with running, it would nice to be good at something.

Kowalski was back, strolling around and tormenting any recruit hapless enough to be having problems, and he had been joined by several other instructors we hadn't seen before. One of them, I noticed, was giving Hardy a particularly tough time. She stood there stiffly, staring straight ahead, as he bellowed at her. Soon, we were running more 10-33s.

By then we were all dripping sweat and wilting from exhaustion, but the instructors sent us right back to the range. "You think you're going to be shooting under ideal circumstances on the street?" demanded one of the new instructors. "Not going to happen. You'll be scared, tired, out of breath, hot, cold, shaky. And guess what? If you've got your gun out on the street, it's probably because someone's shooting back at you. So practice shooting in here while you're tired and hot and stressed, and just be glad no bullets are coming in your direction."

Shortly after that, someone's poorly aimed bullet ricocheted right off the big metal clip holding up one of the cardboard targets, and Garcia, standing off to the side, was nicked by a piece of flying shrapnel. Dripping blood, he headed off to the Police and Fire Clinic. "I'm fine," he assured us. "Just a little ricochet." He was so distracted by the blood that he forgot to make us run another 10-33.

By the end of the weekend, the bruises on my right arm had multiplied, and new bruises had popped up on my left arm. They were strange—they stayed a deep reddish pink color, and never turned the blue or green or yellow color you usually see as bruises age.

My husband told me to stop being stupid and go to the doctor, and my mother told me to drop out of the police academy, since it was clearly making me sick. "I'm fine," I told them irritably. "If I miss any of this training, they're going to make me start all over with a different group, and I'll have wasted a whole week. I just bruise easily. The bruises don't even hurt."

At the range the next week, things stopped going well. Satisfied that everyone could at least fire their weapons in the general direction of the targets, the instructors started to run us through more challenging drills: one-handed shooting, quick-draw drills, nighttime-shooting drills with all the lights out. The more experienced shooters—many of them former military, along with a handful of country boys who had grown up hunting—were separating from the pack. I still felt shaky, sweaty, and sick, even though the instructors had eased up on the 10-33s. And for some reason, all my shots were ending up down and to the left of where I was aiming. They were mostly still in the target, but they weren't going where I wanted them to go.

"Okay, body armor drill," intoned Kowalski from his seat in the range master's booth. "Shooters, you are facing a bad guy who may be wearing body armor, so hitting him center mass might not be enough to stop him. So what you're gonna do, when the target faces, is quick-draw, fire two shots center mass, then one at the head. Two quick ones to the body, then come to sights, aim carefully, and squeeze off one to the head. Got that? Two to the body, one to the head."

I fired two shots at the body. They hit the target, but my head shot didn't go anywhere near the target's head.

We did it again. Again, my head shot landed somewhere near the target's neck. And again. And again. I could not for the life of me make my shots hit the target's head. No matter how many times I fired, my target's un-marred face gazed blankly back at me.

Although we were surrounded by firearms instructors, not much in-structing was taking place. Mostly there was just a lot of yelling. None of the instructors had noticed my head shot difficulties, for which I was grate-ful, since being noticed generally meant being yelled at. In my peripheral vision I saw that Hardy was being berated by one of the new instructors. I couldn't make out much of what he was saying, aside from "Are you fucking stupid?" Spittle was flying from his lips.

Eventually, we were told to break for lunch. Light-headed and dizzy, I retreated to the women's locker room to splash cold water on my face and loosen my ballistic vest. I felt like I could hardly breathe. It reminded me of the childhood song: "I'm being eaten by a boa constrictor."

I started singing softly to myself as I loosened the vest and inspected the proliferating bruises on my arms. "I'm being eaten by a boa constrictor, a boa constrictor, a boa constrictor. . . . I'm being eaten by a boa constrictor, and I don't . . . like . . . it . . . one *bit*."

Then Hardy walked in, sobbing.

"Oh hey . . . hey. You okay?"

She just sobbed some more. Awkwardly, I put my arms around her. I barely knew her. She shook and cried into my shoulder.

"Hey, hey. It's okay. It's okay. What's wrong?"

The new instructor—the guy with all the spittle—wouldn't leave her alone, she finally said. He seemed determined to abuse her for everything she did. He told her she was "fucking stupid," and that she'd never pass the firearms course. And she thought he might be right, because she was having trouble with absolutely everything, not that being screamed at was helping her calm down and learn. When the new instructor started grabbing her arms and shoulders to reposition her body, Hardy said, she finally took his arm in her hand and lifted it off her shoulder, at which point he screamed,

"Don't fucking touch me! You fucking touch me and I am going to fucking kill you!"

I was so dismayed by her story that I temporarily forgot my plan to be a model recruit taking whatever was dished out with an unflappable smile.

"Listen to me, Hardy, that's not okay. Some of these guys down here—what they're doing isn't right. All those sexist and racist 'jokes'? I'm not kidding, it's hostile-environment harassment, and that guy shouting at you was completely out of line. Even from where I was standing I could hear him. If someone sued MPD over this kind of shit, the department would lose. If you want to complain about it, I'll back you up."

Hardy had pulled herself together. She wiped her eyes with a paper towel. She didn't know what to do, she said. She was frightened—she'd never failed at anything before and now she was terrified she would fail at this. We were supposed to start shooting the qualification course the next day. Anyone who didn't pass by the end of the week would be permitted one additional week of remedial instruction. After that, those who hadn't passed would be sent to the police and fire clinic to see if there was a medical reason for their poor shooting. After that, if you had no medical excuse, you were out of the academy—done, dismissed.

"Do *not* let those assholes get to you," I told her. "Seriously, fuck them. It's not you. You're not bad at this; you're just new at this. But instead of teaching us, they're just being assholes. When Garcia comes back, let's talk to him. I bet he'll actually help us. These other assholes, you just have to survive them, and don't let them persuade you that *you're* the one with the problem. Come on. We can do this. We're going to do this."

I was trying to persuade myself as much as I was trying to comfort her.

"We're new at this. So maybe it will take us a little longer than it will take most of the other people. Maybe we'll need an extra few days. But we'll figure it out. We'll pass. Okay? After lunch we're going to go back in there and work on it. We'll be fine."

But after lunch, Hardy wasn't there, and neither was the new instructor who had shouted at her. The rest of us were told that we wouldn't be going back out on the range that afternoon. Instead, the lieutenant who served as the academy's second-in-command would be coming to speak to us.

As soon as the instructors left the room, everyone started whispering at once. No one knew what was happening, but rumors were flying.

Someone said he'd spotted an official with stars on his shoulder storming into the academy. Someone else said Hardy had filed a complaint against the instructor. He was called Williams, one of the recruits had heard. He was, everyone agreed, completely out of control.

"What kind of complaint?" I asked. "Harassment?"

"I heard it was a criminal complaint," Marta whispered.

"That man looked like he was having some sort of fit," Sparta said primly.

"That guy was fucking *scary*," Creatine said. "There was, like, spit all over the place."

Finally the lieutenant came in. We all leapt up and chorused, "Good afternoon, sir!"

"Good afternoon," he said. "Sit down. Relax. You guys didn't do anything wrong, but we need your help. We've got a very sensitive situation."

Officer Williams, he said, was now the subject of a criminal investigation relating to his interactions with Hardy. The rest of us were all considered potential witnesses, and would be required to complete and sign a PD 119 form—a witness statement—providing a full written account of whatever we had seen and heard relating to the allegations against Williams. An internal affairs detective would be interviewing each of us, and we would each be provided with an opportunity to meet individually with a union representative prior to meeting with the detective.

When the lieutenant left, there was more hushed discussion, mostly involving rumors people had heard. Williams had been sent to teach at the academy because he'd been subject to so many excessive force complaints the department wouldn't let him patrol anymore, someone said. No, said someone else, Williams had cancer and was going to be medically retired. But no one really knew anything, and eventually everyone fell silent.

After a while, we were led to one of the computer rooms, where we filled out our PD 119s. Then we were sent to wait in the auditorium, where we were called out one by one to meet first with the union rep and then with the detective.

The union rep was looking unhappy by the time it was my turn.

"Look, what I want you to know is, you don't have to tell the detective anything," he told me. "Okay? Officer Williams is being investigated for making criminal threats. But don't let talking to the detective intimidate you. If you think Williams was maybe just, well, kidding around, or trying to make a point, just, you know, for teaching purposes, that's what you should say."

"But I don't think Williams was kidding around or making a point for teaching purposes," I said. "I think Williams was completely out of control."

He didn't like this answer.

When it was my turn to meet with the detective, I recounted my locker room encounter with Hardy, and told him that although I hadn't witnessed the specific statements that led to the complaint, what I had seen had disturbed me, and went far beyond anything resembling appropriate behavior.

The next afternoon, Hardy was back, but Williams was still gone. Hardy wasn't saying much; she said she had been ordered not to discuss the situation because of the pending investigation. Rumor had it that Williams had been placed on administrative leave.

It was now Thursday, and we were scheduled to finish the firearms course on Friday, but we had lost more than a full day of range time to the investigation. I was starting to feel a little panicky. I needed all the range time I could get. Garcia, back from the police and fire clinic, assured us that if any of us failed to qualify by Friday afternoon, we'd get an extra day the following week to make up for the missed time. "You'll all be fine," he promised. "I'm going to teach you all to shoot."

Back on the range, the instructors started running us through the full qualification course. We started at the twenty-five-yard line and fired from behind a barrier, first from a standing position and then from a kneeling position. We then moved progressively closer to the target, with a different task each time we advanced: one-handed shooting from the strong hand and then the weak hand, quick draw from the holster, shooting from the tuck position, and so on.

To pass, you had to get forty-three rounds on target, out of a possible fifty-one. My problem was that at least two of those rounds had to go into the target's head during the "body armor" component of the course, and I still seemed unable to get any rounds into the head. Worse, you had to successfully pass the "daytime" shooting course three times in a row, then pass the night shooting course twice in a row. Passes had to be consecutive— if you passed the daytime course twice but were a single point short the third time, you had to start all over and get three passes in a row. Each time I passed one course, I'd mess up the next. I was constantly having to start over. I was starting to feel like Hardy. What if I failed? What if I just couldn't do this?

By the end of the day on Thursday, all but five of us had successfully qualified. Those who qualified were sent off to practice "shoot/don't shoot" scenarios using the MILO Use of Force training simulator, a sort of giant interactive video game. Hardy and I were among the five laggards still on the range, together with a bewildered young woman from Uganda, who seemed unable to get a single round into any part of the target, and two male recruits who looked mortified to be stuck with the girls.

Finally, the instructors started to focus on teaching. They had wanted to move along everyone they thought could pass quickly, Garcia told us, so they could now give special attention and coaching to those of us still having difficulty.

My rounds were hitting down and to the left because I was anticipating the recoil, he told me—I was tensing up in anticipation of the noise and the recoil, and jerking my hands down a bit before I finished pulling the trigger. Even if I only moved my hands a couple of millimeters, that would be enough to pull all my rounds down. He took away my magazines and reloaded them with a mix of live ammunition and dummy rounds. My goal, he said, was to keep the barrel steady when I pulled the trigger, no matter what. When I got to an unexpected dummy round, I would see that I was jerking the barrel down needlessly.

Garcia was right, and the drill helped, but I was still having trouble with my head shots. It was maddening.

"Come on, Brooks, stop messing around, we know you can shoot," Kowalski bellowed at me over the loudspeaker.

Suddenly, I loved Kowalski. He wanted me to succeed. I no longer hoped someone would sue him into bankruptcy. I wanted to hug him.

I nodded weakly. Model recruit. Model recruit.

"You got this?" said Garcia.

"Yeah. I got this."

And I did. I got through one of the daytime courses. Then another. Then another. Finally, three in a row. My head shots were just barely in, but they were in. Then I got through one of the night courses. When I finished shooting the second night course, Garcia went over to my target to count the rounds. I closed my eyes and prayed. He pulled down my target and walked back to me.

"Okay," he said with a small smile. "Get out of here."

"I'm done?"

"You're done."

"I passed?"

"You passed. Now get lost. Go do MILO. I'll see you back in the class-room."

The two men had passed as well, but on the other end of the range, Hardy and the Ugandan girl were still struggling. I cast an anxious glance in their direction.

"Stop worrying," Garcia told me. "I'm gonna take care of them."

And he did. Somehow, they both eventually passed.

A fter that, I more or less collapsed. The bruises on my arms started to fade, but I was still shaky and dizzy, and when it finally occurred to me to take my temperature, I found I had a fever. My neck hurt and my back hurt. My knees and hip joints still hurt. There was a strange electrical fizzing sensation between my shoulder blades.

"I think there's something wrong with me," I told my husband. He told me again that I should go to the doctor.

I stared at the fading red ovals on my arms.

"You know, I wonder . . ." We spent as much time as we could out at our weekend house on Maryland's Eastern Shore, where I was constantly getting tick bites. In previous summers, I had twice gotten the classic "bull's-eye" rash associated with Lyme disease, and each time I had imme-diately started a short course of antibiotics. Perhaps because I had always taken antibiotics as soon as I noticed the rash, I had never gotten any other symptoms.

When I started googling "lyme disease rash," it didn't take long to dis-cover that while the bull's-eye was the most common type of rash to appear in those bitten by Lyme-infected ticks, the rashes could take many forms, and sometimes looked much more like . . . pinkish red bruises. Untreated,

Lyme disease could cause a wide range of symptoms, some of them debilitating, from minor flu-like aches and pains to fever, nerve pain, and severe head, neck, and joint pain.

I went to the doctor.

The Fourth of July was coming up, and we had a full week off from our academy classes, our first real break since April. I spent that week shivering and moaning. I couldn't get comfortable; I ached all over. It hurt to stand up, and it hurt to lie down. But by then I was taking antibiotics. Finally, I began to feel better. I was still weak, but things didn't hurt quite as much. I even began, slowly, to run again. I still hated it, but once the antibiotics kicked in, I found that I could run without too much misery.

I had qualified on my firearm, and I could run 1.5 miles within the time limit. I was almost giddy with relief.

With all the new skills and all the stress—all the emphasis on drills and counting rounds—there hadn't been much time to think about why we were being trained to do all this.

Two to the body and one to the head! When my head shots went in I was delighted. It wasn't a real head. It was just an oval printed on a piece of cardboard. It moved, rotating to face you unexpectedly, but it didn't cry out or bleed when you shot it. When it got all torn up, I replaced it with a new target. Once I was no longer sick, and no longer terrified, going to the range was even sort of fun.

One day when I was practicing, one of the range instructors checked my gun. "No wonder your rounds aren't going where you want them," he said. "Look at this, your sights are off center." He showed me. Sure enough, my rear sight was skewed to the side. "Take your gun to the armorer. They'll get that fixed for you." After that, my head shots went right in, leaving satisfying little holes in my target's blank face.

Later, on patrol, I found that I hardly ever thought about the gun in my holster. It might as well not have been there. To the extent that I thought about it, it was mostly because it was sometimes in my way, pinching my skin or banging into my elbow. Sometimes, when I was tired, I used it as an armrest.

But when I got home from each patrol shift, the first thing I'd do was take my gun out of its holster and put it away in its locked metal box. And each time the heavy lid snapped closed, I felt a small wave of relief. It was like slamming the lid on a dangerous viper.

You Live with That Forever

As a law enforcement officer, my fundamental duty is to serve the community; to safeguard lives and property; to protect the innocent against deception; & the weak against oppression and intimidation; & the peaceful against violence or disorder, & respect the constitutional rights of all to liberty, equality and justice. . . . I will maintain courageous calm in the face of danger, scorn or ridicule. . . .

—*The Law Enforcement Oath*

After firearms training, it was back to the classroom. Our class was chugging through the curriculum, covering basic investigation skills, crime scene management, and arrest warrants, along with various practical skills. We learned to use an atrial defibrillator and apply a clotting agent to a bleeding wound, we practiced handcuffing one another, and we learned pat-down and search techniques. (Don't skip the crotch! Everyone feels weird about running their hands over someone else's crotch, we were told, which is why bad guys love to hide everything from knives to heroin in their undies, and why cops need to be willing to get up close and personal while conducting searches. Bras were also said to be favored hiding places. Nonetheless, I noticed, even the instructors were reluctant to demonstrate good search techniques when we practiced.)

We practiced directing traffic, raced police cars through driving courses laid out with traffic cones, lights flashing and sirens blaring, and went through the time-honored police academy ritual of getting a face full of pepper spray.

We had units on handling infectious diseases, industrial accidents, bomb threats, and offenses involving diplomats (a significant issue in Washington, DC, where local law often runs up against the brick wall of diplomatic immunity enjoyed by employees of the city's many foreign embassies). We learned the proper procedures for handling incidents involving members of Congress or government couriers carrying classified national security information—topics similarly not on the typical police academy curriculum, but the kind of thing that comes up in a city that hosts a hundred US senators, 435 members of the House of Representatives, and thousands of Defense Department and intelligence agency employees.

We practiced searching local and national criminal records databases, and operating tint meters to check automobile window tint levels. We covered sex crimes, animal bites, homicides, credit card fraud, theft offenses, assault offenses, domestic violence offenses, and a host of other offenses, major and minor.

Some of the arrestable misdemeanor offenses on the books were minor indeed, or remarkably obscure. We were authorized to arrest people without a warrant for, among other things:

- Digging for bait in Rock Creek Park
- Operating more than five eel traps
- Keeping bees within five hundred feet of human habitation
- Owning or keeping a dog that disturbed the peace (by barking or in any other manner)
- Selling vehicles on public space
- Poster—lewd
- Misconduct in public toilets
- Climbing streetlamps

- Hitching animals to streetlamps
- Landing an amphibian craft without permission

The list of Washington, DC, misdemeanor offenses was long, and included much that I would never have imagined constituted criminal offenses rather than civil offenses. Citizens could be imprisoned for up to ten days for walking their dog on a leash with a length exceeding four feet, an offense of which I had frequently been guilty myself.

The list of traffic violations was even longer. While only the most serious constituted arrestable offenses, we were authorized to conduct traffic stops and issue tickets for people driving too fast; driving too slow; driving with improperly affixed, illegible, or improperly illuminated tags; driving with the front, rear, side, or windshield obstructed; or driving with a sign or other unauthorized item attached to the mirror, window, or window frame. The pamphlet listing moving violations and parking violations ran to thirteen pages.

The academy curriculum was as striking for what it didn't cover as what it did. For instance, we had eight units on vehicular offenses and one unit on use-of-force policies—but nothing at all on race and policing.

Our instructors occasionally talked about race, but only to insist that it didn't matter. As one of the recruit sergeants—an African American former marine renowned for punishing recruits for minor uniform infractions—bellowed at us, "You graduate from *my* academy, you gonna go out there and treat people *right*! You the *police*. I don't care if you got a rich white lady in Georgetown or a black drug boy in Southeast, you gonna put some *respect* on it! And I don't care what color you are, black, white, yellow, brown, or purple. From now on you all gonna bleed *blue*."

Citizens were citizens, and cops were cops. We were legally and morally obligated to refrain from discrimination of any sort, and to assist all citizens who believed they were victims of hate crimes, a category defined in DC broadly enough to include crimes motivated not only by race, sex, religion, and national origin but also by marital status, personal appearance, sexual orientation, gender identity or orientation, family responsibilities, homelessness, disability, political affiliation, and matriculation status.

Officially, we also didn't study the demographic differences between Washington's seven police districts, though those differences were obvious, stark, and the subject of much derisive commentary from instructors and recruits alike. In the Second District, which covered prosperous, mostly white Northwest DC, there were five homicides and 358 violent crimes in 2016, the year I graduated from the police academy. In the Seventh District, which was poor and predominantly African American, there were forty-five homicides and 1,123 violent crimes. We didn't talk about how the city came to be so segregated, or discuss the impact of Washington's growing gentrification on crime and policing, or ask why 80 percent of all arrests and 90 percent of drug arrests were of African American suspects in a city where black residents made up 47 percent of the population.

For that matter, we didn't receive any information at all on overall crime rates, arrest rates, or patterns in crime and arrest rates. Theories of policing (the "broken windows" approach, "hot spot" policing, community-oriented policing, and so on) merited only a single paragraph in one of the early lesson plans, and we didn't talk about what effective policing might look like. If the police did a good job, what would that mean? Was effective policing measured by a high arrest rate? A low crime rate? High levels of community trust? Did it require more cops, fewer cops, or cops who did different things? What kind of policing correlated with what kinds of outcomes?

Over-criminalization and over-incarceration were also never discussed. Throughout the United States, recent decades have seen a well-documented explosion of over-criminalization, at both state and federal levels. Minor civil infractions have been legislatively redefined as criminal misdemeanors, and numerous violations of complex regulatory codes have been criminalized—often creating brand-new and obscure crimes. At the federal level, there are now some three hundred thousand laws whose violation can lead to prison time; at the state level, a recent study found that Michigan legislators created an average of sixty new crimes a year during the six-year period the study looked at, while Oklahoma created forty-six new crimes a year, and South Carolina created forty-five new crimes a year. But we didn't talk about why so many trivial forms of misbehavior—particularly trivial forms of misbehavior more common among poor people of color than among affluent whites—were punishable by jail time, or about the potential relationship between our national fondness for inventing new "crimes" and the nation's skyrocketing incarceration rates.

We didn't discuss the fact that nineteen out of twenty arrests in DC are for nonviolent offenses, or that the vast majority of people arrested for driving without a permit or after a license suspension are African American. We didn't talk about the reasons people might be driving without a license, or the consequences befalling individuals who got arrested, or the impact of high incarceration rates on already challenged communities, or the reasons Washington, DC, has the highest incarceration rate of any state in the country (in a country that has the highest incarceration rate in the world).

We also didn't discuss the national controversies raging over policing, race, and use of force. While I was at the academy, several police shootings made the headlines. On July 5, 2016, while I was still celebrating my successful completion of the firearms qualification course, Louisiana police shot and killed a black man named Alton Sterling. The next day, a Minnesota police officer shot and killed another black man, Philando Castile, during a traffic stop; the officer panicked when Castile told him he was carrying a licensed, concealed weapon, and shot him as he reached for his license and registration. Both shootings sparked mass protests. The day after Castile's death, a black sniper who said he was motivated by anger over police killings ambushed police officers in Dallas, killing five officers and wounding nine others. Three weeks later, there were mass protests in Baltimore after city prosecutors dropped charges against the officers involved in the 2015 death of Freddie Gray. In September, an Oklahoma officer shot and killed Terence Crutcher, an unarmed African American man, and a Charlotte, North Carolina, officer shot and killed a black man named Keith Scott. There were more protests, and the protests sometimes turned violent. In Charlotte, the mayor declared a state of emergency, and the governor sent in the National Guard.

All over the United States, people were talking about race and policing, police violence, and police reform. But virtually none of this conversation made it into the police academy's classrooms. Recruits talked about it, of course, but mostly in the hallways and the lunchroom, and the discussions were hushed and awkward. About half of the new recruits at the Metropolitan Police Academy each year are African American, and it was clear that most recruits weren't comfortable talking about race. We were all blue now, weren't we?

Outside the academy gates, most Americans seemed to be choosing sides: Black Lives Matter, or Blue Lives Matter. Particularly for black recruits, it was a painful dilemma. We all knew that black men make up a disproportionate percentage of those killed by police in the United States. The worst of it was that many of the police officers who fired the fatal shots were also African American. More than once, I heard black recruits offer a wry justification for their decision to join the police: "Why'm I here? Because the safest place for a young black male in this country is behind a badge."

By now, we had watched so many officer-safety videos that most of us, regardless of race, could relate to the officers involved in those shootings.

"There's no such thing as a routine call" had been drilled into us. When you watch enough videos of officers getting hurt because they were too slow to react when a suspect pulled out a weapon, it becomes easy to empathize with officers who pulled the trigger themselves.

And by now, we had all been "killed" during scenario-based role-play practice sessions. In both our classroom practice scenarios and our sessions at the academy's Tactical Training Center, we had been dispatched to mock calls and conducted mock traffic stops. Typically, we recruits would bumble around asking irrelevant questions or falling prey to intentional distractions. At that point, an instructor would pull out a training weapon and splat! Our backs or chests would be covered in bright-colored paint, and we'd trot off sheepishly to be debriefed on our fatal lack of paranoia. ("You were so busy taking nice neat notes in your cute little police notebook that you didn't even notice the guy reaching into his pocket and drawing on you!" "You didn't bother to search the goddamn sofa before you let the 'victim' sit down on it, and you were so busy yapping into your radio you didn't notice when she pulled a gun from between the cushions!")

It became natural to see the officer's side of the story in the wake of controversial police shootings. We watched the same videos the rest of the country was watching, but by now, we had learned to see different things. Ordinary people might see a cop brutally murdering someone who hadn't done anything wrong, but we could see an officer reacting as we had all been trained to react. True, the guy who got shot turned out to be reaching for his cell phone—but it could just as easily have been a gun, right? True, maybe the suspect wasn't responding to police orders because he was deaf or mentally ill—but there was no way for an officer to know the suspect wasn't about to lunge at him with superhuman strength, was there?

Sergeant Flanagan was the only one of our instructors who took any time to talk about this. Somehow, the 2014 Tamir Rice shooting came up during one of our Saturday defensive tactics classes. Rice, a twelve-year-old boy, was shot by a Cleveland police officer as he ran around in a deserted section of a city park, playing with a toy gun.

"I got it, guys, you have to be prepared for anything. And I'm trying to teach you to be ready for anything and to react fast. But fast is not the same as stupid." Flanagan's eight-year-old daughter had come to work with him and was playing a game on the other side of the gym. He kept glancing over at her.

"You have to *think* before you act. You end up killing a twelve-year-old who's playing with a toy gun, how are you going to live with yourself? And why the fuck would an officer run toward someone he thought was an armed man when he had no backup and no one was shooting or in any immediate danger? Think about it."

He seemed taken aback by his own vehemence, and his tone became more apologetic. "Look, I don't want to second-guess anyone. I wasn't there, so it's not for me to say. I'm just saying, from the outside, you have to ask: What could have been done differently in that situation? Maybe wait for backup, take cover, ask the dispatcher a few more questions about the call before rushing in, speak to the kid on the car's loudspeaker and tell him to drop the gun. You rush in, you're scared, you're not thinking straight? Someone gets killed, and you live with that forever."

But the contradictions were baked into the training. Tactical officer safety dicta clashed directly with other precepts of successful policing. To maximize officer safety, you had to be decisive and react quickly. You were supposed to control the situation at all times. You had to watch the suspect's hands and avoid standing too close. You were supposed to put drivers in stopped vehicles at a disadvantage by shining your lights into their mirrors. When you went into someone's business or residence, you weren't supposed to let a suspect sit on the sofa, or talk to you in the kitchen. You never let anyone reach into a place you couldn't see.

But we were also repeatedly told to treat people with respect. ("It is your responsibility as an officer to portray nonverbal signals that are consistent with a positive and professional image," advised the recruit instructional materials. "Officers are human and they will have strong emotions while performing their duties. These emotions must be managed and at times concealed. It is important to avoid nonverbal signals driven by anger, frustration, and inattentiveness because they inhibit your ability to gain an individual's trust and effectively do your job.") A good officer, we were told, is a patient listener who shows empathy and establishes rapport. But it's tough to show empathy or establish rapport when you're staring obsessively at someone's hands, refusing to let him sit down on his own sofa, or shining a bright light in his eyes.

Police departments worry about legal liability, and much of what did and didn't find its way into the academy curriculum seemed to have been dictated more by liability concerns than by common sense. As a law professor, I understood: if an instructor told recruits to relax and stop worrying that every encounter could turn deadly and a young officer was subsequently killed because he didn't take appropriate tactical precautions, his family could sue the department for failing to provide adequate training. On the other hand, if an instructor simply told recruits to use their own judgment whenever they felt any subjective sense of danger, MPD rules be damned, and a young officer subsequently shot an unarmed citizen, the department would be sued then too. But no one was going to get sued or fired for reading a list of rules out loud. If the rules contradicted one another and pushed officers in conflicting directions, that was their problem.

And if a lawsuit threatened, the department would be only too happy to throw us under the bus. Our instructors made this crystal clear: MPD was not our friend. If you were facing an assaultive suspect and called a 10-33 on your radio, your fellow officers would race to your side—but if your actions made the department look bad, you would suddenly find that you were all alone. In the age of body-worn cameras and cell phone videos, we were told, you had to dot your *i*'s, cross your *t*'s, and pay your union dues, because everything you did would be scrutinized by Monday morning quarterbacks.

The contradictions bothered me. Officially, almost no one at the academy was willing to acknowledge that they existed, which bothered me most of all. Here we were, at the police academy in the nation's capital, at a time when the whole country was talking about race, violence, and policing, but you wouldn't know it from our curriculum. We talked about how to attach leg irons and when to contact animal control, but not about the role police should play in a diverse democratic society. We talked about overlapping jurisdictional issues with other federal police agencies, but not about racial disparities in DC arrest rates.

People sometimes speak of the "blue wall of silence," the unspoken rule that cops don't rat out other cops. I had already seen it in action: When the union representative assured me that I didn't have to tell the internal affairs detectives anything about Williams, he didn't have to spell it out. (I'll never know how many of my fellow recruits took the message to heart and stayed mum about what they'd seen and heard.) But the blue wall of silence often extended to internal discussions as well.

A strong norm against asking too many questions has long been part of police culture. Perhaps it stems from policing's paramilitary heritage: Good cops, like good soldiers, follow orders and get the job done. They complain, just as soldiers complain: the uniforms suck, the equipment is shitty, the sergeant is an asshole. But they don't sit around questioning the whole enterprise or pondering the intangibles. Perhaps senior police officials do so, but recruits and junior patrol officers are not, as a rule, encouraged to ask one another if arresting more people makes the streets safer or less safe; or debate whether the training emphasis on officer safety makes cops too quick to pull the trigger; or discuss the impact of midtwentieth-century restrictive racial covenants on the demographics and economic well-being of modern DC neighborhoods.

This is not because cops are stupid or incurious. Some are, of course—stupidity being evenly distributed among all professions, classes, races, genders, and nationalities, as is courage, kindness, creativity, intelligence, and wit. But most police officers are thoughtful and intelligent. They're also far better educated than police officers in earlier generations: within MPD, more than 75 percent of new recruits already have bachelor's degrees when they arrive at the academy.

Recruits come in wanting to ask questions, but they soon learn that there's no percentage in it. The police academy and the roll call room aren't like university classrooms: instructors like Kowalski aren't going to pat you on the head or give you an A for highlighting contradictions and ambiguities. You're evaluated based on your ability to shoot, cuff people, drive fast, fill out forms, write effective reports, and stay out of trouble. No one cares about your views on the nature of the criminal justice system. But the contradictions still troubled me, and I suspected they bothered more of my peers than were willing to admit it.

Despite my determination to keep my mouth shut and focus on being a model recruit, I couldn't entirely hide my dismay. Under the ill-fitting khaki uniform, I was the same person I had always been: too restless, too curious, and too much my mother's daughter to see problems without wanting to jump in and try to solve them. Toward the end of my academy training, I drafted a short memo proposing a new fellowship program for young MPD officers. The program I proposed was designed to create a space for young officers to talk about all the hard issues never discussed at the academy or in the roll call room: race, poverty, mental illness, excessive force, over-criminalization, alternatives to arrest. Through a combination of workshops, projects, mentorship, and community engagement focused on the role of police in a diverse, democratic society, I argued, young officers could be encouraged to ask hard questions and serve as leaders and change agents within MPD.

I shared the memo with my reserve recruit classmates for their comments, then gave it to Ben Haiman, one of our primary academy instructors. Ben was a reserve officer—after graduating, I patrolled with him several times—but he also worked for MPD as a civilian, serving as one of the chief's special assistants. He was young, smart, and energetic, and he struck me as both idealistic enough to think change was possible, and politically savvy enough to know how to get something new through the MPD bureaucracy.

Ben was noncommittal. It was an interesting idea, he said, but this wasn't a good time to float it to the higher-ups. This was the summer of 2016, and Cathy Lanier, MPD's longest-serving police chief and Ben's boss, had just announced her intent to retire. The DC City Council was reportedly interviewing potential replacements, and no one knew who the next chief would be. Until there was clarity about the department's top leadership, Ben said, senior officials would be unsure of their positions, and no one was likely to champion a risky new initiative. It would be better to just wait on this until the tea leaves were more favorable.

I knew that new ideas, like viruses, can trigger the production of bureaucratic antibodies, and I didn't have the credibility or connections within the department to push the proposal forward on my own. I was willing to trust Ben's judgment, and returned to being a model recruit.

Was That Who I Was?

Application of Leg Irons

*Leg irons may be used to secure prisoners who violently resist
arrest, pose an escape risk or at the discretion of the officer to
prevent violence, escape or injury. Leg irons function in the same
way as handcuffs including the double lock.*

*When applying leg irons the officer must remember leg irons
must:*

1. Only be applied to a handcuffed subject.

2. Only be applied from the side.

3. Adjust for fit.

4. Double lock.

—*Recruit Instructional Materials*

O n October 14, 2016, my reserve recruit class turned in our khaki recruit uniforms and received our blues. We took a group photo in front
of the Lincoln Memorial, practiced marching in formation, and memorized
the Law Enforcement Oath. Together with the career recruit class that was
graduating at the same time, we chanted the oath, pinned on our badges,
walked across the stage in the police academy auditorium, and shook the
hand of the newly appointed interim MPD chief, Peter Newsham.

My mother came to our graduation, and managed to be a good sport about it. She summoned up a smile at the appropriate moments, and even complimented Sergeant Flanagan on his impressive physique when the ceremony was over, making him blush. But on the drive back home, she told me she was disturbed by how militaristic the whole thing was—the marching, the chanting, the dress uniforms, and the honor guard. She was particularly upset, she said, by the video played for family members before the recruits marched into the auditorium.

I never saw the video. According to one of our instructors, it was an innocuous pastiche of MPD officers through the ages. According to my mother, it was full of images of officers firing tear gas into crowds of pro-testers. "I might have been one of those protesters," she told me. "*You* might have been one of those protesters."

"Hmm," I said neutrally. "I'll mention that to the instructors. Maybe that video should be retired."

Either way, it was over. Our academy training was done. My classmates and I were sworn, armed officers of the Washington, DC, Metropolitan Police, and we were officially ready to start patrolling.

I didn't feel ready. While I was at the academy, I could still tell myself— and my mother, and any friends or colleagues, if the issue came up—that I was just an observer, only there to find out how cops are trained. But now the city of Washington, DC, had given me a badge and a gun. My science experiment was suddenly becoming less theoretical. Unless I made my mother happy by resigning, I was going to be putting someone in handcuffs at some point, and statistically, that "someone" was likely to be poor and black. Statistically, I knew I was unlikely ever to fire my gun at another human being. I wasn't even likely to use my baton or pepper spray. But it was now a genuine possibility.

Before we graduated, I was someone with a scholarly interest in how other people justified their willingness to use violence. Now I was someone who had to justify my own willingness to do so. I didn't plan to use violence, and I didn't *want* to use violence. But pinning on that badge and going on patrol meant that I was willing to accept it as a potential option, even a potential duty. Was that who I was?

More prosaically, I was also worried about the possibility—indeed, probability—of screwing up. My time at the academy left me keenly aware of all the things I didn't really understand and barely knew how to do. It was the little things that worried me. I was afraid I would fail to hear my call sign on the radio, fill out the wrong property forms, forget to double-lock someone's handcuffs, get lost while driving, be unable to find the phone number for the duty sergeant, and put my body-worn camera on upside down. Out of the academy, among the real police officers, I would be revealed as the fraud that I was: too slow, too soft, too female, too many fancy degrees, too few policing skills. Everyone—the other cops and probably even the local criminals—would look at me with pity and contempt.

At the academy, we usually knew exactly what we were supposed to do at any given time. We might not like it, but it was fairly clear. We had a set and relatively unvarying schedule, we sat in the classroom, we took written tests and practical exams, we did PT and practiced defensive tactics. We knew the next steps. If the rules were sometimes rigid or absurd, they had the benefit of being, on the whole, quite straightforward. And at the academy, I was surrounded by people I had come to know. The instructors knew my name, and I liked many of my reserve recruit classmates. We had done push-ups together, taken exams together, survived firearms training together, been pepper-sprayed together. Now we were about to be separated and cast out of the academy into the big world, and the big world had very little interest in us.

Career MPD officers are each assigned a field training officer (FTO) as soon as they leave the police academy and arrive at their districts, and they spend their first twelve to sixteen weeks of full-time patrol working under the supervision of their FTOs. Typically, new career officers have a different

FTO every four weeks, and work their way through a series of progressively more challenging assignments. For the first month, they focus on honing their radio communications skills, learning their way around the patrol cars' mobile data terminals, learning local geography, handling less-serious calls, and improving their report-writing. Their vehicles are designated as training cars, and aren't generally dispatched to Priority 1 assignments (assaults, robberies in progress, or other urgent calls likely to require more experienced officers). As their training advances in the second and third months, they gradually handle more complex calls and write reports with less supervision. After 480 hours of patrolling, they take a certification ride with a training sergeant who evaluates their readiness for solo patrol. Once certified, officers can operate in either a 10-4 capacity—with a partner, in DC police parlance—or 10-99, all alone.

In practice, the process was often much messier than it was on paper, but the full-time career officers had at least some semblance of a structured field training program. New reserve officers, however, were mostly left to shift for themselves. Like career officers, we were required to complete 480 patrol hours before we could become certified to patrol alone, but we were extras, part-timers. We would set our own schedules, and getting those 480 supervised patrol hours would take most of us far longer than the twelve weeks it took the full-time officers, since we were only obligated to patrol for twenty-four hours each month. Qualified field training officers were in short supply, and with our unpredictable part-time schedules, it made no sense for the department to assign full-time FTOs to each newly minted reserve officer. We were instead instructed to seek out experienced career officers and use them as de facto training officers.

"Just introduce yourselves to the roll call sergeant," our instructors told us, "and ask to be partnered with an officer who likes to work." (Apparently not all officers "liked to work." Instead of patrolling the alleyways and streets, alert for crime, they sought out quiet places to park and chat, or just watch movies on their phones; when calls came in, they pretended their radios didn't work properly, or pretended to be too far away to respond promptly, hoping the dispatcher would decide to assign the call to someone else.) But if we could find good partners—partners who didn't mind riding with a rookie and were willing to seek out challenging situations, let us take the lead, and offer helpful feedback—we would soon learn the ropes.

With no sergeants or field training officers charged with guiding us, however, it would be entirely up to us to make sure we gained enough experience to pass both a district certification ride and a separate reserve corps certification review process. There was no hard and fast rule about what counted as "enough" experience, but we were told to aim for at least eight to fifteen arrests, ten traffic tickets (technically, Notices of Infraction), ten to fifteen offense reports, fifteen or more incident reports, and three or more traffic crash reports. We would need to document all this in our field training binders, which should include printed copies of reports and tickets, as well as copies of all our patrol shift run sheets and copies of at least twenty-five completed PD-348 forms, documenting patrol hours and signed by the career officers with whom we partnered, our de facto training officers. Since we would not be in designated training cars, there would be no gradual introduction to progressively more complex scenes. We would, with our career officer partners, just go to whatever calls happened to come over the radio.

But, I wondered, how did you figure out who the roll call sergeant was for a given shift? Could you just wander into the sergeants' room, or was that forbidden in MPD's hierarchical universe? Was there assigned seating in the roll call room? Where did you put your patrol bag? What did you do if you got close to 480 hours but hadn't made enough arrests?

None of it sounded easy.

PART THREE

The Street

Sweetheart

Unlawful entry; threats: On scene officers were met by Victim who stated that Suspect climbed through the window of her apartment and while inside Suspect asked Victim for a cigarette to which Victim replied no. Suspect then stated "Bitch you hot and I'm a kill you."

—MPD Joint Strategic and Tactical Analysis
Command Center, Daily Report

October 2016. It's a cool fall afternoon, a week and a half after our police academy graduation, and I'm in the women's locker room in Washington, DC's Seventh District police station, already feeling defeated.

Specifically, I'm in a bathroom stall, trying to heed one of the few relatively benign bits of advice dispensed at the academy by Officer Kowalski: "Listen up, boys and girls! Always go pee-pee before you start a ten-hour patrol shift." This dictum was delivered with a contemptuously curled lip, but it seemed like solid counsel.

Now, with twenty minutes to go before the beginning of my first patrol shift, I'm finding Kowalski's advice tricky to implement. Having successfully jammed, tucked, strapped, buttoned, zipped, Velcroed, and snapped myself into my brand-new class B blue uniform before heading to the station, I find myself unable to reverse the process in the tight confines of the bathroom stall. I can't undo the button on my pants without removing my heavy leather duty belt, because the duty belt completely covers the lighter under-belt that's woven through the belt loops of my uniform trousers. But I can't remove the duty belt and its cargo of lethal equipment—gun, baton, pepper spray—without first removing the four belt keepers that tether it to the underbelt.

A belt keeper is a small strip of nylon or leather with snaps or Velcro on each end, designed to be slipped vertically beneath an underbelt, then folded over and fastened on top of the bulkier duty belt. In effect, belt keepers are external belt loops designed to secure an outer belt to an inner belt. For a police officer, having three or four firmly attached belt keepers is a very good thing if you happen to be breaking up a fight or running up five flights of stairs to respond to an urgent assault-in-progress call, since the duty belt holds your radio, gun, handcuffs, flashlight, pepper spray, baton, tourniquet, and various other vital odds and ends. You really want it to stay on your waist and not go flying off as you run—or, worse, fall down around your ankles, snaring your legs in a lasso of your own creation.

But if you happen to be a woman and you happen to need to pee, belt keepers are not your friends.

The trouble right now is this: I've located and removed belt keepers one, two, and three, but belt keeper number four is eluding me. I know it's somewhere behind my back, but with my torso trussed up in a bulky bal-listic vest, both my agility and my ability to see what's around my waist are compromised. I fumble around in the tiny stall, groping blindly for the lost belt keeper. The stiff leather duty belt, almost but not quite freed from its underbelt, swings around wildly, and my holstered gun hits the toilet tank with a loud smack.

By now I've twisted my whole body around so I'm facing away from the stall door. I'm practically straddling the toilet, bracing my legs to try to keep my radio, which now dangles from its holder, from sliding away. (Kowalski:

"That radio cost the department seventy-seven hundred dollars, so do not fucking drop it in the toilet.")

Sweat is pooling under my armored vest as I wrestle, panting, with the duty belt. That's when I hear the stall door (which I recall—too late— wouldn't latch properly) swing open behind my back.

There's a moment of stunned silence, then an appalled voice: "Oh, sweet Jesus, sweet Jesus!"

The stall door slams shut, and agitated footsteps rush away.

I lean my damp forehead against the cool cinderblock of the wall, and begin, helplessly, to giggle.

Finally I turn awkwardly and open the stall door again. There's a young female officer at the opposite end of the locker room, unpacking her patrol bag and clearly working hard not to look at me.

"Sorry," I call. "It's just me. I'm stuck. I can't find the last belt keeper and I'm all tangled up. Could you give me a hand?"

She stares up accusingly. "Girl! I seen you standing facing the wall in there, and I thought you was a *man*! You almost gave me a heart attack!"

"I'm sorry," I repeat sheepishly. My giggles have triggered a fit of hiccups. "I'm female." I hiccup. "I'm just kind of an idiot."

Freed from my duty belt through the aid of my still-wary colleague, and freed from my hiccups through the old childhood trick of hanging my head upside down and drinking water from the opposite rim of a cup, I return to the stall, latching the door firmly this time. I hang my duty belt around my neck as instructed at the academy (putting it on the floor or hanging it on a coat hook is strictly forbidden, because you never know, someone could grab the belt from over or under the stall door, pull the pistol from its holster, then *shoot you with your own gun*, a fate no self-respecting officer would wish to contemplate).

Duty belt properly secured, sharp bits of metal equipment now cutting into my neck, I realize that I don't actually need to pee. Reassembling myself, I carefully reattach the duty belt. One, two, three, four belt keepers, each snapped on tight.

I leave the stall's questionable shelter and make my way to the sink.

With all my gear on, I'm thirty pounds heavier than in my underwear. On *Law & Order* and *CSI*, female cops look svelte and sexy in their uniforms. I look like the Michelin Man, only armed, and less graceful.

Here's what I'm wearing:

- Approved navy blue underwear and socks
- Navy blue T-shirt
- Level III body armor, secured over T-shirt with Velcro straps
- Long-sleeved blue uniform shirt with a Metropolitan Police Department collar pin on each collar point, department patch on the shoulder, a metal name tag displaying a small American flag and identifying me as "R. Brooks" over my right breast pocket, and my shiny silver-colored badge over my left pocket
- Two pens with black ink, as per regulation, properly positioned in my left front shirt pocket
- Police ID card in right front shirt pocket (The card is needed to open the station's magnetic door locks. Since the sensors are at waist height, opening doors requires shimmying down and waggling your chest at the sensor.)
- Axon body-worn camera attached to shirtfront with magnetic holder
- Small clip-on light attached to right shirt pocket flap (not department-issued, but this turns out to be one of my most useful purchases, as it enables me to write in my notebook at night without having to hold a flashlight in my hand, or between my teeth)

- Navy blue cargo pants (New academy graduates are supposed to wear the more formal dress trousers until they finish field training, but I'm gambling that no one in the notoriously lax Seventh District will notice or care. I bought my own cargo pants from 5.11 Tactical, since the department-issued unisex pants don't fit right.)
- Garrison belt—this is the lighter-weight underbelt that goes beneath the duty belt
- Duty belt, snugged up to the garrison belt with belt keepers. Per MPD General Order 110.11, my duty belt contains:

> *Two magazine pouches, each containing a Glock magazine loaded with seventeen rounds of 9-millimeter ammunition*
>
> *Radio case and Motorola radio, with radio microphone cord running up behind my back and through my right epaulet, and the mic then clipped to my shirt lapel. Attached to the mic I have a Secret Service–style earpiece, so I can listen to the radio without broadcasting whatever's on it to everyone around me.*
>
> *Two pairs of Smith & Wesson handcuffs (One issued, one extra. "Handcuffs are always vanishing," the academy instructors told us. "Carry extras.")*
>
> *A handcuff key*
>
> *Oleoresin capsicum spray canister (cops call it OC spray; most people call it pepper spray)*
>
> *ASP expandable friction-lock baton*
>
> *Heavy-duty department-issued flashlight*
>
> *Combat Action Tourniquet*
>
> *Holster containing my department-issued Glock 17 pistol with a full magazine and one round in the chamber*
>
> *Department-issued cell phone case, containing department-issued antiquated Samsung cell phone (which does not*

make calls because MPD did not purchase phone service for the phones it provides officers, but that must be carried anyway, because only the department-issued phone can be paired with the body-worn camera, per regulations, and the phone is needed to tag the body-worn camera videos)

Glove pouch containing nitrile gloves (not issued, but everyone has a glove pouch containing gloves for handling icky things or people soaked with blood, booze, rotting food, snot, urine, feces, or vomit)

Small pouch for personal items (Not issued; I added this myself to carry things like keys, cash, sunglasses, lip balm, disinfectant wipes, mints, tissues, etc. My male colleagues call it my "duty purse.")

- In a leg holster, I carry my Tactical Emergency Casualty Care kit, which contains a chest seal, a CPR mask, a nasopharyngeal tube, a compression bandage, gauze bandages, more disinfectant wipes, wound dressing containing a rapid blood-clotting agent, naloxone nasal spray for opioid overdoses, shears, duct tape, and more nitrile gloves. Also, some Band-Aids, which I added myself. (As issued, the TECC kit is great for catastrophic wounds, but not much use if you get a paper cut.)

- In my back right pocket, I have a pair of black heavy-duty work gloves (for searches and handling broken glass and other sharp objects).

- In my front left cargo pocket I carry my personal cell phone (since the department-issued phone can't make calls, officers carry their personal phones as well).

- In my front right pocket I carry my patrol notebook. (Per General Orders, patrol notebooks must be stored unaltered for a minimum of three years after use, since officers' notes may be discoverable in court proceedings.)

- In my left hip pocket I have a small multi-tool containing a knife, glass breaker, seat belt cutter, pliers, and screwdriver (because I like multi-tools, which make me feel like I'm prepared for all contingencies).
- Black Magnum boots
- Navy blue MPD baseball cap

Giving my uniform a final once-over, I stare unhappily at myself in the locker room mirror. All the mirrors in the Seventh District police station's women's locker room are warped like funhouse mirrors. Some make you look short and squat; others make you weirdly elongated. I prefer weirdly elongated, but the mirror closest to my assigned locker is of the short-and-squat variety. I try to improve things by putting on some lipstick, but this just makes me look like a short, squat cop wearing lipstick.

It's time to leave the locker room. On my way out, I pass one of the elongating mirrors, which makes me feel a little better. I'm no longer a short, squat cop wearing lipstick; now I'm a tall, skinny cop wearing lipstick.

Taking a deep breath, I start down the hall. A burly guy with a bushy red beard ambles past, heading toward the men's locker room. "Hey, sweetheart," he calls over his shoulder. "Your name tag's about to fall off."

Sweetheart?

But I look down and see that he's right. One end of my name tag has somehow come loose, and it's dangling down over my pocket. I return to the locker room, where I find that one of the small metal clutch-backs that are supposed to anchor the right-side pin on the name tag has vanished, probably now buried somewhere inside my bra, waiting to poke me uncomfortably at an inopportune moment. I open my locker and find another clutch-back, having discovered during the academy the wisdom of always stocking extras. I remove my body-worn camera, unbutton my uniform shirt, reattach the name tag, then reassemble myself one more time. My squat reflection gazes reproachfully at me from the mirror.

This time I make it all the way into the report-writing room and through the door that connects the report-writing room to the sergeants' room. I approach the first person I see, a bearded black guy in his thirties. His name tag reads, "Fremont," and he's hunched over a keyboard, scowling at his fingers.

"Excuse me, sir, you know who's got roll call for evenings?"

I've rehearsed this line. I'm hoping it will come out sounding casual, yet respectful. Confident, yet open. Blasé, yet enthusiastic.

Fremont looks up, fingers still on the keyboard, eyeing me. "That's me."

"Oh. Hi, sir. I'm Brooks. I'm new."

"I see that."

Faced with his laconic stare, I start to babble. "Sir, I'm a reserve officer, and I'm working tonight. I just graduated from the academy. So, ah, I just wanted to introduce myself, and ask you to put me in tonight wherever you could use an extra officer. Sir."

Fremont doesn't say anything.

I forge on. "Um, I guess, ideally, put me with someone who likes to work. And . . . who doesn't mind having a partner who's a complete idiot."

His impassive face creases into a small grin. "I got you, Brooks. I'll take care of you. Welcome to 7D. Let's see . . ." He frowns at his monitor. "Tell you what, I'm gonna put you with Murphy. Roll call at 15:00 hours."

"Yessir. Great. Thanks, Sarge."

I turn to go. Not yet accustomed to walking around with all this gear, I forget how wide my duty belt makes me, and bang my radio into the side of a desk. Face hot, extra cuffs clanking, I make my way out the door.

The roll call room presents new challenges. I was told by one of the other reserve officers that newbies—uncertified officers fresh from the academy—are supposed to sit in the front row of tables, so that's where I plunk myself down, but this puts me with my back to the other officers who are starting to wander in. I turn in my chair and introduce myself to the two officers behind me, both of whom just grunt in response. I spot a guy whose name tag says Murphy and introduce myself.

"Hey. I think you're stuck with me tonight."

He gives me a wan smile. "Cool."

Murphy is white, medium height, balding, thirtyish. He looks tired. No one's doing much talking in the roll call room. Mostly, officers fiddle with their phones, or just stare down at the table.

Uniforms at 7D aren't very uniform, I notice. There are several men with their uniform shirts partly unbuttoned over undershirts, and a couple of women with dangling earrings (forbidden) and long false nails (also forbidden). Threadbare MPD ball caps are worn backward or pushed down over eyes. An obese middle-aged woman sprawls in a chair by the door to the sergeants' room, eyes closed. She's wearing stained cargo pants and a T-shirt; over the T-shirt, her uniform shirt is unbuttoned and untucked. (Later, I learn that she is a lieutenant, and widely loathed by the officers. She has lost her duty weapon three times, Murphy tells me. She is nearing retirement and despises everyone; she dedicates her remaining time at 7D to finding minute errors in reports and making people go back and start all over. I am skeptical about this—surely she can't be as bad as people say— until the day she makes me redo a property form three times in a row because she doesn't like the way I abbreviated the day of the week.)

Finally, Sergeant Fremont strides in. He stands directly in front of my table, so close I could reach out and tickle his tummy. I focus my eyes on my notebook.

Fremont has a strong, morose baritone. "All right, attention to roll call, today is Saturday, October thirtieth, this is the evening tour of duty." He reads out the day's code word, names the watch commander and the check-off sergeant, then starts listing assignments.

"Perez and Smith, you're gonna be operating under call sign 7011, utilizing vehicle 7026, take the breach kit."

Perez and Smith each give a desultory acknowledgment. "Sarge."

"Dorry and Fiske, you're 7012, utilizing vehicle 7022, you guys got the M4 patrol rifle."

"Sir."

"Warner and Phelps, you're 7021, in vehicle 7213, special attention to Woodlands; we had three shootings there in the last few days, so look sharp."

"You got it, Sarge."

"Murphy and . . . Brooks, you're 7022."

"Yes, sir."

"Take vehicle 7214, and take the dog pole."

Dog pole? I scribble this down in my notebook, where I'm trying to list everyone's names and call signs.

When Fremont finishes running through the assignments, he goes on to roll call training.

"Okay, roll call training for the day, be advised, 18 DCMR 2405.1(g) prohibits stopping, standing, and parking in bike lanes. Accordingly, members are prohibited from stopping, standing, or parking department vehicles in bike lanes when conducting routine business. In accordance with GO-SPT-301.01 (Vehicle Operation and Maintenance), sworn members may only park or idle in a bike lane in emergency cases, and vehicles must be parked in accordance with traffic regulations as soon as possible. Any questions?"

No one has any questions.

"All right, fall in."

We all stand, and I follow everyone to the side of the room. Fremont gives us a cursory glance.

"Okay. Fall out. Be safe."

Murphy's already disappearing around the corner. Trying to catch up, I push through the scrum of officers standing by the door. One of them, a thirtysomething white guy with dark hair much longer than regulation length, winks at me.

"So, the new reserve officer's kind of hot," he announces to some of the other men.

For a millisecond, I'm brought up short. Is this flirtation? Mockery? Hazing? Some kind of test?

But his tone isn't hostile, and it doesn't seem like a good moment to offer an explication of the laws relating to appropriate workplace conduct. The truth is, I'm grateful that my gender can even be discerned through my bulky uniform. Pathetic.

I wink back. "It's the armored vest, right? Admit it. No man can resist a woman in a ballistic vest."

He laughs. I feel another humiliating surge of gratitude.

I push past and catch up with Murphy, who has somehow acquired both a set of car keys and the dog pole. This instrument is a long aluminum pole with a loop of cable at the end, like a noose. In theory, the loop can be used to snare and temporarily immobilize vicious dogs, while the pole keeps the officer safely distant from sharp teeth and dog drool. Resources are scarce at 7D, so there's apparently only one dog pole for several hundred officers, and on each shift, one vehicle is assigned to drive around with it.

"Carrying this is completely stupid," Murphy mutters as we head out to the parking lot in search of vehicle 7214.

"How come?"

"Because what kind of dog is going to stick its head into one of these things? None, that's what kind of dog. And, what, like we're going to just happen to have this thing handy when a pit bull shows up and lunges at us?"

Murphy shoves the dog pole into vehicle 7214's trunk, where it remains for the rest of the shift.

Your Tax Dollars at Work

Assault with a Dangerous Weapon (bottle): Subject states
Defendant . . . attempted to take his steak and cheese sub at
which point Subject refused and the sandwich fell to the ground.
Defendant became enraged and struck Subject in the head with a
bottle causing minor injury, a ambulance was notified however
Subject refused treatment. Defendant was placed under arrest. . . .

—*MPD Joint Strategic and Tactical Analysis*
Command Center, Daily Report

Then, just like that, I was officially working my first patrol shift.

I offered to drive, per academy instructions, but Murphy declined. "Before we leave, I'm gonna give you the grand tour of the station, and then the whole rest of the district," he promised as he slammed the trunk on the dog pole. "Then after the tour, you can take the wheel and I'm gonna watch a movie, then take a nice long nap. Ha ha, kidding . . . not."

The Seventh District police station was even more down at heel than the academy. It was smaller than most of the other six district stations, and more decrepit. The women's locker room, where I had already spent an unhappy hour, was dank and humid. Neither of the two toilet stall doors latched properly, and the toilets didn't flush unless you held your foot down on the handle for a full five seconds. Unpropitiously, a sign posted near the toilets warned against smearing feces on the wall.

I mentioned this to Murphy. "Is the men's locker room any better?" I asked.

He gave a derisive snort. "This is 7D."

In the report-writing room, several of the ten or so computers were broken, and one of the two printers was out of order. The copy machine was always jammed or out of paper, Murphy said, and the computer keyboards had seen so much hard use that the letters had worn off most of the keys, making report writing a challenge for those who, like me, never learned to touch-type.

The public came in the front door, and waited in an odorous antechamber to gain the attention of one of the station clerks. We officers came in through the rear parking lot and the station's back door, which led to a small landing containing a vandalized, gutted ATM. It looked like someone had taken an ax and a hammer to it, then doused it with gasoline and set it on fire. Down a few stairs, in the basement, were the roll call room, the report writing room, and the locker rooms. The sergeants had their own room, which connected both to the report writing room and roll call room. At the end of the hall were a weight room and some vending machines.

Upstairs somewhere there was a room called the "lunchroom," but Murphy explained that since no one ever had time to sit and eat, it was always empty. The administrative offices were also upstairs, along with the detectives' area and offices for the lieutenants, captains, and the 7D commander.

Upstairs there was also an alcove containing the district Property Book, the archaic, Dickensian object into which all "found property" and evidence had to be entered, by hand and in black ink, with corrections in red ink. The book was enormous, nearly the size of those dictionaries libraries sometimes display on stands, and as battered as the ATM on the landing; it looked like someone had spilled coffee on it and then left it out in the rain for a few weeks before returning it to the station.

The property room itself was in the basement, and even more archaic: like a medieval cabinet of curiosities, it housed scores of moldering Property Books from years past, along with all the items the Seventh District was holding or storing: wallets and cell phones, teddy bears, family photos, wigs, hats, machetes, knives, handguns, Air Jordans, umbrellas, suitcases, textbooks, mops, pillows, jewelry, televisions, bicycles, spent shell casings, crack vials—it was all there somewhere, much of it tucked away in cupboards and ancient storage containers that could only be opened with enormous, heavy metal keys that also looked like they'd been borrowed from a medieval dungeon.

Murphy led me back to Vehicle 7214, and our tour of 7D began.

"That's the big chair. Yeah, it's a giant sculpture of a chair. I don't know why it's there. That convenience store there, it keeps getting robbed; I've been in there, like, ten times in the last few days. Those guys on the left side corner, they're okay. They don't give me any shit usually. That park, though, the kids who hang out in it, they're bad news. They're always up to something. That's what I hate about this PSA, too many fucking juveniles."

He scowled out the window at some teenagers.

"I can handle the older guys, they're pretty straight with me, but the juveniles are another story, and if you arrest them it's, like, two hours of extra pain-in-the-ass paperwork and process because they're juveniles. I *hate* arresting juveniles; it's too much hassle. That's why I liked my last PSA better. Not as many juveniles. . . . Okay, right here, this is where that guy got stabbed last night, you can still see the bloodstain on the pavement, over there, see?"

The Seventh District was divided into eight "police service areas." We were assigned to PSA 702, and we were the second car assigned to that sector; thus our call sign, 7022. Two other officers were assigned to the first sector car in PSA 702, with the call sign 7021. That meant, Murphy explained, that when calls came in, the dispatcher first assigned them to call sign 7021; if 7021 was busy, calls came next to us, call sign 7022, then to 7023, 7024 and so on. "Except there is no 7023 or 7024," Murphy said. "A lot of guys are on leave, so it's just 7021 and us." If our PSA was quiet and we got bored, he added, we could respond to calls in other PSAs as well, and if things got really busy, the dispatchers would start ignoring PSA assignments and send any available 7D car to calls.

I was lucky it wasn't summer, he said. In the summer, when crime tended to spike because the long hot days kept people out on the streets, the department always launched the Summer Crime Initiative, which involved assigning officers to static posts in high-crime areas. "It sucks. You're not allowed to leave your SCI area unless the sergeant gives permission, and you're stuck in the same block or two for ten hours."

By 16:30, the radio started to squawk a bit more. I still had trouble understanding much of what came over it. "You'll get the hang of it," Murphy assured me, "but it takes a while. Anyway, this fuckin' dispatcher's totally ghetto, I can't understand a fuckin' thing she's saying half the time. I don't know where they get these people."

I'd been listening to my police radio whenever I had some downtime, trying to develop what they call "radio ear," and it was true that some dispatchers were harder to understand than others. The best dispatchers spoke slowly and crisply, articulating every word. "Seven-oh-two-one, please respond to the burglary at three-eight-two-one Martin Luther King Ave., apartment number two; repeat, seven-oh-two-one, respond to the burglary at three-eight-two-one Martin Luther King Ave., apartment number two, do you copy?" The worst dispatchers rushed and swallowed half their words, and all you could hear was an indistinct blur of barely intelligible sounds. "—two-one, respond eight-two—King—two—copy?" Usually, assignments also came in over the car's mobile data terminal, but Murphy complained that the MDTs tended to stop working at crucial moments.

Just then the radio crackled, and we heard the steady beep signifying a priority transmission. A garbled, panicky young voice came over the air. "10-33, 10-33! Corner of Southern and South Cap, I'm"—there was some unintelligible crackling and panting—"need additional units!"

Murphy already had his foot on the gas and we were flying down the street, lights flashing and sirens blaring.

If you don't happen to drive an ambulance, fire truck, or police car, you may never have noticed that a high percentage of drivers don't pull to the right and stop when they hear sirens. Maybe they're deaf, or confused, or panicked, or maybe they just choose not to. Either way, Murphy was constantly swerving onto the wrong side of the road to avoid vehicles that were directly in our path. We were on narrow residential streets, going eighty.

I closed my eyes. "God," I thought, "I would really, really hate to die in a car crash on my first night on patrol. If I'm going to get killed in the line of duty, please let me be shot while protecting schoolchildren from an active shooter, not die in a fiery car crash caused by a colleague's overzealous driving." Discreetly, I checked that my seat belt was securely fastened. Murphy wasn't even wearing his, but I decided it wasn't my place to tell him to buckle up. Around us, other patrol cars were also screaming by.

We all converged at the corner of Southern and South Capitol streets. By the time we arrived, there were seven or eight patrol cars there already, slewed out across the road. I had no idea what the emergency was; although there was more crackling and panting on the radio beneath the wail of the sirens, none of it was intelligible to me. Murphy slammed on the brakes, and we both leapt out and raced toward the crowd of people milling around at the corner.

At least fifteen officers were already standing in a loose circle. In the center of the circle, surrounded, stood a middle-aged black man with his hands up in the air. He was dressed conservatively, in khakis and a sweater, and behind his glasses and his trim salt-and-pepper beard, he looked bemused as he surveyed the crowd of blue uniforms around him.

He shrugged wryly, keeping his hands up in the air. "My tax dollars at work."

But already, some of the officers were starting to leave and head back to their cars. There was a lot of muttering and disgusted head shaking.

"What just happened?" I asked Murphy, following him back to our car.

"Aw, that was total bullshit. That fucking guy, Chalin, the guy who called the 10-33, this is the third time he's done that in a week. He totally overreacts. He did a traffic stop and the driver got out and walked toward him instead of just staying in his seat, and Chalin fucking panicked, thought he was being ambushed or something. Fucking idiot. The guy wasn't doing anything; he just didn't know he was supposed to stay in the car. Chalin freaked. People are gonna stop showing up when he calls if he keeps pulling this shit."

I was glad the traffic stop had ended peacefully. A panicky young officer and a subject unexpectedly getting out of the car were common ingredients in too many police shootings. At the same time, I felt a twinge of disappointment as Murphy and I drove away. It was my first 10-33, and after so many practice runs at the academy, I couldn't help wishing for a genuine emergency.

By now the radio was chattering almost constantly, calls starting to come in all over 7D. Suddenly, we were busy. After a few hours responding to disorderly conduct and family disturbance calls, we were sent to check out a case of possible child abuse. An anonymous caller had told the 911 operator that she thought a child was being beaten or hurt in an apartment in her building; she had heard angry shouts and thumps, followed by what sounded like a child screaming in pain.

When we arrived at the address the caller had given, another officer was already in the hallway, and everything was quiet. A television or radio was playing in one of the apartments off the long hallway, but there was no sound coming from apartment 3C, where the caller had said she'd heard a child's screams. The officer already on the scene, a young black guy in the uniform of a mountain bike patrol officer, said he had already knocked on the door, but no one had answered. Murphy knocked again.

This time, we could hear a muffled noise behind the door. It sounded like a child's laughter.

"Police!" shouted the mountain bike officer. "Open the door!"

Behind the door, we heard a child's voice, raised questioningly, followed by a woman's voice.

"Ma'am?" called Murphy. "MPD. Could you open the door, please?"

The sounds came closer. Then, a woman's voice, suspicious: "What do you want?"

"Ma'am, it's the police. Could you please open the door?"

There was a brief silence, broken by the child's voice.

"Police? Mama, is they the police?"

Then the woman's voice again: "I'm not opening this door. What do you want?"

The mountain bike officer was getting impatient. "Ma'am, you have to let us in. We have a report of an abused child in there. We need to come in and make sure that child is safe and unhurt."

"That's ridiculous." The voice on the other side of the door was angry now. "There's no abused child in here. My son is perfectly fine. What kind of busybody told you there was? You just believe every single lie people tell you, and go around accusing people of child abuse?"

We looked at one another.

"Ma'am," I tried, "we're not accusing you of anything. But if we get a report that a child might be in danger, we have to check it out. We can't just ignore it."

Silence.

I tried again. "If your child was with a babysitter or something and we got a call saying that he was in danger, wouldn't you want us to go make sure he was okay?"

"You got a warrant?" she demanded. "If you don't have a warrant, you're not getting into my home."

"No, ma'am. But we really would like to just make sure everything's okay. If you would just open the door so we can see that your child is all right, we'll get out of your hair."

"You don't need to come in. You can tell from right out there that my son is alive and well. He was fussing earlier because he's overtired, that's all, and some busybody with a grudge calls you people to come shout through my door! I want you to leave right now."

"This is bullshit," the mountain bike officer hissed to Murphy and me. "We gotta get in there. We got no idea what she did to that kid. He could be hurt bad for all we know. Or she could have another kid lying dead in there. You got a battering ram in your car? We gotta get that door open!"

"You try to break down this door and I'm calling 911!" the woman shouted.

"We're only here because somebody *already* called 911!" the mountain bike officer shouted back. "We're the *police*, remember?"

"I know exactly who you are," the woman snapped back. "And I know *exactly* what happens to black people when the police come barging into their houses! They end up dead, so I'm not letting you in, and I'm calling 911 and my city councilman to say I got police officers here threatening me for no reason!"

"I'm not threatening you!" The mountain bike officer was indignant. "Now *you're* threatening me! We're just trying to do our job and you're making accusations and threatening to report us!"

Maybe, I thought, a female officer would be more palatable. "Ma'am, we understand what you're saying," I put in. "What if the male officers stand back, and I come in? Just me, one person, just to make sure everyone's okay?"

"No one's coming in here. Not them, not you, not anyone. You people can stand out there all night for all I care, but you're not getting through this door without a warrant."

I looked at Murphy for guidance.

"Come on." He took out his phone and waved us toward the stairs. "Time to call Fremont."

The mountain bike officer was fuming. He looked ready to kick the door in by himself, but he followed us down the stairs, fists clenched.

"The kid sound like he's alive?" Sergeant Fremont asked when Murphy got him on the phone.

"Yeah."

"Okay. Just leave. You got an unconfirmed report from an anonymous caller, and the child's alive and talking? No exigent circumstances. I'll call Child and Family Services so it's logged. They'll decide whether to follow up."

We left, the mountain bike officer still muttering angrily to himself as he rode off down the street.

"He's not a bad officer," Murphy confided. "But he's kind of a hothead. I wouldn't want him in my apartment, either."

"Do you think we're doing the right thing?" I asked. "I mean, if it really was just a false accusation, I totally get why she wouldn't let us in, but . . . what if the 911 caller was right?"

"No," Murphy said. "You can't think about it like that. No exigent circumstances, so no choice. You do what you can do. You think about it too much, you make yourself crazy."

A little while later, we were dispatched to a call for an assault in progress. This time, the door opened instantly when we knocked, and a harassed-looking woman thrust a small boy out at us. "Okay, y'all are finally here, listen, he's going after his brother with a butcher knife and I *need* you to take him *away*."

Murphy put his palm up. "Whoa. Hang on, ma'am, we need to find out what's happening here before we can take anyone away. Can we come in?"

Reluctantly, she backed away, yanking the boy back with her. "Mind your feet."

I looked down. There was a pile of dog shit on the carpet. We stepped over it and into a room that was almost devoid of furniture, just a small table pushed against a wall. Four or five other children were wandering around the room, several in diapers, none older than five. There was also a small black puppy, and several other piles of dog shit.

I took out my notebook. The woman started telling us that her oldest son, who was eight and "has that ADHD and that bipolar thing," was running around with a butcher knife, chasing his little brother. "I can't take this no more. They was fighting over who gets to hold the puppy, and he just went wild and grabbed the knife."

She wanted the boy gone. "You need to put him in the damn hospital, give him some kind of medicine for this; he's all out of medicine. Don't you send him home again with no medicine."

"Ma'am," I asked, "where's the knife now?"

She looked surprised, but turned and went into the kitchen. In defiance of every officer safety lesson, I allowed her to reach into a closed drawer. She pulled out an enormous butcher knife and passed it to me politely, handle first.

I took it gingerly.

"Okay, how about we put this somewhere where none of the kids can reach it?"

We agreed that the top of the refrigerator might make a good temporary home for the knife.

By now two other 7D officers had arrived. One of them stepped in the dog shit and left again, cursing, to wipe his boots on the grass. The other, a woman, picked up the puppy and started cooing to it and waving at the toddlers, who waved back, giggling. The little miscreant at the center of it all just gazed at us, smiling beatifically, not saying a word.

"Come on, you wanna go with these nice officers?" his mother wheedled. "They gonna take you to get some medicine."

The boy looked undecided.

The officer who stepped in dog shit returned, and we all had a discussion about whether we were even allowed to take such a young child anywhere without a parent present. No one was sure, and we debated the wisdom of summoning Child and Family Services. Finally Murphy called Sergeant Fremont again.

"You gonna arrest an eight-year-old?" Fremont asked. "Seriously? Because that would be stupid."

No, no, Murphy assured him, we weren't going to arrest anyone, but in this case we weren't sure about calling Child and Family Services, either.

Fremont eventually said it was okay to just drive the boy to the hospital if we thought we were dealing with a medical or mental health issue rather than a criminal offense, but told us we needed to get the mother to come with us.

The mother was annoyed by this news, and pointed out that the other children couldn't be left alone. She proposed that one of us "lady officers" stay and care for the younger children, and asked the toddlers, "Which one a these ladies you want to have stay, the nice black lady officer, or the nice white lady officer?"

The toddlers all giggled and waved some more at both of us, but we explained that we couldn't stay and babysit. We suggested she call a friend or relative. Reluctantly, she agreed.

Finally, another woman showed up, carrying an additional toddler and a second puppy, apparently a littermate of the first. She looked cross.

"My sister," the mother explained.

Abandoning the sister to manage the room full of toddlers and puppies, the rest of us left. The nice black lady officer, whose name was Warner, said she would drive the boy and his mother to the hospital while we took her still-cursing partner back to the station to wash the dog shit off his boots. Throughout the whole encounter, the knife-wielding boy hadn't said a word, just smiled shyly at everyone.

Our next call was for a burglar alarm at a school. It was dark by now, and we took our flashlights and walked all around the building, stopping at each door to rattle the handles. We shone our flashlight beams through windows and into alcoves, but didn't see anything.

"So what do we do now?" I asked Murphy.

"Nothing. We're done."

We got back on the radio to report the lack of information.

"7022."

"7022, go ahead."

"Ma'am, no signs of intruders or forced entry; the building appears secure. We are 10-8 from that call."

"I copy, 7022 is 10-8."

That seemed to be that, so we went on to another call. There was a female prisoner at the 7D station who needed to be driven to the hospital, and the dispatcher wanted a unit with a female officer to return to the station and take the prisoner. We should probably take that call, Murphy said, since Warner was the only other woman in our PSA right now and she was probably still at the hospital with the little boy.

Back at the station, we were directed to one of the cells, where a morose middle-aged woman lay on a metal bunk, hands over her eyes. She was clad only in beige Spanx-style underwear, the kind of compression garment meant to smooth away all the bulges so your clothes fit better. She was overweight, and her breasts spilled out over the garment's top.

"Okay, Jasmine, these officers is gonna take you to get some medicine for your headache," the officer in charge of the cells called out. With a small moan, the prisoner readjusted her breasts and rose, waiting to be let out.

"You gotta cuff her," Murphy told me.

It seemed absurd to put cuffs on this half-naked moaning woman. *But you knew this was going to happen*, I reminded myself.

When the prisoner came out of the cell, I took a deep breath. I was very aware that both Murphy and the station officer were watching me.

"Okay, ma'am . . . Jasmine. Do me a favor, turn around with your hands behind your back." She obeyed, groaning quietly. I fumbled the cuffs onto her wrists, then glanced back at Murphy. He gave me a quick nod and we led our prisoner out to our car. It was a cumbersome process, because guns can't be brought into the cell area, so we each had to check our guns on the way in, then retrieve them on the way out.

By the time we headed to the hospital, Jasmine was leaning back, eyes closed, in the back seat. "Migraine, huh?" I asked her through the grate that separated her compartment from ours. "That sucks. I get those."

"Yes, this is a really bad one," she whispered, letting out a slow breath. "I just knew I was going to get a migraine."

"How'd you end up in the lockup tonight?" I asked. I wasn't sure of the etiquette when it came to transporting prisoners, but Murphy didn't comment, so I assumed it was okay to ask.

"Domestic violence," Jasmine told me. "I shouldn't have done it, I know I shouldn't have done it to him, but I just couldn't take it no more."

I made a sympathetic noise, one that I hoped combined an appropriate mix of sorrow for her current headachy, imprisoned state with an affirmation that no, she probably shouldn't have done it.

When we got to the hospital and I liberated her from the back seat, she pointed her chin down at her chest. Her breasts had once more popped out of her compression garment. She glanced at Murphy, who had his back to us, and whispered, "Can you help me get these tucked back in?" With her hands cuffed, she was helpless.

"No problem." I stuffed her breasts back into her Spanx, and we proceeded into the hospital. She was checked in and put in a small room, where Murphy told me I had to cuff one of her arms to the bed rail.

This time, I protested. "Seriously? She's not exactly poised to make a run for it, and we're standing right here keeping an eye on her."

"Rules," said Murphy. "Gotta secure prisoners at the hospital."

I shook my head, but lifted Jasmine's wrist and attached the cuffs, as gently as I could. "I'm sorry about this," I told her. "I know you just want to lie down and rest."

"That's all right, officer," she said kindly. "You just doin' your job."

Murphy wandered off to find a vending machine while we waited for the doctor, and I guarded my prisoner. "Can I get you anything? Water, a blanket?" I asked.

"That would be nice," she agreed, voice faint.

Fuck this, I thought. Jasmine wasn't going to try to make a break for it while cuffed to the bed. I recalled Hannibal Lecter pulling off something similar in *Silence of the Lambs*, but Jasmine didn't look like a cannibal, so I left her alone while I went out to find water and blankets. A helpful orderly provided both, and I returned and covered Jasmine with the blanket, placing the water on the table closer to her uncuffed hand.

"You know what, let me turn off that overhead light for you," I offered.

She thanked me again, voice even fainter than before. "I appreciate it, officer."

She was being awfully nice to me, considering. I sat with her, wondering what exactly she'd done to get arrested wearing nothing but Spanx. Hit her boyfriend? Husband? Brother? Son? Stabbed him? Shot him? I couldn't think of a polite way to ask.

After a while the doctor came in and gave Jasmine an injection, and she fell asleep. Murphy made some calls, and an hour later, another officer came to relieve us. We tiptoed away.

In the Wagon

When responding to a Fire/EMS incident, members shall:

- Respond promptly to the scene of all fires to which they are dispatched or observe while on patrol.

- If arriving prior to firefighters or rescue workers, quickly assess the scene to determine: a. What has happened; b. The number of people injured/trapped; and c. The extent of injuries . . .

- Clear the immediate area and prevent interference by pedestrians and traffic. Note: Wear reflective clothing at all times when directing or controlling traffic, regardless of the weather or time of day.

—*MPD General Order OPS 308.11*

One evening in November, I was assigned to "the wagon." Some of the patrol cars in DC are set up for prisoner transport, but most lack a safety grille separating the front of the car from the rear passenger compartment, so when officers assigned to one of these "non-transport" cars make an arrest, they need to summon the wagon—a specially outfitted prisoner transport van—to bring the arrestee to the station for booking. After booking and a short period in the station holding cells, arrestees are transferred, again by wagon, to the city's Central Cell Block to await arraignment.

Many officers hated wagon assignments. "You're just a taxi driver," Murphy complained. The wagon wasn't dispatched to ordinary calls for service, and if you were driving it, you weren't supposed to conduct traffic stops or do much of anything aside from drive prisoners around when needed. Other officers loved the wagon, for the same reasons. "I'm sick of chasing kids over fences and getting in between people who want to kill each other," one older officer told me. "Give me a nice quiet night driving the wagon, anytime."

I didn't mind being in the wagon for a night. For me, just a month out of the academy, everything was still new, so it was all interesting. And I knew I needed more practice handcuffing and searching people. If I was going to be a cop, I needed to get comfortable with applying cuffs, and not every arrestee was likely to be as accommodating as Jasmine.

You might think there's nothing to it, but for the neophyte, handcuffs are not as simple as they look on TV. MPD used the Smith & Wesson Model 100 Lever Lock handcuffs (issued with nickel plating, but available commercially in both nickel and black for the fashion-forward officer). It is possible to put cuffs on someone with a single decisive tap of metal on each wristbone; if you start with closed but not locked cuffs and you get the angle just right, a firm tap will make the arm of the cuff swing around completely and snap quickly into place around the wrist. If you get the angle wrong, your prisoner will instead howl in pain and be left with an unpleasant bruise. (Academy training often left me with banged-up wrists.) Experienced officers make this look easy, but I was nervous about accidentally hurting someone, so I rarely tried the tap-swing method; instead, I'd stand there and painstakingly maneuver the cuffs around to the correct position, then gently close each one. (With real prisoners, this tended to induce cursing, as it often took me longer than it should have to get the cuffs in place.)

At the academy, we were taught an elaborate method for approaching those we planned to cuff. There were different techniques for standing, kneeling, and prone subjects. For a standing subject, you were supposed to begin by standing off at a safe distance—far enough away that the subject wouldn't be able to land a kick or a punch—and order the subject to turn away and bend slightly forward at the waist, with feet spread more than shoulder-width apart and toes pointing outward. This was supposed to ensure that the subject would be in "a position of disadvantage," off-balance and unable to effectively lash out with a foot or arm. The trouble was, the proper position was hard to remember and harder still to explain; in real life, I soon found, even the most cooperative subjects become quickly confused and annoyed by the long series of directions. ("Wait, you want my toes pointing *this* way? Or *that* way?")

Also, though being off-balance undoubtedly made it tougher for a combative subject to strike out at the handcuffing officer, it made it equally difficult for a subject to get his arms into the right position and keep them there. "Place your hands at the small of your back, palms out, thumbs up," you'd command.

This generally led to more questions and/or curses. "You say palms out, thumbs up? The fuck does *that* mean? How'm I supposed to do that while I'm all bent over like this?"

The instructions were complex:

Once the subject is placed at a disadvantage, the officer will remove the handcuffs from the pouch on their belt and approach the subject from the rear at a 45-degree angle. The officer should position the handcuffs in the same hand as the side they are approaching from (e.g. if the officer is approaching from the left the cuffs should be in the officer's left hand). Once the officer reaches the subject, they should:

1. Grasp with the free hand, both of the individual's index and middle fingers firmly to prevent the individual from pulling away.
2. Apply the handcuff to the near wrist.
3. Apply the handcuff to the far wrist.

Just when you finally had palms and thumbs and cuffs lined up just right, however, the subject, being off-balance, would stumble forward or backward, and everything would be off-kilter again.

Getting the cuffs closed around a pair of wrists was only step one. After that, the cuffs needed to be adjusted: too tight and they'd hurt, compressing circulation and causing bruising; too loose and an agile subject could wriggle his wrists out. Then, when the cuffs were just right, you needed to lock them with the tiny, almost invisible lever lock, which was impossible to manipulate while wearing gloves. Failure to set the lever lock would allow the cuffs to tighten on their own, potentially causing injury and lawsuits. Once the lock snicked shut, however, the subject would usually announce that one or both cuffs was digging painfully into his flesh, so you'd then have to find and manipulate the tiny handcuff key, unlock the cuffs, and readjust them.

Once out of the academy, I quickly discovered that no one followed these elaborate directions. Most cops simply said, "Turn around," then moved up behind the subject, heedless of the risk of being kicked or pummeled, grabbed one wrist, cuffed it, grabbed the other wrist, cuffed it, and that was that. When a subject was combative, one officer grabbed and held each arm while a third officer applied the cuffs.

Searching someone is also harder than it looks. At the academy, our instructors would put fake knives, guns, and baggies full of drugs in their underwear, knowing that squeamish recruits would be reluctant to give the groin area more than a cursory inspection. After suffering mock stabbings and shootings due to our failure to conduct proper searches, we all became somewhat more thorough, but here too, searching real subjects was much tougher than searching our peers or the instructors. (Try searching a three-hundred-pound woman who bellows, "You're *tickling* me!" every time you come within six inches of her.) More practice, I thought, could only do me good.

My partner in the wagon was a silent, surly fellow called Yusef. His pale skin was pitted with acne scars. He seemed a little put out to have to ride with me, and offered monosyllabic answers to most of my questions.

"Where you from?"

"Jersey."

"How long you been with MPD?"

"Couple years."

"You like it?"

"S'okay."

I soon gave up.

The only good thing about riding with Yusef was that his near-catatonic state enabled me to get plenty of cuffing and searching practice. The arresting officer puts cuffs on an arrestee and does an initial search, but the wagon officer does a second search before loading a prisoner into the back of the van, and once back at the station, the wagon officer sometimes ends up doing a third search as well if the booking officer is busy, or just doesn't feel like doing another search. Prisoners are uncuffed before going into cells, then re-cuffed before being transported to Central Cell Block or any other location.

Once ensconced in the passenger's seat, Yusef did not budge, leaving the driving, cuffing, and searching entirely to me.

Occasionally he'd offer laconic instructions: "Park," or "Over there." Aside from that, he remained almost entirely silent as we ferried prisoners to and fro.

The prisoners remained mostly silent too. By the time we showed up to transport arrestees to the station, any initial rage or resistance had usually dissipated and been replaced by resignation. They put their hands behind their backs when requested, ducked their heads as advised when climbing into the wagon, and leaned glumly against walls while being searched.

When we had no prisoners, we just drove around.

"Should I go anywhere in particular?" I asked Yusef.

"Whatever."

So I just drove, waiting for the radio to give us something new to do. The streets of 7D were still unfamiliar, and driving around in the wagon was as good a way as any to get my bearings. It was late afternoon and still light out; there were people out on the sidewalks and sitting on steps and porches, but they mostly ignored us as we drove slowly by. I turned a corner and started up a hill.

Suddenly, a man jumped into the road ahead of me, waving his arms wildly. I slammed on the brakes to avoid hitting him. He was shouting and pointing. "That building's on fire!"

And it was. Up the block on the left, flames were pouring out of what seemed to be the back deck of a ground-floor apartment, and thick smoke was rising into the sky. I looked at Yusef for guidance.

"Local. Fire board."

This was more words than Yusef had uttered in the previous hour, but I understood his directive. In MPD-speak, a fire is called a "local," and a fire truck is a "fire board." (An ambulance is just "the board.") I got on the radio and reported that we had a local—Yusef came alive again long enough to provide the address—and needed the fire board.

"Now block the road, lights on, so people don't drive in front of it, but leave room for the fire trucks to get by." Yusef was becoming positively loquacious.

"Shouldn't we, ah, make sure no one's still inside that building?"

Yusef looked at me like I was nuts. "You want to go out there and start knocking on doors?"

"Shouldn't we? I mean, there could be people next door or upstairs who don't know that part of their building's on fire. Shouldn't we tell them, so they can leave?"

"Whatever."

I took this as an affirmative response and hopped out. I was sick of handcuffing depressed prisoners, anyway, and even more sick of sitting next to Yusef. Warning people about the fire seemed like a better way to spend some time.

With a slight groan, Yusef slid out of the passenger's seat to the street. I started running up the hill.

"Hey, watch it," he called after me. "These people don't like us around here."

The flames had created a wall of fire on the side of the building facing the street, but from what I could see, the main entrance to the apartment was on the other side of the building, along with entrances to all the units in the attached apartment block. By now a small crowd had gathered to stare at the flames, but no one seemed particularly perturbed.

"Fire trucks are on their way," I called as I ran by. No one commented.

I ran up the street, around the last unit, and into a large courtyard. On this side of the building, the fire was completely out of sight, and people were milling around casually, chatting and strolling. A few people seemed to be having a picnic.

"The building's on fire!" I shouted as I ran toward the burning unit. Everyone looked at me like I was insane.

I couldn't blame them—from the courtyard, there was no sign of danger. But I kept shouting and shooing people away from the building, and finally even the picnickers began to drift out toward the street.

I ran into the vestibule of the burning building. It was also quiet and empty, though the smell of smoke was starting to drift through. I started up the stairs, pounding on doors as I went. A woman in pajamas opened one door.

"There's a fire," I told her. "You need to get out of the building."

"Fire?"

"Yeah, the ground floor apartment's on fire," I yelled over my shoulder.

I was already running up the next flight of stairs. "Fire department's on the way, but everyone needs to get out."

On the next landing, I could hear a child laughing inside an apartment, but no one answered when I pounded on the door. Shit. I pounded some more.

"Police! The building's on fire!"

No response, though I could still hear children's voices.

I started to wonder if I should try to kick the door in. That seemed melodramatic, but then again, running around shouting, "Fire! Everyone out!" was melodramatic too. And weren't these exigent circumstances? I didn't want any children to burn up because they were too scared to open the door. But I wasn't sure I was strong enough to kick the door in on my own. Maybe I could shoot the lock out like they did in the movies. But no: "Know your target and what is beyond it." There might be small children beyond my target, their heads right at doorknob-level. Yusef could probably help me kick in the door, but where was he? I suspected he was back in the wagon, watching a movie on his phone.

I pounded and yelled some more, and finally, the door was opened by a dreadlocked young man holding a toddler. Two slightly older children hung back behind his legs.

"Yeah?" He was in sweats, and looked like he'd been napping. Everyone in the building seemed to have been napping.

"The building is on fire. You need to get out."

"You want me to *leave*?"

"Sir," I said, using my command voice, "this building is on *fire*. You and the children need to get out. Now!"

He gave me an aggrieved look, but began, reluctantly, to usher the kids out the door.

By now, the smell of smoke was heavier, and I could hear sirens. I banged on a few more doors, but no one else seemed to be home; in a few apartments, I heard dogs barking. I winced at the thought of dogs stuck in a burning building, but there wasn't much I could do. The fire department was coming, and they would either put the fire out and save the dogs, or not.

I was fairly sure I recalled something from one of our academy lessons directing us not to rush into burning buildings, especially not to rescue barking dogs, but to stand back and let the properly trained firefighters rush into burning buildings. Had I been stupid to run into the building? Maybe. But only part of the building was on fire, and I was in the other part. Still. Either the fire was no big deal and it had been unnecessary to get people out, in which case it was stupid for me to have rushed in, or the fire *was* a big deal, in which case it was also stupid for me to have rushed in. Except the fire department hadn't been here when I arrived, and at least one of the apartments in the building had erupted into sheets of flame, and there were children in the building, so perhaps rushing in *was* necessary, even if stupid. And where the fuck was Yusef?

I was still puzzling over all this as I left the building, which was still intact on the courtyard side, at least. Running up and down the stairs and pounding on doors had left me panting and sweating, and the dreadlocked man with the children gave me an unfriendly look when I passed him in the courtyard.

I went back around the corner and found that the cavalry had arrived with a vengeance; I counted at least seven fire trucks. On the street side of the building, water from several fire hoses was gushing into the burning apartment. Soon, the flames were gone, replaced by a billow of greasy smoke.

Down the block, Yusef was leaning against the side of the wagon, looking unruffled. "So, you got, like, a hero complex?" He snickered.

I glared at him.

He looked a little abashed. "Hey, no, I guess that was good, you told people to get out. Yeah. Probably good to have people get out. You know, since the building was on fire." He nodded, apparently just now reaching this conclusion, and let out a small, weird giggle.

I wasn't sure if Yusef was clinically depressed, a jerk, or just an idiot. Or maybe high. "So what do the fire department guys say?"

"Dunno. It was the kitchen, they said. Looks like something caught on fire."

"You *think?*" I asked, but my sarcasm was lost on him.

"Yeah. So, kaboom." Yusef stretched and looked at his watch. "We can go now."

We went back to ferrying prisoners around.

No Plot

Assault with a Dangerous Weapon (knife): At approximately 1145
hours, Victim reports that he was [in] the bathroom shaving when
Suspect came in the bathroom and requested to use it. Victim did
not want to leave at that time. Victim and Suspect got into a
verbal altercation at which point Suspect brandished a knife.
Victim stated that Suspect began swinging the knife at which
time Victim was struck in his right shin. Victim obtained a small
puncture and responded to the hospital. . . .

—MPD *Joint Strategic and Tactical Analysis*
Command Center, Daily Report

Patrol has no plot. I learned this very quickly.

This is why there are thousands of books and movies about detectives, but not many about patrol officers. The work of detectives comes with built-in narratives. Someone killed someone, beat someone, raped someone, stole something—whodunit? The work of detectives involves a mystery, a search for answers, and at least some of the time, a resolution.

Patrol is different. Patrol officers are first responders—they're dispatched by radio, they're flagged down on the street, or they spot a problem and stop to sort it out. Every patrol shift starts from scratch: a full tank of gas in the scout car, and a blank run sheet. The radio crackles and you're off. Sometimes you get boring calls, and sometimes you get interesting calls.

Men hit their girlfriends. Roommates get into fights. Burglar alarms go off; teenagers refuse to come home when they're supposed to; people overdose on drugs. There are car crashes, fires, robberies, and shootings. The next shift, you start over. New people, new problems. Or sometimes same people, same problems. If a crime has occurred and the perpetrator happens to still be on the scene or can be found within minutes, you make an arrest. But patrol officers don't track down serial killers or solve mysteries. If you happen to encounter a mystery—a crime with no suspects, or a missing suspect—you hand it over to the detectives, who may or may not remember to let you know how it all turns out.

One day, for instance, human bones turned up in a basement crawl space in 7D. The construction worker who stumbled onto the bones was part of a crew hired to expand a residential basement, and he assumed he had found the bones of an animal—a raccoon, or just a big rat. Then he saw a human skull, and called the police. A couple of 7D patrol officers arrived and summoned the detectives. By the time the scene had been thoroughly searched, three skeletons had turned up; in addition to the one in the crawl space, there were two in the wooded area behind the building, found by police cadaver dogs.

It was a genuine class A mystery. The skeletons were at least a year old, possibly much older, and once the medical examiner looked at them, it was clear none of them had died of natural causes. All three were female; two had been shot and one had been beaten to death. But though Murphy and I drove by and stopped to chat with the 7D officers guarding the perimeter, it wasn't our business, and it wasn't really theirs, either; they were just standing guard duty. When the remains were finally identified, months later (through DNA samples provided by families of people who had been reported missing years earlier), most patrol officers learned of it through local news reports.

For reserve officers, the experience of patrolling is even more discontinuous, and not only because they're part-timers. Most career patrol officers rarely leave their assigned districts. During major citywide events, such as mass protests, parades, and presidential inaugurations, they might be detailed to civil defense units or parade duty, but the rest of the time, they stay in their home districts. Although each reserve officer is assigned to one of the city's seven patrol districts upon graduation, we were also frequently asked to help out in districts other than our own, especially if they were temporarily short-staffed or expected a surge of problems. I liked patrolling in other districts; it was a good way to get to know the issues police face in other parts of the city, and to see how different each district is. But it added to the disjointedness of patrolling.

Despite this, things soon began to feel more routine. After a few months of patrol, I was starting to feel less anxious. It still took me half an hour to get all my gear on, and I still felt like I didn't know what I was doing, but I was coming to see that often my fellow officers didn't know what they were doing, either, and for the most part, the more experienced officers were happy to help someone new.

During one of my first traffic stops, the driver, a sad-looking middle-aged guy, told me his license and registration were in the back of his van. "Can I climb back and get them?" he asked.

I hesitated, briefly flummoxed. The guy was cooperative; he had asked politely. Should I just let him climb into the back and retrieve his bag? I was about to tell him to go right ahead when my partner Ben jumped in to save me.

"Hang on there, sir," he interjected. "You can just give us your name and date of birth, we'll look you up that way, all right?"

I was mortified. What kind of dimwitted police officer would allow a driver to climb back into the unseen rear compartment of a van to retrieve something? Not for the first time (or the last time), a lifetime of polite habits had trumped every police academy lesson about officer safety.

"That was dumb," I admitted to Ben as we got back into the car to look the guy up.

"I'll give you a few pointers on that one," he said kindly. "We'll talk in a second."

At least I wasn't alone in my cluelessness. Many 7D evening shift patrol officers were young and relatively new to the job. Often, the most experienced officers in each PSA had just two or three years of experience, sometimes less. At complicated scenes, everyone spent a fair amount of time consulting one another by phone. ("You ever handled a juvenile selling weed? Yeah, what's the process? You got a copy of that form? I never even heard of that.")

Scenes were frequently chaotic, and officers were part of the chaos. It was standard procedure for officers to request backup units if a call seemed potentially dangerous, and even when backup wasn't requested, officers not busy on other calls routinely stopped by other officers' scenes to see if they could help out. It was common to end up with half a dozen officers at each call. MPD officials often complained of being short-staffed, but as far as I could tell, there was no shortage of officers. Often, we were tripping over one another.

In theory, the officers assigned to the call by the dispatcher "owned" the scene until a higher-ranking official showed up, but in practice, many scenes seemed to have no one in charge. You'd arrive at a domestic violence call, for instance, and find four or five other officers already wandering around in a house full of people, with no one coordinating their activities. Police culture is hierarchical between ranks but egalitarian within ranks, and officers rarely seemed comfortable telling their peers what to do. This reluctance to take charge meant that several different officers might interview the same victim or witness—not to double- or triple-check their story, but just because no one was keeping track. You'd find five officers in the living room and none at the doors, or four officers searching the yard and no one searching the basement.

It was inefficient and potentially dangerous. On another of my early patrol shifts, my partner and I responded to a domestic violence call. It was an unseasonably warm fall afternoon, and we arrived to find ourselves at a backyard barbecue. At least fifteen guests were milling around, as were the victim and the alleged perpetrator, and everyone was talking at once, most corroborating the complainant's version of events, but a few taking the perpetrator's side. Within minutes of our arrival, half a dozen other officers arrived, adding to the crowd. Several witnesses began an enthusiastic and slightly tipsy reenactment of the assault to illustrate the sequence of events, which had reportedly involved the victim being slammed against the porch door by her boyfriend, and, perhaps, the boyfriend being subsequently hit on the head with a mop handle by a now-absent third party. At some point during the chaotic reenactment, the alleged perpetrator simply walked out the front door and down the street, unhindered by the group of officers standing chatting on the front porch. (Fortunately, he didn't get far; we arrested him halfway up the block.)

Much of the time, however, patrolling involved a whole lot of nothing much. You drove around in circles, waiting for something interesting to happen. Especially in the early part of the afternoon, the radio would often go quiet. You'd head over to the 7-Eleven to get a cup of coffee, stopping to shoot the shit with any other officers who had also decided to spend some quality time in the convenience store parking lot. (Since the Seventh District's 7-Elevens were constantly getting robbed, their employees were usually happy to have a few cop cars visible in the parking lot.) You'd drive around some more, poking the scout car into back alleys and empty lots to see if any bad guys were hanging around. Mostly they weren't, or if they were, they sensibly went somewhere else when they saw a police car roll up.

I soon grew accustomed to certain kinds of recurring situations. Calls reporting disorderly conduct came in constantly, for instance, but rarely amounted to much. When you got a call for disorderly conduct—people yelling in the stairwell, kids standing around on the corner hassling passersby, a noisy party—you had to go check it out, but you knew it would probably come to nothing. Either the disorder would be nowhere in sight when you pulled up—the perpetrators having vanished, or turned orderly— or they would be doing something that didn't in fact constitute a crime, and we would have to explain to the complainant that standing in a group on the corner or playing music at a party does not constitute an arrestable offense. Sometimes we'd go talk to the partygoers or the guys on the corner, just to let them know their neighbors were complaining. Sometimes they'd curse and tell us their neighbors were busybodies, but generally they'd turn down the music or agree to go hang out somewhere else. Only rarely did those calls turn into something more serious.

Cops viewed these as "bullshit calls." You'd respond to a call reporting some kids setting a fire on the sidewalk; you'd arrive and find nothing but a small pile of ash. You'd get a call about a family disturbance, but when you located the address, no one would answer the door and you'd find that the person who called 911 hadn't left a callback number. You'd be dispatched to a convenience store to take a shoplifting report, but the shoplifter would be long gone, and had in any case only stolen a can of soda, so you'd look at the security camera footage, make a few desultory turns around the block in search of your suspect, and shrug apologetically to the frustrated store owner. A woman would call to complain that drug dealers kept hanging around in front of her house, leaning on her fence and dropping their trash in her yard, and you'd have to explain that there wasn't much you could do unless you caught the litterers in the act, and even then, you weren't going to haul someone off to jail for dropping a candy wrapper on someone's lawn. Not in 7D, anyway.

Like most poor minority neighborhoods, 7D was in many ways over-policed—unlike in more affluent areas, police are a constant and visible presence. Activists critical of policing complain, with some justification, that police effectively become occupying forces in poor urban neighbor-hoods. You can't walk for more than a few minutes in 7D without seeing a police car, or two, or three, and when there are more police, there are also more enforcement actions and arrests, further fueling race- and wealth-based disparities.

But over-policing is driven in part by the law of supply and demand—police go where people ask them to go. To put it a little differently: Police don't operate in a vacuum. They are paid by taxpayer dollars; they re-spond to the directives and incentives created by national, state, and municipal laws, policies, and political pressures; and in a day-to-day sense, they respond to whatever calls happen to come in over the 911 lines, whether those calls involve complaints about armed robberies or about disorderly conduct.

In recent years, videos shared on social media have drawn national at-tention to the implicit racial bias that too often leads white Americans to call the cops on black people engaged in innocuous activities, such as barbecuing in public parks, napping in a university dorm lounge, entering their own apartment buildings, or sitting at a Starbucks table without first placing an order. Such bias-driven calls are all too common, especially in demographically changing neighborhoods. They demonstrate the durability of destructive racial stereotypes, waste police resources, and leave people of color feeling harassed and frustrated, knowing that even the most innocent activities may generate hostile scrutiny. But the over-policing of poor black urban communities is also fueled by high demand for police services from members of those same communities. When other social goods and services are absent or scarce, police become the default solution to an astonishingly wide range of problems.

In 7D, overreliance on police services meant constant 911 calls for minor issues. People called the police because their neighbor's TV was too loud, their daughter was sassing them, or they smelled marijuana on the street. They called 911 to report that the kids from down the block kept leaving their bikes in the middle of the sidewalk, the boys on the corner were being disrespectful, or their sister took their favorite scarf without permission. And, of course, there were complaints from the truly mentally ill, who called to report nonexistent crimes and alien abductions. But it didn't matter how trivial or nonsensical the complaint was. When people called 911, the police responded, every time.

I didn't mind the bullshit calls. They were more interesting than sitting around in the 7-Eleven parking lot. In general, I didn't much want to lock people up, but I enjoyed talking to people—even crazy people, lonely people, and people incapable of handling the minor conflicts that are a normal part of life. Many officers complain about having to serve as social workers, mediating family disputes and dealing with people who mostly need parenting classes, drug rehab, or psychiatric care, not police intervention. But though I was keenly aware of the downside of treating police as default problem solvers, I enjoyed the social-work aspect of the job.

Sometimes, the silly things made you feel useful. One cold evening in February 2017, I was patrolling with Ben. We were stopped at a red light when I noticed that the woman in the car next to us was screaming. I rolled down my window.

"Oh my God oh my God!" shrieked the woman. She lifted both hands off the steering wheel. "Oh God oh God!"

"Ma'am," I called. "What's wrong?"

"Oh God oh God there's a spider in my car. Oh God help me." She was hyperventilating.

Ben and I looked at each other. Then Ben hit the blue lights and we both jumped out of the car.

"Ma'am, just come on out of your car," I said. "My partner here is going to take care of that spider."

Ben scowled at me. I smiled sweetly. "I'm scared of spiders too."

Still repeating, "Oh my God oh my God," the woman opened her door and leapt out. Around us, the traffic roared by.

Ben leaned into the car. "Where is it?"

"Oh God. It's enormous. Huge. Can't you see it?"

"Oh, got it, there it is. Actually, well, it's pretty small." Ben swatted the spider with a tissue. "Okay, ma'am. The spider is gone."

"Oh, bless you, officers, bless you, and thank you so much!"

All smiles now, she jumped back into her car.

Back in our own car, Ben looked at me. "Well, that was a first."

High Visibility Patrol. Other item of note: Units observed a female having a panic attack in the middle of Bladensburg Road NE due to a spider on the inside of her windshield. Officers removed a spider from woman's car in traffic and she was very relieved.

—*MPD Reserve Corps Newsletter*

Mothers and Daughters

*Assault with a Dangerous Weapon (Other)—At the listed date,
time Complainant reports to MPD [that she and] Suspect who is
Complainant's daughter were involved in a verbal argument that
quickly escalated to Suspect pushing Complainant into a table
causing Complainant to fall to the ground . . . at which point
Suspect picked up a dumbbell and struck Complainant in the
face causing the listed injuries.*

—MPD *Joint Strategic and Tactical Analysis
Command Center, Daily Report*

One night in the late spring of 2017, we were dispatched to take a missing persons report after a women called 911 to say that her daughter had vanished.

"Oh no, fuck!" my partner moaned. "I fucking *hate* missing persons! This is going to be such a fucking time suck."

No one liked missing persons calls, and this one did seem like a stinker: a sixteen-year-old-girl, missing for several hours. Bad things could happen to missing girls.

There had been a recent missing persons scandal in DC. Local media had noted the high number of police department reports involving missing girls, almost all African American, and for a few weeks, this fueled a social media furor: there was an epidemic of missing girls in DC, activists declared, but because they were dark-skinned, the authorities didn't take their cases seriously and didn't bother to look for them.

The story presented by the media was not entirely accurate. Although more than two thousand missing children and teens were reported missing in DC each year, virtually all of them were quickly located. Many had gone off of their own accord, for reasons of their own, and soon returned home. They were not always promptly removed from the list of missing persons, however, because their families sometimes forgot to let the police know they were back, and police officers sometimes forgot to update the records. The vast majority of children reported missing had not mysteriously vanished or been abducted; they simply were not where they were supposed to be. Sometimes, that was because they hated the places they were supposed to be, and for good reason; many missing children were hiding from abusive caregivers or trying to avoid miserable, overcrowded homes.

Other times, they were just acting like kids.

On one of my patrol shifts, for instance, an eight-year-old boy was reported missing by his mother when he disobeyed her directive not to ride his skateboard in the street; wriggling out of her grip, he managed to grab his skateboard and tear off. The mother was holding a baby in an infant seat and couldn't effectively give chase, so she called the police and reported her son missing.

With mother and baby in the back seat of the patrol car, we drove slowly all over the neighborhood, searching for the young absconder. His mother finally spotted him near a park, skateboarding energetically down the middle of the road. We pulled up alongside and his mother called his name. The boy glanced at us, scowled, and skated even faster, but my partner for the evening, a fit young guy in his twenties, jumped out of the car and tackled him, grabbing him around the waist and hoisting him right off the ground. The boy's feet kicked frantically at the air, but my partner held him firmly off the pavement, then stuffed him unceremoniously into the car next to his mother. I retrieved the skateboard and added it to the now-crowded back seat. The boy was snuffling and bawling, and his mother was threatening him and his skateboard with dire consequences.

We ended up driving them all the way back to her parents' place in a Maryland suburb, getting lost several times along the way, the boy now silent and pouting, his mother loquacious with relief but seemingly unable to recall her parents' address with any certainty. We passed strip malls and made U-turns in a dozen culs-de-sac, the mother squinting at house after house. "I think it's just down that street there . . . no, wait, maybe the next one?" Finally, she spotted a house that appeared to satisfy her, so we let the whole crew off in the driveway, and they vanished inside.

This was an easy one, since the missing boy was found quickly enough to cancel the "missing" designation. But a missing sixteen-year-old girl sounded more troubling, and at first I was taken aback by my partner's cavalier dismissal.

My partner that spring evening was a female officer from Puerto Rico. Like me, she was an older office with teens at home, and I liked her lilting Spanish accent, her empathy, and her calm, no-nonsense attitude toward the macho antics of our younger male colleagues.

Seeing my raised brows, she said, "Yeah, right, *maybe* this girl got kidnapped by a pedophile. But not very likely. I bet this is gonna be bullshit. Just wait."

She was right. When we arrived at the missing girl's home, it was clear that her mother was furious, not frightened.

"I told her, Kenisha, you ain't leaving this house! I said, you grounded!" she fumed. "So I go out to the store, I got errands, she supposed to be staying here doing homework, she got a math test tomorrow. But I come home from the store and she *gone*. She out of control."

"So . . . you reported her missing, Ms. Watkins?"

She harrumphed. "Yes, she missing! She missing from where I told her she got to be, which is right here. So you got to go find her. You got to find her right *now*."

"Are you worried about her safety?" Just because there was no reason to think the girl had been abducted didn't mean she couldn't be in danger. A teen who was fighting with her mother might be angry, depressed, vulnerable to exploitation, even suicidal.

Ms. Watkins snorted derisively. "Oh no. She just acting out. She probably in the park with them friends of hers. She always going there. You just got to go look for her. And when you find her," she added ominously, "I want you to take her *jail*. She need to be taught a lesson about listening to her mother. I tell her to stay put, she need to stay *put*."

All the same, our sergeant insisted that we go through the standard missing persons drill, calling friends, neighbors, classmates, teachers, local hospitals. We sat in the parked scout car, me making calls, my partner—vindicated by the manifest ridiculousness of our quest—watching videos on her phone. I called the girl's friends and teachers; I checked to make sure she hadn't been arrested or taken into the custody of Child and Family Services; I called local hospitals; I even called the morgue to see if any unidentified adolescent female bodies had turned up. Meanwhile, other patrol cars were provided with the girl's description and instructed to drive around looking for her, particularly in the park where her mother claimed she often hung out.

"This is dumb," I finally admitted. "This girl's not really missing. She's just a teenager who ignored her mom and went out with friends."

"You got it. That's how MPD works," my partner agreed, not looking up from her phone. "Gotta look like we're doing something even when everyone knows there's no point and the kid will be home tomorrow."

Two hours later, finally finished with the long list of calls (which were, unsurprisingly, fruitless), I left my partner to her movie and went back and knocked on Ms. Watkins's door.

She looked surprised to see me.

"Ms. Watkins," I said dutifully, "I just wanted to let you know that we don't have any additional information yet, but we're looking all over, and the minute we find out anything, we'll let you know."

"Oh, she's back!"

"She's back?"

"I'm sorry, officer, I meant to call you, but I got so busy yelling at her, I forgot. She come back about an hour ago."

She gestured at a sulky-looking teen sitting on the sofa.

"You gonna arrest her now? I'm sick and tired of this. She won't mind me. Night in jail would do her a world of good."

"Ma'am, she hasn't committed any crime. Going out when you told her not to isn't a thing we can lock her up for."

"Oh . . ." Ms. Watkins looked disappointed. "Okay, I got you. Okay. Can you at least talk to her, try to scare her a bit?" She was suddenly plaintive, an exhausted, worried mother rather than an angry mother.

"I know I sound harsh, but she getting *wild*; she don't listen. She don't understand that I worry about her. This a hard city, you know? She keep up like this, disobeying me, failing math, going with them drug boys, she end up making a mess of her life. Her sister, she an addict. I want better for Kenisha. Maybe you can scare some sense into her."

"I'd be happy to talk to her." I wasn't going to try to scare the girl, and I didn't have much hope I'd be able to persuade her to listen to her mother, but maybe Ms. Watkins was right; maybe a uniformed police officer would have some influence.

I went over to the girl and sat down on a chair so I was facing her. Her hair was dyed a vibrant blue, she had multiple nose rings, and her mouth was set in an expression of mulish teen stubbornness.

"Kenisha, look," I began. "Your mom got really worried about you. I know maybe it seems like she was just mad, but she was so worried about you she called us and reported you missing, because she thought you might be in real danger."

Kenisha gave this the eye roll it deserved.

I tried again. "I'm not kidding. She was really worried about you, and we were too. We had police all over the neighborhood, searching for you. We called every hospital in the city in case you got into some kind of bad accident and were lying there hurt or unconscious. We even called the morgue to make sure you weren't lying there dead on a slab."

My mention of the morgue generated a brief flicker of interest, but it was quickly replaced by another eye roll.

"So do me a favor, Kenisha," I concluded. "Listen to your mom. I know how she's feeling. I've got two kids too. I've got a teenage daughter. I worry about her too. That's what moms do. So I know it's annoying when your mom says don't do this, don't do that, don't go here, don't go there. But she's your mom, and it's her job to worry about you. Okay? So can you try to mind her, make sure she knows where you are, listen to her when she says to stay home? She's not saying it just to be annoying, even though I know it can feel that way to you. She wants you to go to school, study, stay out of trouble, grow up, live a good, safe life. She loves you."

Kenisha inspected her fingernails. "Whatever."

We got a lot of calls involving conflicts between mothers and daughters. Or maybe it just seemed that way to me.

On my next shift, we got a call for a family disturbance, and when we arrived, we could hear a woman shouting, "Out! I want you out!" Objects were flying down the stairs from the townhouse's second level: a pair of jeans, a book, a shoe.

The man who opened the door shrugged his shoulders and rolled his eyes, but didn't say anything. It's unfortunate, his body language suggested, but what can you do?

Behind him, in the living room, a girl was huddled on the sofa, crying.

"Out! Gone! *Git!*" The voice was coming from the top of the stairs.

A backpack flew down at us.

"Whoa! Police!" My partner headed toward the stairs, and I headed toward the girl, both of us shouting and dodging flying objects.

"Please stop throwing things!"

A woman's head and torso appeared at the top of the stairs.

"Officers, you need to take her away." The woman pointed at the sobbing girl on the sofa. "She is *out* of control!"

"Ma'am, could you please come down and tell us what's going on?"

As in most family disturbance calls, the story was garbled because people kept interrupting one another, and no one would stay still.

The woman at the top of the stairs refused to descend, but the rain of objects from the upstairs landing stopped.

"She try to bite me," she called down. "The little bitch try to *bite* me. You need to get her out of here."

I looked at the "little bitch." She *was* little, maybe fifteen or sixteen.

"You try to bite her, like she says?" my partner asked.

She wiped her cheeks. "Nah." She looked both defiant and resigned. "I just pretended to try to bite her."

I went over to the girl and gestured with my head to my partner. He nodded and headed up the stairs. The man who had answered the door busied himself making coffee, carefully keeping his back to us.

"So what happened here?" I asked the girl.

She looked down. "Me and my mother got into it."

"Okay . . ."

"That her new boyfriend." She gestured at the man making coffee. "They got a baby."

She sniffled, starting to choke up again. "She want him around, she want the baby around, she want my sister around. The only person she don't want around is me."

Upstairs, I heard raised voices again, and an entire twin-size mattress came sliding down the stairs.

"Here's your bed! Take it and *go!*"

The girl collapsed into tears. "She want everybody around except me."

All over Washington, it sometimes seemed, there were girls whose mothers wanted them arrested, and girls whose mothers wanted nothing to do with them.

I thought of my own mother, whose disapproval still rankled. But I was lucky, so undeservedly lucky: even during those painful years before I left for college, when our house felt like a prison, each of us trapped in separate, solitary cells, I never doubted my mother's love for me. The prison bars I chafed against as a teenager were constructed from my own emotions, not from cold, hard metal.

On another evening in the spring of 2017, I was patrolling with an officer called Reid, a self-declared Second Amendment nut. ("I'm a single issue voter," he informed me. "And my issue is gun rights.") Reid collected weapons, and in his spare time, he took every commercially available course on defensive tactics, room clearing, and active-shooter situations. He never allowed his two young sons to enter a store or restaurant without first determining all exit locations and looking through the windows to determine the position and threat posture of all occupants, he told me earnestly: "I want tactical room entry to be second nature to them."

To his credit, Reid took his role as my ad hoc training officer seriously. He spent an hour drilling me on safe traffic stop tactics and another hour showing me the websites of training schools where I could further my tactical education. He was delighted to have a law professor as his partner, and spent another hour offering an explication of the drafting history of the Second Amendment, an exercise that only ended when we were called to an assault in progress.

Lights flashing and sirens blaring, I drove to the scene Code 1, under Reid's watchful eye. When we arrived a minute or two later, we were greeted at the apartment's outer door by a tearful woman in a black T-shirt.

"I need you to take my daughter before I kill her. I'm serious, she's breaking up my shit, swinging on me . . ."

She sat down on the stairwell, put her head in her hands, and started crying.

"She mad, she keep asking my boyfriend for money, calling me, 'Fuck you, bitch!'" She shook her head. "I'm like, 'Get the hell out of my house, now!'"

Reid told me to interview her while he went to the apartment to talk to the daughter. "It's unlocked," the mother called after him. "Just go in."

I stayed out on the landing, trying to get the details: Who, what, why, when, where, how?

She gave me the basics, but mostly just sat there crying, holding her head, defeat plain on her face.

"I can't even think. She slamming my lamps, breaking my lamps, biting me, breaking up shit in my house, breaking my fan."

She took a gulp of air and looked up at me. "She need to learn. I want her to go to jail. I want her to be in some type of home. I don't even have custody of her; my mother did. My mother keeps sending her over here."

"So, she's seventeen, she lives with her grandmother, your mother, but your mother keeps sending her back here? Why's that?"

She shrugged, indifferent, or exhausted. "They be going through whatever. So my mom keeps sending her over to my house. She is fucking disrespectful. She try to pull my hair out. Look at this shit!"

She examined a livid bruise on her arm, but she seemed more sad than outraged, and she declined the offer to have a medic check her out.

"She wanted money from my boyfriend, I'm telling her to wait, he going to get her some money, but she calling me all types of bitches, 'fuck you,' all that."

"I'm going to go inside, check in with my partner, okay?" I gestured to her apartment door. "I'll be back in a few minutes."

Inside the apartment, I found I had interrupted a tense scene. A slender girl sat slumped on a folding chair in the middle of the room, and Reid was speaking to her sternly.

"I can't see what you're doing and you might try to hurt me; that's why I raised my voice."

The girl looked offended. "I'm not trying to hurt you!"

"I don't know that," Reid retorted. "I never met you before and I don't know that. You *could* be trying to hurt me."

"But if I'm trying to hurt you, sir, *you* got a gun!"

"*Plenty* of people with guns have been killed," Reid informed her. "Plenty of police officers. All I'm trying to explain to you is, in the future, if something like that happens, now you understand why we react like that."

What had happened? I stood at the door, looking from Reid to the girl and back again.

"I was looking for my phone out of my bag when you came in the door," the girl protested.

Reid was unmoved. "Am I a mind reader? I didn't know what you were looking for."

"Well you didn't have to grab me out," the girl said indignantly. "I know how to cooperate. I would've just sat down!"

"But you didn't. So I told you to put your hands out, and show me where they were."

"I did that *already*, sir!"

Reid evidently decided that his explication of sound officer safety tactics was falling on deaf ears, so he changed the subject. "Okay, please tell me, in your own words, exactly what happened."

The girl was having none of it. "I don't want to tell you. I want to talk to another officer," she said sulkily.

Good for you, kid, I thought.

"Okay then," Reid said brightly. "Would you like to speak to Officer Brooks?"

"Yes."

Reid looked at me and pointed at the girl. "She's seventeen years old, name is Imani, the boyfriend and a baby are in the back room."

"Got it."

Reid retreated to the stairwell.

"How you doing, Imani? Sounds like you had a bad morning," I offered.

Imani sat quiet in a chair, wiping her eyes with the hem of her shirt. The room was a wreck, almost entirely empty of furniture, just a few folding chairs, with clothes all over the floor. The walls were bare—no decorations, nothing.

Imani's story matched her mother's, more or less. She and her mother had started to argue, and somehow things got out of hand.

"It started getting wild, she yanking my hair, and I *did* start swinging back," she acknowledged. "Then I just wanted to leave. I started looking for my phone, I'm looking for my school uniforms, I gotta go to school on Monday. But she screaming at me and she keep on yanking at my hair, it hurts all over my head. I'm the one who called the police."

It was shortly after this, apparently, that Reid came in, and spotted Imani reaching into a bag. She was searching for her phone again, she told me, so she could show Reid that she was the one who had called 911. But Reid, seeing her suddenly reach into her bag, assumed the worst.

"He just grab me, he put me in the chair, he just jumped at me!"

I thought Reid had acted like an ass. By now, after more than six months of patrolling, I was starting to trust my own instincts. Yes, people reaching into bags sometimes pulled out weapons, but the people who pulled out guns and shot at cops were virtually never young girls in their mothers' living rooms. Letting the girl reach into her bag would have involved a level of risk that was statistically insignificant, and the alternative was to further spook an already traumatized girl, as Reid had done. This girl had a rough-enough life to start with. She didn't need a jumpy cop screaming at her for reaching into her own backpack.

But I couldn't say any of this to Imani. Instead I said, in an apologetic tone, "Yeah, cops can get nervous. You go to an apartment and you don't know who's there, you kind of want everybody sitting still . . . he probably just got a little nervous."

Imani was back to worrying over the fight with her mother.

"I wasn't raised by her; it's like I don't know her, and she don't even *want* to know *me*." For a moment, she looked lost and sad. "She and her boyfriend, she and Grandma, they always fighting about something."

"What kinds of things?" I asked.

"Stupid stuff, they're always taking it out on me." She looked at me, plaintive. "I just want to go."

She did go too, but not in the way I'd have liked. While I was talking to Imani, Reid summoned the sergeant, and somewhere along the line, while Imani and I sat there making small talk about her favorite school subjects and the things she liked to do on weekends, Reid and the sergeant decided that Imani was the primary aggressor in what had now been rede-fined as a domestic violence assault situation, triggering a mandatory arrest.

Imani was heading to the juvenile processing center, and since it sounded like her grandmother was unable or unwilling to keep her, odds were high that Imani's mother would get her wish, and the girl would end up in a court-ordered group placement.

It fell to me, as the only female officer present, to cuff Imani and pat her down. She didn't complain or struggle. In her short life, I suppose, she'd already gotten used to things turning out badly. But it was one of my worst moments as a police officer. This girl was a victim, not a criminal. I thought of my own children, and imagined how my daughter would feel if both I and her grandmother seemed to be rejecting her. Would she want to lash out at me or hit me? If she did, I wouldn't blame her. Adults are supposed to take care of children. Instead, I was attaching heavy metal handcuffs to Imani's thin wrists. I felt a little sick.

A few months later, with a different partner, I responded to another assault-in-progress call. The MDT described it as involving *"serious bleeding."*

It was dark when we arrived, and the address the dispatcher gave us turned out to be wrong, so for a while we wandered around in the housing project's parking lot, looking for signs of a bloody assault. After a few minutes a young girl came tentatively up to us, accompanied by a small boy in a Redskins football jersey.

"We the ones who called," she confided. "'Bout our mom."

"It's your mom who's hurt?" I clarified.

"Mmm-hmm." She looked down at her toes. She was no older than twelve or thirteen, and the boy with her looked to be nine or ten.

"What happened?"

"Um, somebody hit her."

"Someone you know? Or a stranger?"

"A stranger. Somebody going around saying something, then he came to her and punched her in the face. But she don't like the hospital and she tell us if the ambulance comes she won't go."

The girl was called Zari, and her little brother was Darius. We followed them into a building, where Zari went up to a door and began to knock. No one answered. She knocked again, and rang the bell. We all waited.

Zari put her ear to the door. "She in there with someone."

"You live in there too?" my partner asked.

Zari looked down. "No. She live there without us. We live with my sister."

She knocked again, glancing hopefully at the door.

Finally, the door swung open. A man glanced at us, then walked away, indifferent, but a woman, beer can in her hand, leaned into the doorframe.

When she saw the children and several police officers, she looked surprised, then a little annoyed.

"Are you the person who's hurt?" I asked.

"*I'm* not hurt," she replied, giving Zari a look.

"Yes you are," Zari insisted.

"No, I'm not."

Zari looked at me, then pointed at her mother. "She's hurt."

She turned back to her mother. "Your lip is swollen."

It was dark in the stairwell, but I could easily see what Zari was pointing at. Her mother's lip was swollen to twice the normal size, the flesh red and raw.

Still holding the beer can in her right hand, the mother put her left hand on her hip and tried for a stern expression, undermined by the fact that she was having trouble staying upright.

"She say, 'Your lip swollen.' I tell her, 'Oh no, I'm not hurt!'" Her voice was slurred and distorted, maybe partly from the swollen lip, but mostly, I suspected, from the beer and whatever else she was on. She scowled at Zari. "So why you call the ambulance?"

There was a short pause, then her daughter spoke quietly. "Because, Mom, we care about you."

"Okay. But I'm not hurt, though."

"Yes you are. He hit you right in the mouth."

For a moment, mother and daughter just looked at each other.

Zari won the battle of wills. Her mother turned to us, resigned, and nodded.

"He outside in the street. He probably still outside."

We asked his name.

"His name is . . . Kent," the mother said.

"Ken," corrected Zari. "*Kenny.* She can't remember."

"Ken," echoed Darius, coming up to stare at his mother's swollen lip. He touched it gently.

"There's an ambulance coming," my partner put in. "They don't need to take you to the hospital, but they should just check you out."

The mother stepped back and gave a vigorous head shake. "I don't need that."

"She need to get checked out," corrected Zari.

Once again, Zari prevailed. Darius ran outside to show the medics in, while their mother just stood there, shaking her head.

I started running through the usual questions: names, phone numbers. The mother ("Deandra, with a *D*, and an *E* and an *aaaaandra*")—pursed her lips and started reciting a string of numbers, then stopped and laughed uproariously.

"*Wait* a minute, wait a minute. I'm fucking drunk! You ask for my phone number, and I give you my date of birth, not my phone number." She chuckled at herself some more, then gave me another number.

She didn't know Kent or Ken or Kenny's last name, she maintained, nor what he looked like, nor where he lived, though she gestured vaguely to her left: "This way, I think."

Once again, the children provided most of the missing details. *Kenny* had a beard and a mustache, they told us. (Deandra interrupted: "A what? A what?" but the kids ignored her.) He was short, and was last seen wearing a fluorescent yellow shirt "with some black or gray on it."

Just then, another door popped open, and a neighbor in a bathrobe stuck her head out into the hall.

"What happening out here?" She gave Deandra an accusing look.

"Everything's fine, ma'am," my partner told her. "Please go back inside."

Reluctantly, the neighbor complied.

This triggered a flurry of comments from Deandra, Zari, and Darius: Kent or Ken or Kenny had staged his assault because of something the neighbor lady had said. The story was garbled and I couldn't quite make out the causation.

"Kent and me, we just friends," said Deandra. "I used to smoke coke, I be stupid sometimes. But *that* bitch, she smokes, she *still* smoke crack."

The medics arrived, and Darius tapped his mother on the arm. "Ma, you gotta get your lip checked out."

His mother rounded on him. "Would you *please* shut *up*?"

Darius and Zari exchanged a look. Her moods kept shifting.

Deandra glared at them for a moment, but then allowed the medics to look at her.

"She's been bleeding since it happened, and she's still bleeding," Zari said softly. "I already told security, I told her she should get a warrant or something."

"Were you there the entire time they were arguing?" my partner asked Zari.

"No," she said, looking down at her toes again. "If I did, I would have pushed him off her."

"Me too," whispered Darius.

"It's good of you to take care of your mom," I told them. "Even if she doesn't want it."

The children watched gravely as the medics cleaned and disinfected their mother's lip, Zari with her hands clasped in front of her, Darius nibbling on a fingernail.

There was little more we could do. We would investigate, we promised. We would talk to the security guard, and see if we could find out the identity of Kent/Ken/Kenny; if we could locate him, we'd get a warrant. In the meantime, we'd write a report.

I didn't bother giving my card or the report numbers to Deandra, who was humming to herself, eyes glazed. I just handed everything to Zari, since she appeared to be the responsible party.

"You see him again, anytime, you *call* us, okay?"

She inspected my card solemnly. "You gotta go now?"

I nodded.

She looked again at her mother.

"Mom, they say with you being hurt, you shouldn't be drinking all evening."

Her mother wasn't having it. "They didn't say anything about that."

Zari just inclined her head a little, like she hadn't really expected that gambit to succeed. Her cheeks were wet with tears, and for a while she just stood there, wiping her face with her sleeve.

"You're lucky," I told Deandra. "You've got kids who love you a lot."

For a moment, this seemed to penetrate Deandra's chemically induced haze, and she looked genuinely moved.

"Yeah. I do. I do." She thought for a minute, then added, "I have eleven kids."

"Eleven kids," my partner said. "That's a whole lot."

"Mom," interjected Zari. "Will you go inside and put an ice pack on?"

"I don't need no ice pack! What you doing? Get on out of here."

Zari and Darius exchanged looks again, then both started slowly down the stairs, away from their mother's apartment, the apartment that wasn't their home.

"Bye y'all!" Deandra called, cheerful now, taking a long swallow from the can of beer.

"I'm not going, Mom," Zari said over her shoulder. "I'm gonna be standing here. Right here."

Officer Friendly

Victim . . . reports that while attending a Halloween event . . .
he was assaulted by an unknown female. . . . Victim reports that
while at the bar area in the club he had words with the suspect.
Victim reports that the suspect then threw her alcohol drink in
his face. Victim reports that he was unable to see out of his right
eye at that time. Victim reports that the suspect then threw her
drinking glass at him hitting him in the right eye. Victim
describes the suspect as a black female . . . wearing little brown
bunny ears on her head . . .

—*MPD Joint Strategic and Tactical Analysis*
Command Center, Daily Report

Sometimes, the Seventh District just seemed so unremittingly sad. Even as a part-time cop, and even early on, there were days when it was hard to summon up the energy for one more shift's worth of large and small tragedies. In 7D, the perpetrators usually seemed as lost and desperate as the victims, and I soon discovered that many of the victims doubled as perpetrators, and vice versa: the same guy whose wallet was taken on Monday by a kid with a handgun was the guy you had to arrest on Tuesday when he took his frustrations out on his girlfriend with his fists.

The main occupational hazard of policing is not assault or injury, but cynicism. Almost by definition, the typical patrol officer gets a one-sided view of humanity. People whose lives are going well don't spend much time with the police. No one calls the police to say, "Hey, officers, just wanted to let you know that it's a beautiful evening, and when I got home from work I had a relaxing barbecue with the whole family and then we went inside so I could help the kids finish their homework." You're not there to see parents reading to their kids, or hosting birthday and graduation parties. You're not there to see all the large and small moments of joy and affection and triumph. You only get called when things go wrong—when Dad hits Mom or Mom pulls a knife on Dad or Junior runs away or Grandma gets robbed by Junior's friends or Junior's sister overdoses. Sometimes, it seems like everyone you meet is crying or yelling.

It can make even well-intentioned officers cynical; it's easy to start to think that *everyone* on your beat is nothing more than a criminal-in-waiting. This is not true, of course—even in the most dysfunctional, crime-ridden, drug-ridden neighborhoods, the vast majority of people are simply trying to get by, often working two or three jobs just to hold things together for their families. In 7D, there were old people like the Carters, living off pensions after a lifetime driving the city's buses or teaching at local schools. There were girls like Zari and boys like Darius, trying to take care of the adults who should have been taking care of them. There were soccer coaches and youth groups, church choirs and entrepreneurs, community organizers, high school boys who wrote poetry, and girls who wanted to go to medical school. There were men who helped single mothers fix broken toilets and busted sinks, because who else was going to help? There were middle-aged women who brought blankets out to the drug boys on the corner on cold winter nights, because even drug dealers shouldn't have to sit out there and freeze. There was plenty of kindness and courage and generosity amid all the misery.

But if you were an outsider, you had to look hard to find it sometimes. I made a point of searching for the good things, however small, in the bleakest situations: the drug-addicted mother whose apartment contained almost no furniture, but who still proudly displayed her children's school report cards on the refrigerator; the older brother who put his arm around his younger brother's shoulder and hugged him close each time their mother shouted or cursed.

Still, sometimes it was nice to get out of 7D. From time to time, district officials would ask reserve officers to help out on dates they expected would be particularly busy. We helped staff the annual High Heel Race, the Special Olympics, and assorted protests and parades. Parades, special events, and holiday details offered a chance to be Officer Friendly for a change, to see people looking healthy and cheerful rather than miserable and angry. I smiled, waved, gave people directions, helped them decode program schedules and Metro maps, and posed obligingly for photos with out-of-town tourists who were thrilled to meet a police officer in the nation's capital. At the St. Patrick's Day parade, people kept trying to give me plastic shamrock necklaces and offering me sips of green beer. (I accepted the necklaces, but declined the beer.) At the two-day Barbecue Battle festival, I couldn't get a single merchant to take my money; everyone kept insisting that I have a cold bottle of iced tea or a hot dog on the house, and thank you for your service, officer.

You're not supposed to accept freebies, and when people told me there was no charge, I'd generally put some cash down on the counter and ask them to consider it a donation to their favorite charity. Sometimes, they would still refuse to take the money, and insisting seemed rude, so I just accepted the free iced tea. Often, people offered spontaneous thank-yous, and every now and then, spontaneous hugs.

Those hugs reminded me that despite everything, most Americans like the police. In Gallup's annual survey of public confidence in institutions, police consistently fare quite well: In 2019, 53 percent of Americans said they had "a great deal" or "quite a lot" of confidence in the police, and only 17 percent had "very little" or no confidence in police. Among public institutions, only the military fared better than police, with a whopping 73 percent of those surveyed responding that they had "a great deal" or "quite a lot" of confidence in the military. The criminal justice system as a whole had the confidence of only 24 percent of those surveyed, and public schools didn't do much better, garnering positive reviews from only 29 percent of respondents. The Supreme Court and the presidency clocked in at a modest 38 percent confidence level, while Congress fared the worst, with only 11 percent of Americans expressing "a great deal" or "quite a lot" of confidence in their elected representatives.

These figures hide significant racial and ethnic disparities. White people are more likely than African Americans to express confidence in the police, with Hispanics somewhere in between. Republicans are more likely to have a favorable opinion of police than Democrats, and across all partisan lines and all racial and ethnic groups, older people are more positive about police officers than younger people.

I knew all this. But the occasional hugs were still nice.

My first holiday shift was on December 31, 2016, when I was just two and a half months out of the academy. I was temporarily sprung from 7D to provide extra New Year's Eve manpower to the Third District's Nightlife Unit. It was an unseasonably warm night, with temperatures in the midforties, and the sergeant was effusive in his thanks to the five reserve officers who turned up to help out.

"It's gonna be crazy," he warned us. "It's too warm. Everyone's gonna be out. We really appreciate your being here—we have a lot of guys on leave, so we need all the help we can get. All I need from you is, try to focus on the big stuff. No bullshit arrests; we're too busy and I don't want you tied up back at the station for two hours locking someone up for a POCA." POCAs—possession of an open container of alcohol—would be everywhere tonight. "Just try to help keep things from being out of control."

I was paired with an experienced 3D Nightlife officer, a big friendly guy called Maloney, who seemed pleased to have the company. "Normally I'm ninety-nine," he explained. "Gets kind of lonesome out there." Our beat would be a five-block stretch of Ninth Street, with Nellie's Sports Bar at Ninth and U at the epicenter.

This was a different kind of policing. For one thing, two-thirds of the people on the streets were white, unlike in 7D, where cops, teachers, social workers, and the occasional foolish suburban kid trying to score some drugs were often the only white faces. Most people in the crowd looked happy and affluent, and absolutely everyone was either drunk or well on the way.

Maloney parked the patrol car in an alley, since the crowds in the street were too thick to drive through, and we started walking up and down. Within minutes, a blond kid wearing cargo shorts and a button-down shirt had attached himself to us.

"Hi, officers!" He had the bonhomie of the extremely inebriated. "Hey, Happy New Year! Isn't this a great night? Man, this weather is something else! It's like, it's like . . ." He paused, frowning, unable to decide just what it was like. "Like, it's like when it's really warm. Like . . ." It came to him. "Summer!" He leaned in confidingly. "Listen, officers, do you know the best place for me to get a taxi? I'm trying to hook up with some friends over in Adams Morgan and I can't remember where I left my car, and"—goofy smile—"I'm thinking anyway that probably I shouldn't drive, but I thought maybe you could help me out. Man, it's so . . . nice out. So . . . warm!"

Maloney gave him a curt smile and suggested he try Uber. The boy beamed. "Oh wow, that's . . . a really good idea! Except . . . I can't find my phone. I was thinking, could you guys maybe give me a ride? Maybe if you just drove me a little ways I could remember where my car is. I promise I won't drive it! Maybe I'd just . . . nap in it for a few minutes."

I advised him to walk down a few blocks and try for a cab where the crowds were less thick. He nodded, thanked us effusively, then spent the next hour following us around, coming back over to us every twenty minutes or so to smile some more. I was the nicest police officer he'd ever met, he said. Seriously, would it be possible for him to just sit in our police car for a few minutes? He liked me very much, and he liked my partner too, and he thought maybe if he could just sit down with us for a little while, he'd be able to come up with a better plan for the evening. Or maybe he could buy us a drink? No, of course not, he totally understood, we couldn't drink on duty, of course not! Another time, then? If I would give him my phone number, he would call me as soon as he found his phone, and then we could really spend some time getting to know each other. He squinted hopefully at me until Maloney urged him, somewhat less gently, to get lost, at which he fell back to trail us from about fifteen feet away.

Soon we were hailed by one of the servers at Nellie's. They had a drunk woman who was causing trouble and refusing to leave. "No problem," Maloney said. We made our way through the crowd to gleeful cries of "Oh shit, it's the pigs!" mixed with "Happy New Year, officers!" Inside, you could barely move; by now, the drunk woman had collapsed onto the bar, weeping. "She was cursing at everyone," the server told us. "And she kept asking for more drinks, and we said she'd had enough, and then she took a swing at Todd." Todd, the bartender, looked quite able to take care of himself, but we took the sobbing woman by the elbow and half led, half carried her outside, several of her friends following along. She didn't look pleased, but she didn't resist, and outside we told her it was time for her to go home. Her friends promised they'd take care of her, and we moved on.

In the next block, two men were scuffling. "What the fuck, man, what the fuck!" they bellowed at each other. Maloney grabbed one guy and I grabbed the other, and we pulled them apart. They stood scowling and huffing at each other, but once they were separated they stopped struggling and agreed to head off in different directions, with only an occasional "What the *fuck!*" tossed back over their shoulders.

Everywhere, music was thumping, and between the music and the noise of the crowds, our radios were inaudible. "Let's take a break and go sit in the car for a bit," suggested Maloney. "Check the MDT and the radio, see if we're missing anything."

As soon as we sat down in the patrol car, the drunk boy popped up again, knocking at the window.

"Are you *sure* I can't just sit in there with you for a little while? It's getting cold," he added sadly. "Maybe just for a few minutes? I probably shouldn't have worn shorts tonight, you know, except it was warm, like summer, only now it's not so warm."

We told him again that he could not join us in the car, and urged him to go inside somewhere warm, like a restaurant. He brightened again immediately.

"Oh, that's a really good idea! I'll just go back inside! But listen, officer, can I give you my phone number? You could call me and I could buy you a drink sometime. I'd like to do that, because I really, really appreciate what you're doing. I mean, it's just so . . . so wonderful, so . . . nice . . . what you do, I mean, it's so great, like, your being out here, and, you know, keeping us safe, and everything!"

He started to tear up, so I accepted a receipt with his phone number scribbled on the back, then told him to go inside and get warm. "Right! No problem! That's exactly what I'm going to do! Thanks, officer! Okay, Happy New Year! Bye! Thanks!" He retreated, waving enthusiastically.

The mobile data terminal apprised us of a call for damage to property, so we drove a few streets away. "The PSA guys are supposed to be handling the routine calls," Maloney explained, "but if it's within a block or two of the clubs, we might as well take it." We drove to a deserted lot behind a small theater, where we found a young woman standing by a car with a shattered windshield. Someone, she said, had thrown a rock through the windshield, maybe from the roof of the theater. The front seat of her car was littered with broken glass, and a large rock sat in the middle of it. We took her details and got a case number from the dispatcher, and I started writing the report on the car's mobile terminal.

Maloney decided we should spend some time driving around in the alleyways behind the clubs. We found several men skulking in various spots, and interrupted one probable robbery, but the probable robber hadn't had time to take anything, and the probable victim seemed disinclined to provide us with any details. "I just want to fucking go home, man," he said, so we escorted the probable robber to the end of the alleyway and told him we didn't want to see him again. In another alleyway, we found a guy peeing against a wall, and Maloney, who was angry that we hadn't had enough basis to arrest the would-be robber, told him, rather aggressively, to get the fuck out of there. "I'm going, man, I'm going!" the guy protested, zipping up his pants. "Shit! Sorry, man, I just had to take a piss, for fuck's sake!"

In the next alley, we found a young woman sitting curled on the ground, her head in her hands. At first she was unresponsive, ignoring us completely when we asked if she was all right, but after a while, she looked up. "He cursed at me. I can't believe it. All I said was that I was getting tired, and then he started yelling at me and—" Her left cheek was swollen.

"Did he hit you?" I asked.

Just then a man appeared. "Come on, baby, I'm fucking sorry, let's just fucking leave, okay?"

"Hold it, asshole," Maloney told him. "Come over here. We need to talk to you."

I crouched down next to the young woman, who now had a frozen expression on her face. "Listen. Did he give you that bruise on your cheek?" I asked quietly.

She blinked and looked away. "No. It's fine. I just had too much to drink. I walked into a door. I'm fine."

"Ma'am, if he hit you, it's not okay. We can help you, get you to a safe place."

She scrambled up. "I'm fine! It's fine. Nothing happened. We just argued. I'm just tired. I just want to go home."

Reluctantly, we let them go off together, the man holding her arm too tightly as they walked away.

"Nothing we can do," Maloney said. "Can't force her to tell us what happened. We arrest him, it'll get thrown out tomorrow if she denies it and won't testify. She wants to stay with that shithead, there is abso-fucking-lutely nothing we can do."

American Carnage

On January 20, 2017, the District of Columbia will host the 58th Presidential Inauguration. The designated uniform of the day for the Metropolitan Police Department (MPD) for this historic event is as follows:

- Members the rank of Sergeant and below: Class "B" Service Uniform, Eight point hat or "Trooper-Style" winter hat, light blue uniform shirt, tie, uniform slacks and the MPD issued Class "B" Jacket or Leather Jacket.

- Ear Covering/Ear Muffs—Members may wear ear coverings or ear muffs as long as they are black or navy blue in color.

- No Bullet resistant vests shall be worn as an outer garment. Bullet resistant vest shall be worn under the uniform shirt.

- No skull caps, beanies, or knit hats shall be worn by any members on this detail.

—MPD Teletype: "2017 Presidential Inauguration Uniform Requirements"

There was abso-fucking-lutely nothing I could do about quite a lot of things.

On January 20, 2017, I found myself nominally—and temporarily—in charge of forty shivering police officers from Cincinnati. Together with several thousand other officers from around the country, our job was to safeguard the parade route down which the newly inaugurated President Trump and his motorcade would soon drive, followed by dozens of marching bands.

The inaugural festivities had gotten off to an inauspicious start for the DC Metropolitan Police: one of our own reserve corps officers, Mark Kirwan, was run over by Vice President Elect Mike Pence's motorcade. Officer Kirwan was hospitalized only briefly with minor injuries, but dark rumors immediately started spreading through the force: Pence's motorcade hadn't even stopped! The vice president elect had left our officer lying prostrate in the street! He might have been dead, for all Pence knew!

Whether this account of the accident was true, I don't know, but it was all anyone could talk about. "That car was driven by anyone else, we'd charge 'em with hit-and-run and arrest their asses," one of my colleagues said grimly.

Most of the time, policing in the nation's capital is probably no different than in any other American city, but at moments like this, everything changed. I had never seen anything like the controlled chaos of the inauguration planning process. Imagine the most complicated event you ever organized—your wedding, maybe, or a major conference. Think of all the complexities of the planning process: Who will be invited? Where will guests park? Will there be a vegetarian option for lunch? How many microphones should you set up? What if it rains? What time will the dancing begin? Multiply those complexities by about a million, then throw in mass protests and potential terrorist threats. That will give you some idea of what goes into preparing for a presidential inauguration.

Washington's small size often surprises out-of-town visitors, who expect something on the scale of New York, Hong Kong, or London. But at under seven hundred thousand, the population of the nation's capital is smaller than that of Jacksonville, Florida; El Paso, Texas; Indianapolis; Columbus, Ohio; or Memphis, Tennessee. No one knew how many people would flow into the city to attend President Trump's inauguration, but an estimated 1.8 million spectators showed up for President Barack Obama's 2009 inauguration, and city planners had to assume the numbers could be similar for Trump.

The expected crowds would place enormous strain on everything from the Metro system to the police department. The parade route had to be cordoned off, with streets closed off for dozens of square blocks to ensure a safe buffer zone around the presidential route. Hundreds of tour buses needed places to park, and hundreds of thousands of people would need hotel rooms, food, and toilets. Some would need directions; others would need medical assistance; some would pick up souvenir T-shirts; others would have their pockets picked by enterprising local criminals. And some people would come to DC not to admire the Washington Monument or cheer on the new president, but to join protest rallies and marches. Most of those would be peaceful, but some would not. Antifa activists were assumed to be planning violent disruption, and militant pro-Trump groups would likely square off against them. The day after the inauguration, the planned Women's March was expected to pull in hundreds of thousands more protesters and counterprotesters.

To cope with the anticipated extra demand, the inauguration planning team—a sprawling interagency group made up of officials from MPD and the city government plus the Secret Service, the FBI, the Department of Homeland Security, the military, the intelligence community, the Transportation Security Administration, and dozens of other agencies—put out a call to police departments around the country, asking them to contribute officers to help out during inauguration. Under a complex cost-sharing agreement, outside agencies providing inauguration personnel would be reimbursed by the federal government. Dozens of departments from all over the United States responded, and it was MPD's job to manage the thousands of extra law enforcement personnel.

Within MPD, the reserve corps was tasked with serving as the liaison for all these visiting police officers. This in itself involved substantial logistical challenges. The extra officers—and their weapons—needed to get to the DC area a few days early for briefings, tourism, and beer drinking. They needed hotel rooms and local transportation, so reserve corps officers were assigned to pick them up at area airports in MPD vans and buses hired for the occasion, bring them to their hotels, get them all checked in, show them around, and generally make sure they got to the right places at the right time with the right equipment, and not too much of a hangover.

The day before inauguration, we shepherded our armed, uniformed charges into the DC Armory. Built during World War II for the DC National Guard, it was one of the only structures large enough to contain the thousands of visiting law enforcement officers. Bleachers and folding chairs had been set up in the vast, echoing building, and each agency occupied several rows. There were Tennessee Highway Patrol officers in green and tan; sheriff's deputies from Brazos County, Texas, in black and tan; and police officers from dozens of cities—Miami, Baltimore, New York, Phoenix, Minneapolis, Seattle, Los Angeles—in a hundred different shades of blue. There were national guard troops too, assigned to help with crowd control. A series of officials thanked the uniformed crowd on behalf of MPD, the Mayor, the FBI, Homeland Security, and the Secret Service, then all the out-of-town officers were sworn in en masse as deputy US Marshals, with limited, temporary jurisdiction to provide security. In the sea of uniforms, you couldn't easily distinguish the cops from the soldiers. Everyone was armed and cheering, eager to leave the Armory and get in a few hours of tourism or drinking before the next day's long tour of duty.

It was quiet and cold on Pennsylvania Avenue the next morning. By the time the sun rose over the dome of the Capitol, painting it pink in the slanting morning light, I had already been standing in front of the FBI building for several hours. At 11:47 a.m., nine blocks from where I stood, John Roberts, the chief justice of the Supreme Court, was scheduled to swear in Donald Trump as the forty-fifth president of the United States.

The temperature was mild for mid-January, but already most of my Cincinnati officers were hopping up and down to keep their toes from going numb. As a liaison officer I was free to roam around, but they were stuck at static posts, staring at nothing, trying to stay upright and awake. No one had slept more than a few hours before heading out to our posts in the small hours of the morning, and it was going to be a long, cold day.

I walked up and down the line, offering hand warmers and granola bars. "Welcome to Washington, DC, guys. A grateful nation thanks you. You need to pee, break room's two blocks north. Having fun yet?"

It was strange to see such a familiar place, utterly transformed. No morning commuters, no tourists or hot dog stands or bicyclists weaving in and out of traffic. Everyone in sight wore a uniform of some kind. Soldiers and sailors were lined up facing the road, while my Cincinnati charges were positioned facing the opposite direction, toward the crowds of spectators we expected would soon appear.

I walked out into the middle of the empty street, just to see how it felt. No one stopped me; my uniform, badge, and temporary Secret Service credentials allowed me to be anywhere on the route. I could have done cartwheels down the center of Pennsylvania Avenue, or taken a nap on the yellow center line. I imagined how the street would look a few hours later, with spectators and protesters pressing in on both sides.

Our role was to make sure no one unauthorized entered the parade route—no overenthusiastic Trump voters hoping for autographs, no protesters eager to throw eggs at the new president, no terrorists or armed assassins. According to the detailed inauguration procedure handbook distributed by MPD, "Members assigned to [the] fixed cordon posts shall be responsible for the area ten feet to the left and ten feet to the right." If a spectator or protester attempted to cross the fence line onto the parade route, we were directed to "take the necessary action to prevent a breach of the cordon."

For a moment, I wondered what I would do if an assassin popped up in my small section of Pennsylvania Avenue. Was I really prepared to use lethal force, or risk my own life, to protect Donald Trump? It was a question my mother and several of my friends had posed to me. I concluded that I would have no choice—I had sworn an oath, and my colleagues were depending on me. But I didn't feel very enthusiastic about it.

In the end, we stood there on Pennsylvania Avenue for sixteen hours straight, fingers going numb and feet swelling up. Through my radio earpiece, I heard the sounds of chaos and struggle in other parts of the city: Antifa activists were throwing bricks and MPD's civil defense units were blasting them with tear gas. "Hold the line! Hold—the—line!" a voice shouted in my earpiece.

My brother Ben was out there somewhere, commissioned by a magazine to write a story about the inauguration protests, and every now and then he called me to ask if anything exciting was happening near the parade route. But my patch of Pennsylvania Avenue remained quiet, devoid of Antifa, assassins, and Trump fans alike. At ten-thirty a.m., the streets were almost as deserted as they'd been at sunrise.

Around eleven, a handful of tourists in "Make America Great Again" caps materialized just beyond our cordon, looking as if they thought they might have come to the wrong city by mistake. They kept checking their maps and asking anxiously if this was really the right place for the parade. Down the block, a few hundred anti-Trump protesters appeared, but they were just waving signs and chanting, not throwing bricks or Molotov cocktails.

Finally, around noon, we heard the far-off sounds of a powerful public address system coming to life. Nine blocks away, the ceremony had begun.

One of the Cincinnati cops started live-streaming the speeches on his iPhone, the volume turned up as far as it could go. President Trump's distant voice floated through the empty streets and echoed through the small iPhone speakers, high and tinny.

"Together, we will determine the course of America . . ."

"What's he saying?" someone called from farther along the parade route.

"Some kinda crap," replied one of the cops.

"A small group in our nation's capital has reaped the rewards of government. Washington flourished—" Trump's voice intoned.

He should visit 7D, I thought.

Maybe he was reading my mind.

"But for too many of our citizens, a different reality exists: mothers and children trapped in poverty in our inner cities . . . and the crime and gangs and drugs that have stolen too many lives. . . . This American carnage stops right here and stops right now."

"You hear that, guys?" said one of the Cincinnati sergeants. "It stops right here! Right now. No carnage. At least, not today, not on this block. Got it?"

A light, cold drizzle had begun to fall.

"I think it's raining on his parade," observed one of the Cincinnati cops.

"Couldn't happen to a nicer president," I agreed.

"—America first—winning like never before—"

From the direction of the Capitol, there were scattered cheers.

"—We all bleed the red blood of patriots—"

"Blood? Fuck this shit," said the Cincinnati officer with the iPhone. "I'm turning this shit off."

He thumbed the volume button on his phone and Trump's voice disappeared.

When the parade finally started and the endless speeches were replaced by familiar marching songs, my Cincinnati flock perked up a bit. The sergeant began to whistle, and some of the officers started singing loudly: "Oh be *kind* to your web-footed friends, for a duck may be some-body's mo-ther . . ." Everyone was getting a little punchy.

I felt sorry for the high school bands with their scantily clad young baton twirlers, marching through the damp and empty streets. I could see the goose bumps on their bare arms and legs. They had traveled to the nation's capital from all over the country to be part of a presidential inauguration— part of history—and there was almost no one here to see them. Most of the anti-Trump protesters had drifted off, and the soldiers and sailors lining the route weren't much of an audience: they were required to stand there at parade rest, hands clasped behind their backs, so they couldn't even clap. By the time the last half dozen bands marched by, each looking more miserable than the last, only soldiers, cops, and a few Make America Great Again stragglers remained. I cheered for the bands as loudly as I could, trying to make up for the lack of crowds. I didn't want the visiting high school kids to leave with bad memories of the nation's capital.

"Aren't you the little cheerleader," said the Cincinnati sergeant.

"MPD," I said, pointing to the slogan on the patrol car parked at the corner. "We are here to help."

Bad Things Happened

Felony Threats [Domestic Violence]: (Known Suspect)
Complainant reports her boyfriend poured gasoline in her front
and rear yard. The Suspect then called the Complainant and
stated he would return to light the gasoline.

—*MPD Joint Strategic and Tactical Analysis*
Command Center, Daily Report

No question about it, bad things happened in the nation's capital. Mothers fought with daughters. Men fought with women. Gangs fought with rival gangs. People stole from each other and threatened each other. They punched, stabbed, raped, slapped, and bit one another. They hit each other with shovels and bats and bricks, or, when these were unavailable, with brooms, plates, vases, bottles, shoes, and even the occasional vacuum cleaner or snapping turtle.

Washington is divided into seven police districts, and they might as well be seven different cities. In every district, the majority of calls for police service involve reports of disorderly conduct. This can mean anything: an aggressive panhandler, kids smoking weed in the park, a loud drunk staggering around in the middle of the road, someone peeing in an alley. But after the ubiquitous disorderly calls, the seven police districts diverge. In the wealthy Second District, the most common calls after disorderly conduct complaints involve burglar alarms and business alarms going off, followed by accidental property damage (usually minor fender benders) and traffic complaints. In 7D, after disorderly conduct calls, most calls for service involve "family disturbances," assaults, and "other," with burglar alarms coming in fifth. It's similar in the Sixth District, also east of the Anacostia River, and in parts of the Fifth District, which encompasses some of the poorest, most crime-ridden areas west of the river.

Washington's tonier districts—1D, 2D, and 3D—get their fair share of "glamorous" crimes, the kind that generate media buzz, conspiracy theories, and daytime TV specials. There was the attempted assassination of President Ronald Reagan in front of the Capital Hilton in 1981; the anthrax attacks in in 2001; the DC sniper attacks in 2002. There was the murder of intern Chandra Levy, whose body was found in Rock Creek Park in 2002 and whose affair with Congressman Gary Condit lent her death a scandalous cast. There were the 2015 mansion murders, in which a wealthy DC family and their housekeeper were tortured, then killed. There was the shooting of Democratic National Committee staffer Seth Rich, whose 2016 murder continues to fuel right-wing conspiracy theories centering around Hillary Clinton's alleged role in the affair, and the Comet pizzeria gunman, not to mention half a dozen thefts of valuable artifacts from the city's museums. And, of course, there were the famous political crimes—the Watergate burglary, the Iran-Contra scandal, and the special counsel investigations that have dogged presidents from Bill Clinton to Donald Trump.

This is not the kind of crime you see in police districts in the poorer parts of the city. In 7D, as in 6D and 5D, you don't tend to get serial killers, terrorist bomb threats, daring bank robberies, or jewel heists. Instead, you get the small, sad crimes of the very poor. Whole families live in dark apartments with piles of trash in the corner and no furniture except a few mattresses. They steal doughnuts and chicken wings and cans of Red Bull; they burglarize houses and make away with vacuum cleaners, TVs, and the occasional iPhone. They hold each other up at gunpoint for six dollars or a pair of Air Jordans. People are shot or stabbed over a few bucks. Sometimes they are killed. It's enough to make you cry.

Items used to inflict injury during assaults in Washington, DC, 2018:

AA battery
Acid
Bar stool
BB gun
Belt
Bicycle
Bicycle lock
Bleach
Blunt object
Book
Book bag
Bottle
Bottle of cologne
Bottle of soda
Bottle of soy sauce
Box cutter
Brass knuckles
Brick
Broom
Bug spray
Butter knife
Cane
Can of air freshener
Can of paint
Can of veggies
Cell phone
Chair
Chemical agent
Chip rack
Cigarette

Computer printer
Computer stand
Crate
Desktop computer
Dog repellent spray
Exercise machine
Fire extinguisher
Firework
Fist
Flowerpots
Food tray
Fork
Frying pan
Gasoline
Glass mug
Golf club
Gun
Handgun
Handheld blow-dryer
Handheld speaker
Hands and feet
Hard plastic object
Headbutt
Heavy display case
Heavy plastic bin
Hot cider
Hot coffee
iPad
Key chain
Knife

Lamp
Lawn chair
Log
Mace
Machete
Mason jar
Metal pole
Milk crate
Mug
Nail file
Paintball
Paintball gun
Paint pole
Pellet gun
Pepper spray
Phone cord
Pick comb
Pipe
Plastic bat
Plastic bin
Plastic broom
Plastic hangers
Plate
Pumpkin gourd
Purse
Remote control
Rock
Rubbing alcohol
Scalding hot food
Scalding hot liquid

Scissors	Taser	Vacuum cleaner
Screwdriver	Teeth	Vase
Shoe	Television	Vehicle
Shovel	Traffic cone	Video controller
Spatula	Trash can lid	Water bottle
Spray deodorant	Tree branch	Water from fire hose
Squeegee	Umbrella	Wheel lock club
Stick	Unknown irritating	
Stool	substance	
Table	Unknown object	

Like soldiers, doctors, and others who see a lot of misery, police officers survive by making jokes. Bleak, absurdist humor predominates. On a bulletin board in 7D, someone pinned up a drawing of Eeyore the donkey holding Winnie the Pooh's decapitated head in his mouth. The caption read, "If Pooh lived in 7D . . ."

Cops cherish encounters with weirdness, and you could always count on the citizens of Washington, DC, to offer up plenty of weirdness. You could generally count on cops to see the absurdity of their own lives too. In the report-writing room at the Fifth District station, officers had annotated the sign that identified Computer No. 3.

COMPUTER #3

Not working!

Nothing works here.

You work here

Unfortunately.

Debatable

222

Given the bureaucracy's tendency to introduce typographical errors into all official documents, it was sometimes difficult to distinguish between sly cop humor and the unintentionally absurd. One day a report alerted officers to a hate crimes investigation into the distribution of flyers containing "wording of anti-semantic nature." (I imagined linguists all over the city living in fear.) Another day, I found a notice posted at the station, informing officers of upcoming mandatory professional development training (PDT):

2018 PDT:

—PDT is starting two (2) months early, on January 23, 2018
—PDT consists of three (3) days of ten (10) hours shifts
—Two (2) days of training will occur at [the Metropolitan Police Academy] and one (1) day of tanning at the African American Museum.

I let out an involuntary snort of laughter, and soon half a dozen other cops were also in stitches. For the next few days, I overheard black cops teasing their white colleagues: "Man, you lookin' a little pale. Good thing they got PDT coming up. I think you're overdue for your day of tanning."

Each day, an email went out from what was still quaintly called the teletype office to let everyone know the code word, which was to be used to demonstrate authenticity when requesting sensitive information by telephone rather than over the encrypted radios, or, in an emergency, to prove that you really were a police officer. I was familiar with military and intelligence code words, which always managed to strike a tone of high seriousness; they tended to be phrases like *eagle fire* and *tempest dune*. MPD code words were more prosaic, and often silly: *backpack, optional, happy, love, fun, rocket, urology,* and *waffle* featured among recent entries.

It was hard to imagine a desperate undercover officer trying to identify himself as a "friendly" during an armed police raid by yelling, "Waffle! Waffle!" and shouting "Rocket!" struck me as a recipe for dangerous misunderstandings. At one point, the police code word was *police*, which seemed both redundant and unpersuasive. Sometimes, code words appeared to be nonsense words, or maybe just typos: there was *clop*, for instance, along with *cartop*, *ultimacy*, *unpurely*, and *uncrazy*. One day, the code word was *Zombi*, but that was duly corrected in a subsequent teletype message to *Zombie*.

"Zombie," said Murphy. "They got that right. It's like Night of the Fucking Living Dead around here most of the time . . . and I'm just talking about the *officers*."

Portraying a Person

Sick Person to the Hospital: MPD units received a disorderly
call. . . . The Complainant was inside the church acting
erratically and aggressively, at which point he began jumping
from the second floor choir balcony onto the first floor. A couple
minutes later had climbed onto the roof . . . Complainant
initially refused to communicate with officers, as he continues to
demonstrate unusual behavior. Moments later, [a medic] was able
to get the Complainant to safe grounds without incident. The
Complainant was transported to [the emergency psychiatric
clinic] for evaluation. . . .

—MPD Joint Strategic and Tactical Analysis
Command Center, Daily Report

Officially, there are no crazy people in Washington, DC. There are only what the Metropolitan Police Department refers to as "mental health consumers"—although much of the time, this label describes those who *should* be consuming mental health resources but are not, for one reason or another. According to official estimates, only about 3 percent of DC residents suffer from schizophrenia or severe bipolar disorder. Within the city's homeless population, 13 percent suffer from severe mental illness, and another 15 percent suffer from chronic substance abuse problems.

Encounters with mental health consumers could be sad and frustrating, but they were also treasured by officers for their comic potential. Only with a mental health consumer, for instance, was an officer likely to encounter someone deploying a snapping turtle as a weapon. This happened to a 7D officer I know. Arriving at the scene of an assault call, he found an incoherent woman brandishing a snapping turtle in her estranged boyfriend's face. Each time the boyfriend protested, the woman shoved the turtle a little closer to the boyfriend's nose. "Everyone's yelling and screaming and acting crazy, and the turtle's going snap, snap, snap!" the officer told me dreamily. "It was such a great call. I loved that call. Arrested her for domestic violence—Assault with a Dangerous Weapon. ADW-Turtle."

One evening in the fall of 2017, my Academy classmate Lowrey, who now worked in the Fifth District, texted me a screenshot from his scout car's mobile data terminal: "C1 stated he was being sexually assaulted by monkeys."

"So what happened with the complainant who was assaulted by the monkeys?" I asked when I saw him next.

Lowrey grinned. "Well, when we arrived there weren't any monkeys. I said, 'Sir, you reported that you were being sexually assaulted by monkeys, but I don't see any monkeys.' The guy got really, really mad, and said, 'Well, what did you expect? They flew out the window just as soon as they heard you knocking!'"

A few months after that, I was patrolling with Lowrey in 5D when the car's mobile data terminal pinged. We were directed to "check on the welfare" of a man in Northeast DC. Typically, welfare check requests come from concerned neighbors or relatives. ("Mail's piling up on old Mr. Smith's doorstep and he's not answering the phone or the door, even though his car's in the driveway, and I'm worried that maybe something's happened to him.") This particular request came through a more circuitous route.

According to the dispatcher, the San Francisco Police Department had received a call from a man asking them to initiate a tap on his phone lines. The caller provided the San Francisco police with his address—in Washington, DC—and his name, which he gave as Dracula. He explained that he was being abducted by aliens and tracked by the Mafia, and needed the police in San Francisco to help by tapping his phones. The San Francisco police called the DC police and suggested that someone might want to check on Mr. Dracula's well-being. That night, Lowrey and I were the lucky officers.

"Oh, wow," Lowrey said, looking at the address on the screen. "I think this is the 'sexually assaulted by monkeys' guy. You're in for a treat."

I was happy to be patrolling with Lowrey. He was big and slow moving, which had sometimes exasperated our academy instructors, but his measured thoughtfulness made him an excellent officer. He didn't rush people, and he listened more than he spoke.

It was getting dark when we arrived at Mr. Dracula's home, which was not a forbidding black castle, but a nondescript two-story brick apartment block. Mr. Dracula had done his best to make up for the building's drab ordinariness by covering his apartment door with unusual decorations. Among other items, the door was graced with a laminated photo of Bela Lugosi in the movie *Dracula*, with a hand-lettered caption that proclaimed, PLANET EARTH. Beneath this was another hand-lettered sign: PORTRAYING A PERSON IS AGAINST THE LAW.

More signs were posted up and down the doorjamb.

ELF, declared one.

TREE, read another.

Mr. Dracula himself was a fortyish black man. He wore jeans and a white T-shirt on which was written, in shaky black marker, KKK over a five-pointed star and the word POLICE.

Initially, however, he seemed pleased enough to see us.

"Like I say," he explained, "I want my phone tapped."

I nodded encouragingly. "You want your phone tapped. . . . How come?"

Mr. Dracula became immediately agitated, his face a rictus of anxiety and distress. He glanced around suspiciously. "Word of honor! It ain't about what somebody did or said, or just playing or laughing, see what I'm saying?"

His voice had gone up several decibels. "Word of honor!" He pointed accusingly at Lowrey's chest. "I want *you* to stand by your word of *honor!*"

"We just wanted to make sure everything is all right," Lowrey put in placatingly.

"And I'm telling you now, I want my phone tapped!" insisted Dracula. "I want my phone tapped, because *I don't like* your Nazi state!"

Lowrey and I made soothing noises.

"We're going to try to help you, all right?" Lowrey said.

"Ain't *nobody* gotta help me!" Dracula looked at us like we were the dumbest police officers he had ever encountered. "*I* didn't call you, San Francisco did!"

He scowled at us. Then, losing patience, he shouted, "It doesn't matter! It doesn't matter, brah! Word of honor! First of all, I *don't* want you spying on my *house!*"

Lowrey frowned. "But—" I cut him off before he could remind Mr. Dracula about the phone-tapping request.

"We're *not* doing that," I said firmly.

Dracula folded his arms, a picture of outraged skepticism.

"Oh you're *not?* So you're telling me that you *wasn't* listening over that smoke detector?"

"No, sir. Not us." There was still a lot I didn't know about MPD, but I felt quite confident about this one.

Dracula narrowed his eyes and leaned forward. "You're wrong. You're *absolutely* wrong. I *know* that you're listening to me over the smoke detector. And . . . the *light*bulb."

His tone became suddenly confiding. "Matter of fact, they got a law, with the lightbulb. Called 'Make a difference.'"

He gave us a sly smile and chuckled. "And you're sitting and talking like 'I don't know!' Well *I* know, my man. *I* know, all day long!"

Suddenly he was shouting again.

"I don't care what y'all do. Just don't come on my property. *Don't* come in my house!"

"You got it, sir," Lowrey and I chorused, both taking a rapid step back.

This still did not satisfy Mr. Dracula. "I got family and friends, and they do *not* like the United States, they want *nothing* to do with it, and you are *in* the house, *and* the water spigot, *and* the wall socket, *and* the smoke detector. I have *in*formed the president, and I'm telling you, I don't like it! Okay?"

We made affirming murmurs.

"And that," Dracula added triumphantly, "is why I went up to the Secret Service, just yesterday, and I told them. I'm waiting for the president to tell me what he's going to do about it. Because if you want to know, if you want to know what happened to me at this location, I was abducted by aliens. I stepped out of my door, and *off* I went, that way." He pointed up, toward the sky.

His voice grew hushed and conspiratorial. "You ain't safe in your house. You ain't safe at all. Your kids . . . I even had to close down the toy factory. Because they were messing with the toys. They were doing *very* abusive things. I called Mickey Mouse and told him."

"Well," I said, stymied. "That does sound bad. It's a scary world."

Dracula was affronted by this. "It's *not* a scary world. Not to me. And I'm telling you, all I need is for you to get off my property."

"Okay, sir." It seemed like a good time to bring our conversation to an end. "Well, thank you for telling us about all this. We appreciate it."

"No, no, no," Dracula countered. "If I do something for you people, I'm *not* doing it for free. I mean, you *pay* me! And I'm *not* joking."

With that, he stepped back into his apartment and slammed the door.

There wasn't much we could do. We consulted with Dracula's neighbors, who affirmed that he was off his rocker and most likely off his meds, but that he was generally no bother to anyone in the building, aside from his odd rants and unusual door decorations. DC offers emergency psychiatric services for the flagrantly crazy, but without voluntary consent, police can take someone to the clinic only if they appear to pose an imminent threat to themselves or someone else. Mr. Dracula was clearly psychotic, but aside from that, he didn't appear to be sick, hungry, or even unkempt. He had a home, he appeared to have some means of support, he wasn't threatening anyone, and he had made it pretty clear he wasn't interested in our assistance.

A few weeks after that, we responded to a call for a "suspicious person." A resident had complained about a man hanging around the back stairs to her apartment unit. We split up to look around, and after a few minutes of searching, shining my flashlight into alleys and behind dumpsters, I spotted a heavy-shouldered man with a long black beard beneath a set of wooden stairs. He was sitting, hands around his knees, head down, rocking slowly and rhythmically back and forth, and he didn't even lift his head when my flashlight beam played across his face.

On the landing at the top of the stairs, a door opened and a woman stuck her head out. "Officer! If you see a guy with a big black beard who looks like Jesus down there, that's him!"

"Hey there," I greeted the man. He kept rocking but his head drifted up, and he offered me a gentle smile. He did look a little like Jesus. His clothing was rough—work boots, jeans, and sweatshirt—but his eyes were soft and dreamy.

I didn't want to provoke or panic him, so I kept my voice low and friendly. "Hey there. . . . How you doing?"

He smiled and gave me a dignified nod.

"You think you could come out of there for a minute and talk to me?" I suggested.

He nodded and smiled a bit more, but didn't get up. He just continued to rock back and forth.

"Sir . . . I need you to come out here for a minute."

This time, he spoke, in a soft, apologetic tone. "Lo siento, no entiendo."

Spanish. I tried again. "Hola, señor. No habla Ingles?"

"No, no habla Ingles," he agreed.

I summoned up my minimal Spanish. "Ah, entiendo. Cómo se llama?"

"Jesús."

Of *course* that was his name.

"Hola, Jesús. Me llama Rosa. Cómo estás?"

"Estoy bien, gracias." He gazed at me, rocking, his eyes wide and trusting.

I had now exhausted my small supply of Spanish phrases, and turned to my cell phone. Pulling up Google Translate, I typed in "Do you live near here?"

Google suggested that I say, "Vives por aquí?" so I gave it a try.

Jesús gave a small but decisive head shake. "No, no. Estoy esperando."

He was waiting, Google Translate informed me.

"Para quien?" For whom?

"My friends. Me recogoran."

"You're waiting for your friends to come pick you up?"

"Sí, sí. Me recogoran. They come."

"Qué trabajo haces? What work do you do, Jesús?"

"Construcción."

Jesús didn't seem at all bothered by my continued questions. His Christ-like demeanor was unruffled, his gaze direct, calm, forgiving.

"Ah, entiendo."

I was starting to think I understood. I assumed Jesús was part of the region's army of Spanish-speaking day laborers, one of the men who waited outside Home Depot each morning hoping to be picked up by contractors looking for a pair of extra hands. Now, at the end of a long workday, he was waiting to be picked up and brought home again. It made sense.

My radio chirped. A Spanish-speaking officer was on his way over to help, the dispatcher said.

While we waited, I tried again with Google Translate.

"Jesús, entiendo qué estás esperando, pero no puedes sentarte aquí. I know you're just waiting for your friends, but you can't sit here under these stairs. You're making the people who live here nervous. Estás poniendo nerviosos a los residentes. Could you wait for your friends somewhere else?"

He shook his head courteously, and said something in a mix of Spanish and English that sounded like "waiting for aliens."

Ah, I thought, he's saying he's an illegal alien, or his friends are illegal aliens? This was possible; many day laborers are undocumented. Perhaps he was nervous about standing out in the open, or worried about talking to the police.

At this point, Gonzales, the Spanish-speaking officer we had requested, appeared, and I briefed him on what I had learned so far.

"He says he's waiting to be picked up, and I think he said something about illegal aliens? I didn't really understand."

Gonzales turned to Jesús and began an exchange in rapid Spanish, then looked back at me again.

"He says he's an alien. He's waiting for the other aliens to pick him up."

"Yeah, okay, the other undocumented workers?"

"No, the other aliens. The aliens from outer space. He says they dropped him off here this morning, and he's waiting for them to come back with their spaceship so he can return to his home planet."

"Crap."

From under the stairs, Jesús continued to rock and smile.

Gonzales politely asked him if he'd mind going to talk to some doctors—specifically, the doctors at the city's emergency psychiatric clinic.

Jesús considered this for a moment. I thought he would decline, but after a bit of thoughtful rocking, he agreed. "Sí, I go with you."

With an effort, he pulled himself up and came out from under the stairs, murmuring softly to himself as he approached us.

I looked at Gonzales for a translation. He grinned.

"He says the aliens can just as easily meet him at the doctor's."

L̲ater, we responded to an assault call. When Lowrey and I arrived, we found a heavyset bearded officer standing on the porch, looking disgruntled. His name tag read "Lamar." As we got closer, the reasons for Lamar's displeasure became clear: sitting on the doorstep was a slender, wriggling young man, his hands cuffed behind him, and next to the young man was a small pool of vomit.

"He punched his aunt and uncle," Lamar told us.

"They pushed me first! They got they hands on me first!" the youth interjected. He looked upset, and he was wiggling his legs around. "I gotta go, I gotta see my son, my baby mama gotta go to work tomorrow. This is so *sad!*"

Lamar looked at me, then pointed at the vomit. "Watch that, watch that there."

"Yeah, I see it."

The boy interrupted. "That's *my* throw-up!"

"I know," said Lamar, disgusted. "And now *we* gotta deal with it. Just stop moving around like that, or you gonna end up sitting in it!"

"My baby mama's pregnant," the boy said defensively, continuing his nonstop squirming. "What you want me to do?"

This seemed like a non sequitur, and Lamar ignored it.

"So tell me again what happened?"

"Well," said the boy, "I just came in to use the phone, 'cause I gotta call my baby mama—" He shifted position again. "Can I just pull up my pants?"

He rose to a crouch, his cuffed hands down behind his knees, and turned so his backside was facing us. His wriggling had caused his baggy jeans to fall down his hips, partially exposing his buttocks. He started to giggle.

"My pants, could you—?"

"Oh, *really*?" Lamar's mouth twisted in disapproval.

"My pants are down, man," the boy said plaintively. "I can't, I can't—"

"You're killing me, kid!"

"You're having a bad day," I put in.

"I *am*! This is so sad!" The boy waggled his butt at Lamar. "Awright, come *on*!"

Lamar opened his palms and gazed up at the sky, as if hoping for some heavenly intercession. "Dude, what were you *doing*?"

The boy looked sheepish and giggled some more. "Brah, I was trying . . . I was trying to do the little thing—" He gestured with his head toward his cuffed hands.

"You were trying to work the cuffs down and under your feet so your arms would be in front," I suggested.

"Yeah, yeah!" he agreed. "I seen it on TV. But when I did that, my pants . . . It's not as easy as it looks on TV. My pants fell down."

He still looked embarrassed, but he was laughing uncontrollably now. "I'm sorry, I'm sorry y'all gotta see me like this. Please, brah, please . . . help me here. *Please*, brah!" he appealed to Lamar. "You gotta help me, or everyone in the whole city gonna see my butt!"

By now Lamar was laughing too, reluctantly. "Aw. Man. I can't believe I have to do this."

He put his gloves on, then started tugging the boy's waistband up, the boy still half-crouched and giggling. "Man, you are killing me here! Stop wriggling! Whoa, watch it, watch it! Don't get in the throw-up!"

"I got this, I got it!" the kid said. "Okay, I'm good!"

He sat back down, shaking with giggles.

"Oh, man," he said rhetorically, glancing back up at Lamar, then smiling up at me. "He lookin' at me like, 'Oh my God!'"

"You're probably having the worst night of anyone I've met so far," I told him, smiling back.

"I am, actually," the kid said, growing suddenly somber. "I just need to get outta here and go get my son from my baby mama, she gotta go to work tomorrow, I don't want her to lose her job."

"You keep an eye on this clown for me for a minute?" Lamar asked. "I wanna go see what's going on inside with my partner."

When Lamar was gone, I looked back down at the handcuffed youth.

"I just don't want her to lose her job," he said again.

"I know. Just hang out. Give us some time to see if we can sort this out. You wanna tell me what happened?"

The kid, animated again, launched into a complex and not very coherent tale. "It's my grandma's house, I just went in to use the phone, and my aunt, she starts saying, 'Get out, get out,' and I'm like, 'I'm just using the phone, and why you saying that, it ain't even your house!'"

His voice was getting faster and faster, and rising with excitement. "Then she and her boyfriend, they're both pushing and shoving me! And I'm like, 'I'm too small for your big ass, you stop pushing me!' And I squared up at them!" He tried to reenact this, but since his hands were cuffed, all he could do was twitch his body rapidly back and forth, which he did several times, adding a few comic-book sound effects—"Oof! Pow!"—for good measure.

He looked over his shoulder toward the house and called out, "Grandma! You tell the police, they put their hands on me first!"

I pointed to the vomit. "So when'd you throw up? How'd that happen?"

He looked surprised. "Oh. See, my girlfriend's pregnant. So I just . . . you know what I'm sayin' . . . " He gave me a knowing little wink. "I got . . . symptoms."

I must have looked puzzled.

"I mean, we eat, and sleep together," he added. "And throw up together! It's my second time too. . . . But," he added thoughtfully, "I didn't throw up with our first child. So . . . I bet we're having a girl, this time."

I didn't know what to say to this. It was starting to occur to me that this kid was somewhat crazy. "Well," I offered, "maybe that just shows you're emotionally involved with you girlfriend's pregnancy. That's good, I guess."

"I am!" He nodded eagerly. "I *am* emotionally involved. I spend all my time with my son. I tell my girlfriend, 'I'm not going to let you go through this alone.'"

He looked down at the ground, and the pool of vomit.

"I just . . . I want to be a good man."

"I hear you."

"My family is fucked up, though," he confided. "The only time they wanna see me is when I got money. It's fucked up. Aw . . . my stomach's balled up so tight. I feel like I might throw up again."

I liked this kid. He was a weird kid, mercurial and probably more than a little bit nuts, but appealing.

"Are you sick? Do you want me to call the medics? If you want, we can get them to come check you out."

"No, no, it's nothing, it's just what I said, my girlfriend's pregnant—"

Just then, a man came up the walk from the street and started up the stairs.

"Whoa, whoa!" the boy and I cried in unison, but it was too late. He stepped right in the vomit.

"Ew!" cried the boy. "Ew, sorry, brah, it's my fault, man."

The man cursed, gave the kid a pissed-off look, and backed off, wiping his shoes in the grass.

"Aw, shit," said the kid. "Everybody be looking at me. Everybody looking at me like I retarded." He gazed up at me. "Could you put my hood up over my head so people can't recognize me? Please?"

I complied, pulling his hood as far forward as I could.

The boy lowered his head to his knees. "It's not even funny no more. I just want to see my son." He started to cry. "I ain't seem him in so long."

I was about to remind him that he had said, just moments ago, that he spent "all his time" with his son, but the kid was sniffling forlornly into his hood, and I didn't have the heart.

He stared down at his knees. "I just want to be able to make money so my baby boy and my baby girl can look sweet. I want—I want my son to go to college. I ain't gonna let him get into no trouble, not like me. I see him mess around with drugs, I gonna whup his ass. *Whup* his ass. . . . I mean, me, I was a problem, from when I was ten, twelve. Not my son! I'm gonna whup his ass."

He glanced up at me from under his hood, and added hastily, "I mean, I'm not lookin' *forward* to it, I hope he be a good boy, but if he ain't, I whup his ass to teach him to be better. He too little now, you can't hit him, he into everything but he just a baby, he don't understand, but when he bigger . . . I gonna tell him, don't be like me. You be like me, you end up with the police, in handcuffs, you little butt hanging out."

Parallel Worlds

*Homicide—Murder 1—MPD was dispatched . . . for reports of a
shooting. Once on the scene, officers observed V-1 laying on the
ground suffering from multiple gunshot wounds . . . Victim was
unconscious and not breathing. . . . Victim was transported to a
local area hospital . . . where he was pronounced deceased.*

*—MPD Joint Strategic and Tactical Analysis
Command Center, Daily Report*

It was a strange way to live.

During the hours I spent immersed in the world of the Metropolitan
Police Department, everything else faded away. Policing was immediate
and raw—sometimes tedious, frustrating, or absurd, but often wrenching,
and always absorbing. When I was patrolling, it was hard to remember that
I had another, quite separate life, one in which I was Rosa or Professor
Brooks, not Officer Brooks. But that other life—my "real" life—existed in a
parallel universe.

I was on sabbatical from my job as a law professor during my first
months at the police academy, but I still went to occasional Georgetown
workshops and faculty meetings. I wrote articles and reviews for newspapers
and magazines, worked on law journal articles and chapters for scholarly
books, and participated in conferences and panels on national security, international law, and civil-military relations. The book I finished right before

applying to the reserve corps—*How Everything Became War and the Military Became Everything*—was published in August 2016, when I was about halfway through the police academy, and in the months that followed, I combined my life as a model police recruit with the usual things authors do when they're trying to promote a book, speaking at bookstores and doing radio interviews.

By August I was also back at Georgetown full-time, serving as one of the law school's associate deans for graduate programs. Unlike the "real" dean, who presides over faculty meetings, sets budgets, and represents the school to students, the community, and big-money donors, law school associate deans function much like department chairs in other parts of the university. No one covets these positions, and the dean generally has to do some arm-twisting to persuade reluctant faculty members to step up. I was no exception—I agreed to become an associate dean mostly because I couldn't think of a good enough excuse to say no.

As an associate dean, my days were a whirl of meetings and memos. From nine to five, I'd meet with disgruntled staff members unhappy about their budgets, soothe the nerves of anxious students worried about their postgraduation job prospects, and review proposals for new courses. Then I would change into my uniform—first, my khaki recruit uniform, and after graduation, my blues—and head to my MPD life.

My two worlds could hardly have been more different. Academic culture—even in law schools—is theory-oriented and full of polite, passive-aggressive circumlocutions; police culture is pragmatic, profane, and largely indifferent to norms of political correctness. In 7D, no one bothered to be passive-aggressive—there was no need, since open aggression, both verbal and physical, was accepted and often praised. No one cared about theoretical constructs, and "Don't *ever* be such a fucking moron again" was considered an appropriate form of workplace feedback. Sometimes this rattled me, but other times, I found it almost refreshing. In the academic world, I was accustomed to tiptoeing around difficult issues lest someone take umbrage. At 7D, no one ever tiptoed—and perhaps the conversations, though often jarring, were also more honest.

Initially, my separate worlds never overlapped. Often, each was completely immersive: during my two weeks of firearms training, for instance, I was at the police academy every day from six thirty in the morning to two thirty or three in the afternoon, then home for a few hours, then back at the academy again for regular recruit classes in the evenings, and back once more every Saturday. The law school and my life as an author might as well have ceased to exist. After graduating from the academy, there were similar periods of near-total immersion—weeks when I would do several patrol shifts back-to-back and my "other" life, my "regular" life, would start to feel almost imaginary.

This was true the other way around as well: when I was sitting in a Georgetown faculty meeting or traveling to give a talk about my book to an audience in Ottawa or Vienna, my police life seemed equally unreal.

Every now and then, though, when I was overtired or distracted, I'd forget for a moment which world I was in. In 7D, I'd lose track of the context and offer a casual comment about the social construction of crime and the otherization of communities of color. My fellow officers would look at me with consternation, then remind me that the guy whose plight had prompted my burst of academic blather was "a fucking animal, and if he doesn't want to go to jail, he can just stop selling crank." Other times, sitting in a frustrating meeting back at Georgetown, the academic niceties would slip away from me, and I'd find myself telling my horrified faculty colleagues that the motherfuckers on the university budget committee needed to get their heads out of their asses.

Despite these occasional slip-ups, few people in either of my worlds knew about the other. It's not that either world was a secret, exactly—a handful of my friends and Georgetown colleagues were aware of my life as a police officer (and as I had predicted, they were variously stunned, dismayed, amused, and intrigued, sometimes all at once). And when police academy instructors or, later, my various patrol partners asked about my day job, I told them. But in both worlds, most people didn't ask many questions. Maybe they didn't know what to ask.

Or maybe they just weren't interested. Usually, when someone in the policing world asked about my day job, I'd say something vague, like "I'm a lawyer." This was not entirely accurate, but it was simple, and it had the virtue of being both boring and off-putting (most cops dislike lawyers), so few people pursued the subject. Sometimes I said, "I teach," which usually led other officers to assume that I taught elementary or high school kids. Almost no one bothered to ask any follow-up questions.

Mostly, I was glad. As much as possible, I wanted my partners to accept me as just another officer. But sometimes it created an almost vertiginous sense of double vision, of two worlds existing in uneasy juxtaposition, with, at any given time, one of those worlds invisible to everyone but me.

I'm probably overdramatizing. Everyone inhabits multiple worlds: our families, our homes, our workplaces, our neighborhoods, our present, and our past. If my multiple worlds were unusual, it was only because they so rarely intersected, and because they were, in so many ways, mutually unintelligible.

My mother—one of the few who knew about both my worlds—still wasn't happy with me. She rarely raised the subject directly, but periodically she'd send me links to news stories about police abuses, and whenever we were together, she'd make a grim reference to the latest travesty:

"So, how about those cops in Utah who arrested a hospital nurse because she wouldn't let them draw blood from an injured suspect?"

"Uh-huh, I saw that," I'd say. "Terrible." And I'd change the subject.

A few days later, she'd look up from the newspaper again. "It's outrageous how the NFL is treating Colin Kaepernick. But thank goodness someone's raising the issue of racism and police brutality."

"Mmmm, yeah," I'd say.

Occasionally, she was less indirect. "Well," she'd say, "I was *going* to tell you that smoking marijuana is really helping with my back pain, but I remembered I'd better not say anything, because you'd probably arrest me."

I've never found it easy to confront my mother about conflicts or tensions between us. But after months of this, I finally lost patience.

"Mom, would you please cut the crap!"

She gazed at me wide-eyed, all injured innocence.

I ground my teeth. "I understand perfectly well that there's a lot wrong with policing, and that it's very, very easy to read the news and find examples of cops doing awful things. I don't need you to constantly remind me of that. I read the news too."

She sniffed. "I'm just mentioning a few issues."

"Mom, I get that you don't like that I'm doing this, but why do you trust me and respect me so little? You act like I'm uncritically joining 'the enemy,' and you keep making nasty cracks about it. It's offensive, and it's hurting my feelings."

She stared at me. I expected her to be defensive, but for a moment, she just seemed taken aback.

After a long pause, she said, "I'm sorry."

We were both silent for a few minutes.

Then she said, "My encounters with the police have all been bad. I mean, very bad. Traumatic. So I can't help finding it upsetting that you're doing this."

"Just *trust* me a little bit, okay?" I wasn't sure how to make her understand. "Please, just trust that I'm the same person I've always been. I haven't become blind to any realities or abandoned any values. But I think the world is complicated, and people aren't all one thing or all another. I'm trying to learn something. I don't *know* where I'm going to go with this, or what I'm going to do with this." I hadn't yet told my mother about the proposal for a new fellowship program I had put together while I was at the academy, the program that I hoped would create a space for young officers to talk about racial justice, over-criminalization, alternatives to arrest, and all the other issues resolutely ignored in the official recruit curriculum. I didn't know if my program proposal would go anywhere, so I hadn't mentioned it, but I was still hoping it would eventually come together. "Just trust me, whatever I do with this, it won't be something bad. Okay?"

She looked at me again, a little uncertain. "I love you, and I'm always proud of you. I'll try."

It was something, at least.

Like a Sparrow

Many lay responders worry about hurting the person (for example, by breaking the person's ribs or breastbone) while giving CPR, but a person who is in need of CPR is clinically dead (i.e., the person has no heartbeat and is not breathing). It is very unlikely that you will injure the person while giving CPR, but even if you do, consider this: any injury you may cause is secondary when compared with the person's current circumstances.

—*American Red Cross, First Aid/CPR/AED*

"Clear!"

We all stood back, leaning away from the elderly woman on the floor. The medics had ripped her shirt open to apply the defibrillator pads to her chest, and her body jumped slightly as the machine buzzed and electricity coursed through her.

"Resume CPR," ordered one of the medics.

My partner that night, Adam, was a full-time paramedic when he wasn't working as a reserve officer, and the DC medics who arrived a few minutes after us seemed content to defer to his expertise. Now, Adam looked over at me. "Your turn."

I knelt by the old woman's side, adjusted my hands, and started chest compressions. Her skin was warm and soft and crinkly. I was flooded by a sudden memory: sitting on my grandmother's lap as a small child, running my hands wonderingly over the soft, wrinkled skin of her arms. She died of a heart attack when I was eight.

You're supposed to aim for thirty compressions at the rate of a hundred compressions per minute, followed by two rescue breaths, then more compressions. In training, they told us to sing the lyrics to the Bee Gees song "Stayin' Alive" while doing chest compressions, because the aptly titled song turns out to have precisely a hundred beats per minute. But it didn't seem right to belt out "Ah, ha, ha, ha, stayin' alive, stayin' alive!" over the body of a dead or dying woman, so I tried to just keep the song going inside my head while I counted compressions out loud. "One!—Two!—Three!—Four!"

It's a terrible thing to do to someone, slamming the heels of your hands repeatedly into their chest. There's nothing decorous about CPR. It's undignified, exhausting, and violent. By the third or fourth compression cycle, I was breathing hard. The old lady was still unresponsive, her body tiny and vulnerable, her wrinkled breasts shifting slightly with each compression.

"Fourteen!—Fifteen!—Sixteen!"

Under my hands, I felt the brittle bones in her rib cage shift and crack, and it took all my willpower not to cry out and jump back. Instead, I kept slamming my hands down on her chest.

"Seventeen!—Eighteen!—Nineteen!"

More bones cracked.

Fractured and broken ribs are considered an acceptable by-product of CPR, since it is better to be alive with some cracked bones than dead with an intact rib cage. But it felt like sacrilege. The old woman was like a tiny injured bird. Like a sparrow, I thought. And I was crushing her soft, fragile chest.

"Switch," Adam finally ordered, and a medic slid in beside me and took over the compressions. I pulled myself up, relieved.

We continued the CPR for another few minutes, but finally the senior medic with the ambulance team gave a small shake of his head. "I don't think there's any point continuing. I'm calling it," he said. He looked at his watch and made a note on a tablet. We all stood back, breathing hard. It was crowded in the small bedroom, with four or five adults hovering over the little body on the floor.

Outside, there was an awful wail of rage, or pain. Then a male voice, cursing, and thuds and crashes, and more cries of pain. It sounded like someone was taking a beating. Adam and I looked at each other and, stepping as carefully as we could over the body, rushed out to the hallway.

In the short corridor running between the living room, bedroom, and bathroom, an enormous man appeared to be trying to smash down the wall. He cursed and howled and smashed his fists into the drywall, shouting and kicking and clawing at it. His long dreadlocks snapped back and forth as he flung himself at it, and tears streamed down his cheeks.

We had rushed out prepared to intervene in an assault, but it took only an instant to understand that what we were watching was simply grief, raw and angry. Adam sighed and went back into the bedroom. I stayed where I was, watching the man howl and writhe until finally, exhausted, he slid down onto the floor and wept.

After a few minutes, I cleared my throat. "I'm so sorry."

"Yeah." His voice was ragged and muffled. "That's my mom. . . . I came right over. I was bringing her dinner. I saw you all doing CPR and I thought she was going to be okay, then I heard him say—I heard him say—" He stopped talking and sobbed some more.

After a few minutes, he stopped crying, stood up shakily, and walked into the living room. I trailed after him.

He wiped his eyes on his sleeve. "Can I go in and see her?"

"I'm sorry, not yet. A doctor or a detective might need to come in and take a look first." I held my hands out, palms up, trying to preempt his incredulous questions. "I know, it's crazy, but even when it looks like clearly it's natural causes, we still have to do that. I'm sorry."

"Can we at least put a blanket over her?"

"I'm sorry, but not yet." I felt like the worst person on earth. "For now, we need to leave everything the way it is. I'm really sorry. I know this is hard."

He nodded, looking down. "So what happens now?"

"Good question. Let me go check in with my partner, okay? I think he's calling this in."

I went back to the bedroom. The medics were packing up their equipment, and Adam was on the radio. I waited.

"Detective has to come," he confirmed. "He should be here in half an hour or so, maybe a little more. He's on the other side of town."

Which left us with nothing much to do but wait. I went back out to explain it to the dreadlocked man.

"So everyone just waits here?"

"I'm afraid so."

"Aw, Christ. I fucking can't stand this." But his anger had been taken out on the wall, and he just sounded sad. "She was fine just a few hours ago. I was over earlier today. She was completely normal."

I took out my notebook and started running through the usual questions. Name, age, health history, occupation.

The dreadlocked man was Thomas, and his mother was Ernestina. She was in her seventies, but had still been working as an accounts clerk at a school.

"That's what I hate," said Thomas. "She worked her whole goddamned life. Her whole life. She brought me and my siblings up alone and she worked the whole fucking time. She worked three jobs sometimes. Now, I was always on her to retire, but even though she had money saved up, she kept saying she couldn't afford it."

I thought of my own mother, also in her late seventies, also still working. She too had worked all through my childhood, writing books and articles, traveling to give lectures, organizing protests, marching on all those picket lines. Somehow, she had managed to support her family that way, and though money was tight throughout my childhood, eventually the success of her books left her financially comfortable. Now she didn't really need to work anymore, but like Thomas's mother, she kept at it anyway, still writing and speaking and organizing, even though she was becoming frail, her once-strong frame shrinking and growing brittle.

By now two more people had come into the apartment, a young man and an older woman. Both sat at the kitchen table.

Thomas gestured at them. "That's my boy. He's autistic. My mom kept saying she needed to keep working because his care's so much money, and I'm out of work. That's why we've been staying with her." He gestured with his chin at a mattress on the floor at the opposite end of the room.

Tears flooded down his cheeks again.

"I told her I could handle it, I'm gonna find a job, I got some savings too. I told her she needed to take a break, enjoy life a little for once, she didn't need to be helping me. She said maybe next year she'd retire, travel a little. She worked her whole goddamned life. Her whole goddamned life. I never could get her to just take it easy."

We waited for a while, in silence. I was tired and wished I could sit down. But if my own mother was lying dead on the floor, I wouldn't want a bunch of cops sprawling lazily around on my living room sofa, so I just shifted my weight from one leg to another.

Finally Thomas waved listlessly at the kitchen. "That's my son, Robert, and Mary, a neighbor."

Mary made a little harrumphing noise and gestured at the bedroom with her chin. "She gone to Jesus."

Thomas scowled at her. "She's not with Jesus. She's just fucking dead. She spent her whole fucking life working and she never got to rest, and now she's dead."

Mary harrumphed again and looked away. Robert didn't say anything.

He just rocked his body back and forth in his chair and made a quiet keening sound. He looked to be in his late teens or early twenties.

"Shit." Thomas stood up. "I guess I better start calling people to let them know. I'm gonna go outside and make some calls, okay?"

He left. Through the window, I could see him out on the sidewalk, pacing and talking into his cell phone.

After a few minutes, Mary made more harrumphing noises and walked out too.

That left me and Robert, who continued to rock and moan softly. From the bedroom, I could hear Adam and the medics talking quietly. They were standing in a dead woman's bedroom, her still-warm body cooling on the floor. I knew they were trying to keep their voices low and respectful, but every now and then there was a muted snort of laughter from one of the medics, quickly suppressed.

After a while, I said, "Hey, Robert. You okay?"

He made a little high-pitched noise.

"Your dad's going to be back soon, Robert. In just a few minutes. Can I get you something? Maybe a glass of water?"

Robert didn't make eye contact, but he nodded his head and said, "Glass a water, glass a water."

I rummaged around the cupboard and found a clean glass. I filled it at the sink and offered it to Robert. He took it and drained it in quick gulps.

"Wow, you were pretty thirsty, huh?"

"Glass a water, glass a water," he said to the floor.

"Another?" I asked.

"Glass a water, glass a water, glass a water."

"No problem. Can you give me the glass back? I'll go fill it up again."

Robert looked at the wall over my head, but he handed me the glass.

I filled it up and gave it back to him, and he gulped it down again.

"You hungry, Robert? Looks like there's some crackers here too." I handed Robert a box of crackers I'd spotted on the kitchen counter, and he wolfed a few down, then shoved the box toward me, making a mewling noise. "For me? No, I'm good. Thanks." He took the box back and ate more.

Time was passing agonizingly slowly. Where was the detective?

"Adam," I called out. "What's the story?"

"Just gotta wait," Adam called back.

I wandered around the room. It wasn't a bad apartment; if there hadn't been a queen-size mattress taking up floor space at the end of the living room, it would have seemed comfortable and open. On the walls, there were framed travel posters and African art, along with some bright paintings of flowers and birds.

By the time Thomas came back in, Robert had gone through two more glasses of water and the whole box of crackers. "Hey, buddy," Thomas said, crouching in front of his son. "You're going to your auntie's house, okay? She'll be here in a minute." Robert made a noise that sounded happy.

"That's a really beautiful painting," I said, pointing at the wall.

For a moment, Thomas's face brightened. "Yeah, it's nice, isn't it? My mom loved African art. She collected it. She always wanted to go there, you know? See what it was really like." His face crumpled again.

"I like that one too." I pointed at a painting of birds.

"Robert did that one."

"Robert? He painted that?"

"Yeah. He's a real good artist. Aren't you, Robert?"

Robert nodded and grinned and made a little yipping sound.

"Wow, Robert. That's amazing. You're a really good artist."

"He goes to this program for autistic people, they do a lot of art there. They keep saying he could sell his paintings."

"He could. This is great."

"You want to see some of his other stuff?"

"Sure."

Thomas opened a big wooden chest and rummaged around a bit, coming out with a large scrapbook. We spent the next ten minutes going through Robert's paintings and drawings. Until Adam came in and cleared his throat, I almost forgot about Thomas's mother lying dead in the next room.

"It looks like the detective got held up at a crime scene, sir. But the medical examiner talked on the phone with the ambulance team and says that since everything looks okay—in the sense that this was natural causes, I mean—they don't need the detective to come after all."

Thomas looked unsure. "So, okay, no detective, but what do we do now?"

"Well, it's okay to release the bo—your mom—to a funeral home. Usually, they come pick people up. You got a funeral home you like?"

This was too much for Thomas, who started to cry again. "A funeral home that I *like*?"

"I just mean, one your family uses."

"Yeah, I know what you mean. Let me call my sister. Had an uncle died last year. She'll remember."

Thomas got back on the phone, and the medics finally emerged from the bedroom, carrying their gear. They made apologetic gestures at Thomas and Robert, and left.

"We can go," Adam told me quietly.

"We don't have to wait for the funeral home people to come?"

"Nah, could be a couple hours. I guess they changed the procedure. Used to be you always needed a detective, but looks like they're saving money or something."

"So we just . . . go?"

"Pretty much. Nothing for us to do here now."

"Let's just wait till he's off the phone, then."

Thomas finished his calls and looked over at us. "My sister called the funeral home. They're sending people over."

"Thomas, we need to get back out on patrol," I said. "We're going to get out of your hair and leave you and your family to it. We're so sorry about your mom. She sounds like she was a wonderful woman. I wish I had been able to meet her."

"Yeah," said Thomas. "She really was."

"You guys gonna be okay?"

Thomas looked at Robert. "We gonna be okay, bud?"

Robert moved his head from side to side and made a noise like a dolphin.

"Yeah, we're gonna be okay."

Globally, someone dies roughly every half second. In Washington, DC, almost 5,000 people die each year, translating into an average of 13.6 deaths each day, or one death roughly every hour and forty-five minutes. In 2018, there were 160 homicides in DC. Ninety-two DC pedestrians died after being hit by cars, 36 vehicle occupants died in crashes, and about 400 other people died in accidents of one sort or another (they drowned in rivers and swimming pools; got crushed in construction site accidents; fell off balconies, trees, roofs, and ladders; toppled down Metro escalators; froze to death on cold nights; suffocated from smoke inhalation in house and apartment fires; or overdosed on drugs). The remaining deaths—the vast majority—are from natural causes.

Regardless, this translates into lots and lots of dead bodies for police officers. Within a year of graduating from the academy, even as a purely part-time, twenty-four-hours-a-month officer, I had seen at least six or seven dead bodies, including one homicide victim and two overdose victims. Full-time officers see ten times as many dead people. Like everything else, repetition makes it routine. People die all the time. There's nothing special about it.

Even so, for weeks after that, my mind kept veering back to the feel of those birdlike bones shifting and cracking under my hands.

The Secret City

*Officer . . . reports the arrests of an ATV operator driving
recklessly with a juvenile passenger and the seizure of his ATV.*

—MPD Joint Strategic and Tactical Analysis
Command Center, Daily Report

There's a thrill to it. I can't deny that.

It's not the thrill of power, exactly, although I am certain that for some cops power is the lure. For me, it was more the thrill of getting to do things others couldn't do, go places they couldn't go, see things they couldn't see. As a police officer, you get a view of what things look like backstage—the realities behind the illusions, the machines that keep it all going. The secret city.

The secret city mostly comes out at night. For the commuters who arrive in DC each morning from Maryland and Virginia, Washington's a nine-to-five sort of place (or, depending on the commute and the nature of the job, a six a.m. to nine p.m. sort of place). For residents, DC starts a little earlier and ends a little later each day, but unless they're hard-core partiers (and DC is not a hard-core-partying sort of city), most people are tucked safely into bed by midnight or one a.m. But even at three in the morning, while the rest of the world is sleeping, the secret city's still bustling. There are cleaning crews going floor by floor in fancy K Street lobbying firms, doctors and nurses and orderlies staffing hospital wards, medics playing cards in ambulances and firehouses, tired security guards manning desks at museums, emergency repair crews fixing Metro track problems.

And there are cops, lots of cops, driving the quiet, empty streets. You still get occasional calls at three or four a.m.: burglaries, domestic violence. But most nights, things quiet down after one or two and stay quiet.

There's a fair amount of camaraderie among residents of the secret city. It's like going out right when a big snowstorm ends: in the sudden silent whiteness, neighbors who normally only exchange polite waves become chatty and amiable, helping each other with shovels and snow blowers and trading stories about other big storms they've known. Night-shift people are the same—even complete strangers act like they've survived something together.

Here is one of the hidden joys of being a cop: You can go virtually anywhere you want. No one will stop you; you're the police. You want to know what it's like to walk around in the Smithsonian Museum at two thirty in the morning? Just wave to the security guard and he'll let you in. No one minds if a uniformed police officer wanders around the galleries with a flashlight for a few minutes. Or—need a bathroom break? Stop by the brand-new luxury apartment complex with the fountain in the lobby. The guard there will be happy to let you use the elegant restrooms with the cloth towels. Museums and luxury apartment complexes often have kitchens and break rooms for staff, and if you need a quiet place to eat your dinner, the guards are usually happy to let you sit around for a bit.

And the hotels! Many of the fancier DC hotels will give police officers free meals, waving them back to the employee-only dining area. I never experienced this—7D does not run to fancy hotels—but on more than one occasion, academy classmates assigned to the Second District sent me selfies as they dined for free at the Ritz or the Four Seasons.

In the middle of the night, even the mundane gets a frosting of magic. One night, I got stuck guarding the perimeter of a homicide scene. This may sound exciting, but it's not; you string crime scene tape all over the place until you run out of tape, then you just stand around for the next few hours, making sure no one wanders in and stomps all over the evidence. Every so often someone shows up and asks what happened, and you tell them there's an investigation underway, and that you don't have any information. (You say this no matter what, since it would be bad form to start telling passersby that there's a dead body just up the street, but most of the time you're telling the truth when you say you don't have any information; the detectives don't go out of their way to walk the perimeter and offer updates to patrol officers.) But this night, I didn't mind the tedium. My little corner of the crime scene was at the top of a hilly street in Southeast DC. When I turned around, my back to the dead body and the bustle of detectives and crime scene technicians, I could see all the way across the Anacostia River, across rooftops and parks and city streets, all the way to the glowing dome of the Capitol and the spotlighted Washington Monument.

Strange magic! Blood and squalor and misery behind me; the monuments of the nation's capital in front of me, bright and glittering in the still night air.

Southeast DC boasts some of the best views in Washington. There's a parking lot behind a church on Morris Road that offers a panoramic view of the city and its rivers and monuments. The residents of the beleaguered Seventh District know about it, and it's a popular spot for weddings and picnics, but I'd bet the majority of Washingtonians never dream such spots even exist.

Mostly, I'm just nosy. Sometimes I think that's the whole truth of it. I liked having license to poke around in other people's lives. When you're a police officer, people invite you into their homes and kitchens and bedrooms. You see beautifully decorated apartments in dysfunctional neighborhoods, and trashed apartments in wealthy areas. You see unvarnished lives: angry people, weeping people, frightened and hurt people. They answer the door wearing the oddest garments: pajamas, their underwear, elaborate kimonos. Once, we got a guy wearing a gorilla costume. (My partner and I both yelped and did a double take, which made the gorilla yelp and do a double take too, before taking off his gorilla head. "Sorry, officers, forgot I was wearing this," he explained.) People tell you strange, often incomprehensible stories. ("Well, you see, Jeff decided to dress as Dian Fossey, so I thought it was a good time to get the gorilla suit out from the attic. . . .") You hear about their no-account boyfriends and their ailing mothers and their son who is going to grow up to be a famous artist.

My nosiness about people and their stories was rarely shared by my partners. Maybe it was the age difference—many of my partners were young enough to be my children, and they had little patience for people's long, rambling stories about how a once-happy relationship fell apart or a good job failed to work out, or why cousin Fred was really much nicer to be around when he was on crack. Mostly, my partners wanted to be somewhere else, doing something more interesting. The young men in particular often craved action. They didn't want to talk to senior citizens with long sob stories about how their diabetic husband only stole those cookies from the 7-Eleven because his blood sugar was all messed up and he wasn't thinking right. They wanted shootings, stabbings, and high-speed car chases.

Much to the chagrin of many of the young officers I knew, high-speed chases were officially prohibited in DC, except in rare circumstances and with the authorization of senior officials. The reasoning behind the prohibition was straightforward: the risks outweigh the benefits. Nationwide, most of those pursued in high-speed police chases are suspected of only minor crimes; often, police are simply chasing people who failed to pull over for traffic stops. But high-speed police chases are dangerous, killing several hundred people a year. Most of the time, it's the suspect who ends up crashing and dying—a high price paid for what are usually minor offenses. But about a third of those killed in high-speed police chases are innocent bystanders, and each year, several police officers are also killed in vehicle chases.

Still, many officers chafed at the no-chasing prohibition. In 7D, what particularly rankled were the kids on dirt bikes and ATVs. It's illegal to ride them on city streets, but every so often, small packs of kids on dirt bikes and ATVs (which had often been stolen from local dealers) would take over roads and even highways, popping wheelies, spinning doughnuts, laughing and hooting as other drivers slammed on the brakes and cursed. The ATV gangs caused traffic snarls and accidents, but there was little the police could do. By the time someone called 911 and patrol cars arrived, most of the ATVs would be gone, and the kids who remained would veer off in different directions, cutting across yards and empty lots where patrol cars couldn't follow. Even the kids who stayed on the roads usually got away— the ATV drivers all knew the cops weren't allowed to chase them, so they just ignored the lights and sirens and sped off.

The antics of the ATV gangs were often covered on local news, with unflattering commentary from citizens and city officials about the apparent inability of the police to do anything about them. Sometimes, the police helicopter would track the ATVs from above and direct officers on the ground, but it was still nearly impossible to catch them. It drove cops crazy, and many officers did everything they could to circumvent the no-chasing rule.

One hot June evening in 2017, about eight months after my academy graduation, I was partnered with a young guy called Jeremiah. He was small and slight, with very dark skin and round, boyish features; he couldn't have been more than twenty-two or -three, hardly older than the ATV riders themselves. He was a good-humored, friendly soul; whenever he saw me, he greeted me with an enthusiastic hug. He hugged everyone—crime victims, witnesses, even suspects—and everyone, even the people he put in cuffs, seemed to respond to his infectious joy. But the ATVs drove him nuts—"It's dangerous; these kids could cause an accident and kill someone, you know?"—and he was obsessively dedicated to catching them. As we drove around, waiting for a call, we heard loud chatter on the radio. An ATV gang had been spotted on Interstate 295, which cut through the western side of 7D.

The police chopper was in the air, narrating their movements for earthbound colleagues.

"Okay, a bunch of them just hung a U-ey and are heading south, and a couple others broke off onto Malcolm X. Ah, okay, looks like two of them are turning onto MLK northbound—"

Jeremiah gave a whoop. We were just a block south of the intersection of Malcolm X and Martin Luther King Avenue. He stepped on the gas, and sure enough, we could soon see two ATVs ahead of us. Jeremiah drove faster. The ATV drivers glanced over their shoulders and sped up. Jeremiah sped up too. "I wanna catch those little bastards so bad," he said happily. "Sooooo bad."

The ATVs sped up some more. So did Jeremiah. By now, we were going about sixty miles per hour on a residential street.

"Hey, Jeremiah," I said, "aren't we not supposed to chase them?"

He shot through an intersection. "We're not chasing them," he said. "We're *following* them."

"Ah, what's the difference, exactly?"

He grinned maniacally at me. "Well, see, I don't have my lights and siren on. If I had them on, it would be a chase, and we're not allowed to chase them. So I don't turn on my lights and siren! Because we're not chasing them. We're just following them."

The speedometer now read seventy.

"So, high-speed chases with lights and siren are prohibited because they're too dangerous, but you're thinking that driving just as fast after the ATVs *without* your lights and siren on is totally fine?"

"Um . . ." For a minute Jeremiah looked uncertain. "Um, yeah? Because if there's no siren, there's no chase?"

I almost never talked to my young patrol partners about my day job, but this seemed like a good moment to mention it. "Jeremiah, you know I have a law degree, right? That I teach at a law school?"

He gave me an anxious glance. "Oh yeah, that's cool."

"Yeah, so listen, I don't think the distinction between 'chasing' and 'following' would go over real well with the department's lawyers if you had to explain why one of those kids crashed into a telephone pole."

Jeremiah took his foot off the accelerator, crestfallen. "But then how are we going to catch them?"

The ATVs vanished over a hill.

"We're not," I said. "Not right now, anyway."

In some parts of DC—especially in the prosperous, low-crime neighborhoods of the city's northwest quadrant—bored cops turn to traffic stops when there's nothing else going on. I know officers who take great delight in traffic stops and enjoy issuing multiple tickets. With nearly two hundred moving violations to choose from, it's easy enough to do: "Well, ma'am, I stopped you because you failed to signal prior to changing lanes, but now I see that your window tint is excessive, the light over your license plate is broken, and those dice hanging from your rearview mirror are obscuring your line of sight." If an officer wants to ruin someone's day, it's easy to find lawful ways to do so.

Traffic stops were too easy, like shooting fish in a barrel. You'd tuck your car into a nice sheltered spot, turn off your lights, and wait. It never took long—soon someone would shoot a red light, or go the wrong way on a one-way street, or merge into the next lane without signaling, or drive by while yakking into a handheld cell phone. Bingo! You'd turn on your lights, give the siren a little whoop, and pull them over. You'd run their plates and their license; if everything checked out, you'd give a warning or write a ticket and send them off, relieved or disgruntled.

I didn't like traffic stops. Most of the time, I felt like they were just harassing people who were only trying to get to work or get home. When I had to stop someone, I almost always issued warnings instead of tickets with fines.

Fortunately, patrol officers in 7D were under no pressure to make traffic stops, and most 7D officers shared my aversion to them.

"Do you guys do a lot of traffic stops?" I asked Murphy the second time I patrolled with him.

"Nah," he said. "Not unless, you know, someone's shooting out their car window or something. Not worth it. We're too busy."

Part of the problem was that in 7D, traffic stops tended to lead to arrests, and traffic arrests were boring. It was standard procedure to run plates, check licenses, and check for warrants during traffic stops, and the Seventh District's extreme poverty more or less guaranteed that every second or third driver would be driving on a suspended license, have no license at all, or be driving an unregistered or stolen car, in which case they would have to be arrested.

Driving without a valid permit, or even in a stolen car, didn't make someone a criminal mastermind—people forgot to renew their licenses, or they didn't possess the right documents to get one, or they had their licenses suspended for unpaid fines. And the very poor, whose lack of bank accounts and even home addresses often forces them to operate in the cash economy, sometimes unknowingly bought stolen cars, or borrowed them from friends or relatives. All the same, driving without a permit and operating a stolen vehicle were arrestable offenses, and in a district that saw several violent crimes each day, few 7D officers wanted to waste their time arresting people over such trivia. Each arrest meant a minimum of two or three hours trans-porting the arrestee, writing a report, and filling out forms. It was just too much paperwork. Anyway, Murphy said, "If we stopped everyone we could stop, and arrested everyone we could arrest, there'd be practically no one left around here."

No one in 7D liked traffic accidents, either. In part, this was because they sometimes involved gory injuries, but mostly it was because they in-volved so much time and paperwork. You had to stand around waiting for ambulances and slow-to-arrive tow trucks, and then there were extra reports to fill out. Traffic accident reports had to include a pictorial diagram of the accident, showing all involved vehicles, street signs, the direction and speed of travel, the location of any damage to vehicles or other objects, and so on.

There was special software that allowed this to be done electronically, with a lot of clicking and dragging. You'd draw the road, click and drag tiny cars into place, and add whatever embellishments were required. You could click on tiny stop signs and speed limit signs and drag them into place, or add a tree, a motorcycle, or a small explosion icon to your diagram. For some reason, there was also an icon that appeared to depict a llama. No one was ever able to explain why the software designers had included a llama as an optional traffic accident icon, but because everyone liked it, quite a few accident diagrams included a tiny llama somewhere in the frame. It took forever to get the diagrams just right, and often they'd be bounced back by sergeants demanding additional details, or the deletion of a stray llama.

I was okay with traffic accidents. They were complicated, but they of-fered a window into the many forms of expertise it takes to keep a city going: police, medics, firefighters, 911 dispatchers, tow truck drivers, road repair crews, crews to fix damaged signs and streetlights. Sometimes it was like being a child again, or like living inside a Richard Scarry picture book: *What Do People Do All Day?* Or *Cars and Trucks and Things That Go* (not to mention *A Day at the Police Station*).

One night, my partner and I responded to a one-car accident on the Suitland Parkway. A guy had driven his car off the road and into a ditch. He was drunk but had somehow walked away without a scratch. His car wasn't as fortunate—it was nose-down in the ditch, tail end sticking up almost vertically, and bits and pieces of the car were scattered across the highway for a hundred yards. Another officer took the drunk guy off to the station for booking, and my partner and I set up flares and waited for the tow truck (or, in DC parlance, the tow crane). When the tow truck arrived, we had to shut down the parkway's westbound lanes altogether, since the tow truck needed to back into the traffic lanes while pulling the car from the ditch.

I am shutting down a highway, I thought. What a strange thing to be doing! I went over to speak to the drivers of the first few cars to explain what was going on, and though no one was very pleased about being stuck on Suitland Parkway at midnight, they were pretty polite about it. After that, I went back to watch the tow crane guy at work.

His job looked nearly impossible: pulling an almost vertical car out of a ditch and onto the flat bed of his truck. But he knew just what to do. He dashed around and attached hooks here and chains there, and within ten minutes, the damaged vehicle had been pulled, creaking and groaning, onto the truck. So that's how you do it, I thought. It was a minor miracle— the kind that happens a hundred times a day in every city but is usually invisible.

Other times, of course, the secret city revealed itself as less benign— more Dickens than Richard Scarry.

Half a mile from the White House and the offices of the high-priced lawyers and lobbyists, there's a guy passed out on the sidewalk, almost dead from fentanyl-laced heroin. On the next block over, there's a woman scream- ing, running away from the man trying to slam her head into the wall. Across the street, there are four kids in a one-bedroom apartment, their mother too high to remember to buy food. The kids get by on a mix of school-provided lunches and petty shoplifting—a bag of chips here, a can of soda there.

Here's the ugliest, most Dickensian thing of all: If my colleagues and I catch them, those shoplifting kids might end up in handcuffs. If we catch them several times in a row, odds are they'll spend much of their adult lives in a cage.

Cages

Burglary: On today's date between the given times, MPD received a 911 call for a Burglary in progress. Upon arriving on the scene, MPD was met by witnesses who . . . pointed Officers to the room where Defendant was hiding. Defendant was placed under arrest for Burglary 1. While in police custody, Defendant on multiple occasions flashed his penis to MPD staff. Defendant also poked his penis through the cell block doors and proceeded to masturbate in front of MPD staff. Soon after doing that, Defendant was placed inside a closed door cell where he broke a water pipe, causing a flood in the cell block.

—MPD Joint Strategic and Tactical Analysis
Command Center, Daily Report

You can call them cells if you want, but cages is what they are. Most cops prefer other words, because they don't see themselves as people who put humans into cages. Ask a dozen police officers what made them go into law enforcement and most will tell you they wanted to help people. Many of the officers I got to know in DC had been crime victims themselves at some point in their lives, or were close to someone who'd been a victim; stories about mothers, sisters, or brothers who were mugged, beaten, stabbed, or shot were common. A few credited positive encounters with a police officer as having changed their lives. It's a cliché, but clichés are clichés because they reflect common experiences, and I've had more than one young officer tell me, eyes wide with emotion, that he would have ended up in prison instead of wearing a badge if Officer So-and-So hadn't shown interest and compassion at a crucial moment in his life.

What research exists on the reasons people choose law enforcement careers bears this out: in both older and more recent studies, police officers tend to rate the opportunity to help people as the single largest factor in choosing their job; pay, power, and authority are near the bottom of the list.

True, some people are attracted to law enforcement because they're bullies who like the idea of having a badge, a gun, and a license to order people around. I have met a few officers like that—those who gleefully arrest kids for stealing candy bars and have no qualms about locking up a single mother for driving to work on a suspended license—but they aren't common, and they tend to be disliked by their peers. The vast majority of the police officers I met in my time with MPD were decent, well-intentioned men and women.

Policing tends to attract practical people with little patience for ambiguity, and it's probably fair to say that the average officer is not much given to pondering abstractions about crime, guilt, and the nature of society. But the best officers—and I met many excellent ones—combine practicality with a willingness to seek solutions that seem compassionate and just, rather than merely expedient.

And contrary to popular belief, cops don't spend a high percentage of their time putting people into cages. In 2017, 3,837 sworn MPD officers made a total of 34,136 arrests. That's a lot of arrests, but for each individual officer, it averages out to fewer than nine arrests per year. Granted, arrests are not distributed evenly. Some officers serve as station clerks or are assigned to headquarters and may make no arrests at all in a given year, while others, particularly those assigned to a Gun Recovery Unit or one of the city's Crime Suppression Units, may make far more arrests than typical patrol officers. But these differences come out in the wash; a typical full-time patrol officer will average well under one arrest each month.

For better or for worse, police officers spend most of their time serving as medics, mediators, and monitors. They break up fights, shoo away aggressive panhandlers, write accident reports, search for missing persons, take sick people to the hospital, encourage abuse victims to seek protective orders, respond to burglar alarms, and do a dozen other things that don't generate arrests.

But sometimes, police officers do put people in cages.

It is possible to say this in a nicer, more euphemistic way: sometimes, police officers arrest those whom they have probable cause to believe have violated one or more criminal laws. But we should be clear just what it is we are talking about. In the United States, arresting people involves locking them behind metal bars, and this is an inescapable part of what police officers do. It is entirely possible to be a police officer who rarely arrests people, and I know many officers who go far out of their way to avoid arresting people for minor offenses. But there is no way to be a police officer who *never* arrests people. If you are a police officer, sooner or later you will put another human being into a cage.

Here's what happens when you get arrested. First, your arms are locked together behind your back with metal cuffs. If you don't cooperatively place your hands behind your back when told to do so, police officers will yank your arms behind your back, and they won't hesitate to cause some pain while they're doing so; if you resist being handcuffed, "control holds" and nonlethal force are in order.

Then you're searched. The first time, you're searched by one of the arresting officers. It's not a strip search, but it's plenty intrusive. The searching officer goes through your pockets and, if they're doing their job properly, runs their hands over every inch of your body, including your private parts. If the searching officer feels anything untoward—a weapon, or a baggie containing drugs—they may search inside your clothes as well as outside. They take your shoes off and search inside, and do the same with hats, gloves, jackets. All your personal possessions, including belts, shoelaces, and jewelry, are removed and bagged.

If the arresting officers aren't driving a transport car, you then stand or sit around for a while, waiting for the wagon to arrive. Everyone who passes by stares at you, and if you're arrested at home, your family and your neighbors watch you standing there in cuffs. When the wagon finally shows up, the driver searches you all over again, and then you find yourself sitting on a hard metal bench seat in the back of a van on the way to the police station. No windows, no cup holders, no iPhone chargers, just a metal seat.

At the station, you're searched a third time by the booking officer, and you're put in a holding cell. Everything's made of metal: bunks, toilet, sink. There's no privacy; anyone walking by can see into your cell. And there are no comforts—no blankets, no pillows. No phone, no TV, no books or magazines. You can stare at the wall, or yell at the cell-block officer, or try to nap, but there's nothing else to do. You might have the luxury of a cell to yourself, but if it's a busy night, probably not.

After a while you'll be put back in the wagon and brought over to the city's Central Cell Block. Here, it's more of the same. If you're lucky and got arrested on a weekday morning, you could be arraigned within a few hours. If you're not so lucky and got yourself arrested on a Saturday night, you'll be spending a couple of nights in jail before you're brought before a judge.

Luck also plays a role at the next stage of the proceedings. If your crime was minor and your record is clean or reasonably clean, or if the arresting officer was sloppy and wrote a report that prosecutors find lacking, you may simply be released; prosecutors don't even bother to pursue many cases. Even if they plan to go forward, you'll probably be released and given a date to reappear. In DC, only a small fraction of arrestees are detained for more than a few days pending trial, and no one is detained as a result of inability to pay bail. In this sense, DC has a remarkably progressive approach to pre-trial detention; only those charged with the most serious offenses are held.

If you're released, you get your possessions back and you get to go home, assuming you have enough money for transportation, or your phone has enough juice to call someone for a ride. But don't imagine your problems are now over. Your employer may be angry that you missed work while you were cooling your heels in jail; depending on the employer, you may find you no longer have a job. At a minimum, you've probably lost a day or two's wages, and you now have an arrest on your record. If charges weren't dismissed, you'll have to go back to court, which will mean missing more work.

You'll probably be offered a plea deal, and your lawyer (most likely court-appointed, if you're the average arrestee, which is to say poor) will probably urge you to take it. Here again, if you're lucky, there will be no prison time involved, just probation, community service, or payment of fines or restitution. But if you're poor, paying fines may be impossible, and finding the time for community service—and getting transportation to the place where you're supposed to undertake it—may be difficult or impossible, which may mean you fail to meet your release conditions, which may, in turn, make you subject to rearrest.

By now you have a criminal conviction on your record, which makes it harder to get a job and access certain other services. Here too, DC is relatively progressive: in 2014, the city council passed legislation prohibiting employers from asking about criminal records prior to making conditional employment offers. But the law is regularly flouted, and in practice, even a misdemeanor on your record may make it tougher to get a job or be admitted to educational programs.

If you end up serving time, things get even worse, both for you and for your family. If you had a job, you don't have one anymore, and any family members who depend on your income are out of luck. If you have children, they're now missing a parent, and studies suggest that children with an incarcerated parent are six times more likely to end up incarcerated themselves, compared to children whose parents stay out of prison. They're also more likely to suffer from emotional and behavior problems, and if your imprisonment leaves them without a responsible parent or guardian, they'll end up in the care of Children and Family Services, which means placement with a foster family or in a group home, both of which increase their odds of getting subsequently involved in the criminal justice system. If they run away from a court-ordered placement, they can be arrested for absconding. And if their behavior lands them in juvenile detention, this also ups their chances of finding themselves incarcerated as adults: 40 percent of kids in juvenile detention are incarcerated again by the age of twenty-five.

Even when you're released, your troubles aren't over. Your criminal record will make housing and gainful employment a challenge, and the odds won't be in your favor—once you've served time, you'll probably serve more time. A recent Justice Department study found that 68 percent of released prisoners had been rearrested within three years, and a whopping 83 percent had been rearrested within nine years. Maybe your difficulties finding a job will drive you back to crime, but you may also find that the conditions of your release carry the seeds of re-incarceration with them: nearly 30 percent of prison admissions are for acts that are not inherently criminal, but that involve technical parole violations (such as failure to check in with a parole officer at the appointed time, changing residences without permission, failure to complete mandatory programming, etc.).

So try hard not to get arrested. Especially for the poor and for people of color, getting arrested is like getting sucked into a lethal riptide: You *might* be tossed back out again and find yourself washed up on the sand, bruised and frightened but essentially unharmed. But most of the time, the tidal pull of the criminal justice system drags you farther and farther away from shore, and you drown.

Baked into the System

*On the listed date and time, at the listed location, MPD
responded for a call for theft of property. . . . Victim reported that
Defendant had been inside of the store buying a slurpee. Victim
stated that Defendant handed him $2.00 to pay for the slurpee,
which was $1.86.*

*Victim reported that when the cash register opened
Defendant reached over the counter and into the cash register
and grabbed a handful of U.S. currency. Victim was able to grab
some of the U.S. currency back out of Defendant's hand.*

*Victim then yelled to Witness, who was outside, and told
him to keep the door closed. . . . Defendant never made it outside
of the store and officers pulled on scene shortly after. . . .
Defendant was placed under arrest for Attempt Robbery of
an Establishment.*

—*MPD Joint Strategic and Tactical Analysis
Command Center, Daily Report*

Washington, DC, is a small city, but it has lots and lots of cops. The
Metropolitan Police Department alone has about 3,800 sworn officers, for a ratio of roughly 55 MPD officers per 10,000 DC residents. In
contrast, New York City has about 42 cops per 10,000 people, Atlanta has
39, and Dallas and Los Angeles have about 25, giving DC one of the highest
ratios of police to residents of any large American city. And MPD officers

are only part of the story. DC also has the US Park Police, with jurisdiction over the National Mall, the monuments, and the vast expanse of Rock Creek Park. It has the Secret Service Uniformed Division guarding the White House, the Vice President's house, and foreign embassies. There are Metro Transit police, housing authority police, the US Capitol Police, FBI agents, and more than a dozen other police forces with limited jurisdiction, including Amtrak police, Supreme Court police, and even Bureau of Engraving and Printing police.

Having all those cops around doesn't necessarily reduce crime, but it does ensure that lots of people get arrested. In 2017, 31,560 adults and 2,576 juveniles were arrested by MPD, and other law enforcement agencies in the city arrested an additional 19,054 people, mostly adults, bringing the total number of annual arrests in DC up to 53,090. (If that number doesn't seem large, remember that Washington has a total population of less than 700,000. In New York, a city with a population of more than 8.6 million, police arrested just 239,064 people in 2017.) The high DC arrest rate ensures a high incarceration rate. In 2018, for instance, 7,654 DC residents were in local and federal prisons, giving DC one of the highest per capita incarceration rates in the country, in a country with the highest incarceration rate in the world.

The criminal justice system doesn't affect all DC residents in the same way. A 2019 ACLU report found that 86 percent of those arrested by MPD were black, while black residents make up just 47 percent of the city's population. Nationwide, minorities, and particularly African Americans, are also stopped by police and arrested at rates disproportionate to their representation in the US population. Black Americans are also more likely to be convicted if arrested, and more likely to receive a harsh sentence than white Americans convicted of the same offenses. Overall, black men have a one-in-three chance of landing in prison at some point in their lives, while white men have only a one-in-seventeen chance. African Americans make up just 13 percent of the overall US population, but they constitute 40 percent of US prisoners.

The racial disparities in American prisons are so glaring that many scholars and advocates, influenced by Michelle Alexander's 2010 book, *The New Jim Crow*, see mass incarceration as just the latest manifestation of the same white supremacist impulses that once allowed enslaved black people to be viewed as chattel. In this school of thought, the primary function of the US criminal justice system is to prevent black people from ever gaining access to the same privileges white Americans take for granted.

This is not a view that's popular among police officers.

"That's just bullshit!" Murphy objected when I described Alexander's work one night during a particularly slow period. "It's crap, and it's offensive. Race has *nothing* to do with the decisions I make." He was indignant. "I get it—people who don't know me might think, 'Oh, you're a white officer and all you ever do is arrest black people,' but I don't, like, profile people or something. I don't stop or arrest people because they're *black*; when I arrest them it's because they're committing *crimes*. Crimes against other black people! Anyway, practically everyone who lives here is black, so any profiling I do goes the exact opposite way—I see a white person around here who's not a cop, and I think: Either that's some kind of social worker or that asshole is up to no good. Buying drugs, mostly. Because trust me, white people don't come here to admire the fucking view."

Auguste was just as insistent: "It has *nothing* to do with race. My skin's black too, but you don't see *me* fucking people up for a few bucks. These people here, they're just messed up. It's like they *like* being bad, like they think being bad is good. Nobody makes these people act like they do. They don't like it here, they should fix their neighborhoods, or leave."

Jeremiah, another black officer, also didn't think much of Michelle Alexander's theories. "That lady's just wrong. I'm sorry, I'm sure she's really smart, but she's wrong. She should come out here and ride with us some-time. She should check out ShotSpotter."

ShotSpotter is a gunfire detection system that uses audio sensors to detect the distinctive acoustic signature of gunshots in real time, and it's tied into the DC police dispatching system.

"When ShotSpotter sends out an alert for sounds of gunshots, we go to where the gunshots are. How is that racist?" Jeremiah demanded. "ShotSpot-ter can't tell the color of the person firing the gun. And what does she want us to do, ignore the 911 calls from black neighborhoods because if we go, we might have to arrest black people? The people calling 911 are black too. Don't black people have a right to have us come when they call?"

Such views aren't unique to police officers. In his Pulitzer Prize–winning 2017 book, *Locking Up Our Own*, James Forman Jr. wrote about the evo-lution of criminal law in Washington, DC, and the ways in which many of the city's black leaders led the call for "tough on crime" measures. "To understand why," he writes, "we must start with a profound social fact. . . ." Beginning in the 1960s, "black communities were devastated by historically unprecedented levels of crime and violence." In response, DC's black lead-ers "exhibited a complex . . . mix of impulses." Though some had "sympathy for the plight of criminal defendants, who they knew were disproportion-ately black," that sympathy "was rarely sufficient to overcome the claims of black crime victims, who often argued that a punitive approach was neces-sary to protect the African-American community—including many of its most impoverished members—from the ravages of crime."

The result, writes Forman, was a majority-black city led by mostly black elected officials—who nonetheless passed laws and pursued policies that led to the arrest and imprisonment of mostly poor black people, in the name of protecting other black people from crime. But although the tough-on-crime policies advanced by many black leaders were motivated by a desire to pro-tect black crime victims, such policies did nothing to address the grinding poverty that fueled DC's high crime rates—and that was itself substantially caused by centuries of racially discriminatory laws and practices.

This is why racism seems like a nonissue to many street cops; it's baked so deeply into the system that it's invisible. Cops in DC's Seventh District see the poverty, hopelessness, and the crime, but they don't see that 7D is a mostly black neighborhood because the segregationist policies of previous decades forced blacks out of many other parts of the city (and today, rapid gentrification west of the Anacostia River is pushing still more poor African Americans into southeast DC, the last part of the city with anything close to affordable home prices). Cops see 7D's battered liquor stores and convenience stores, but they don't see the decades of tax rules and subsidies that gave supermarket chain stores an incentive to locate in wealthier, whiter parts of town. They see the joblessness that drives people to drugs and crime, but they don't see the decisions about the placement of bus and subway lines that leave many of the city's poorest people facing long, complex, costly commutes to get to where the jobs are.

Nationwide, centuries of overt discrimination have left African Americans still struggling to overcome enormous race-based disparities in educational attainment, employment, health, and economic well-being. In recent decades, the United States has seen the rise of an increasingly visible black middle class, but on average, African Americans still have shorter life expectancies than white Americans. They're more likely to be unemployed, less likely to finish high school or college, more likely to live in poverty, and more likely to end up in prison. Black Americans are also some three times more likely than white Americans to become homicide victims or victims of other violent crimes.

It's not just a matter of the long-term structural impact of slavery and segregation. There's still plenty of active and virulent race-based discrimination in American society. Some of it is overt—antiblack hate crimes have risen in recent years—but much of it comes from deeply rooted stereotypes or from what researchers call implicit bias: prejudicial attitudes we may not even consciously know we hold.

Thus, employers are less likely to hire job applicants with "African American–sounding names" than applicants with "white-sounding names," even when their résumés are otherwise identical. Similarly, studies have found that young white males with felony convictions on their records are more likely to get called back after a job interview than young black males with identical qualifications—and no criminal records. Even African American children often don't receive the benefit of the doubt. The death of twelve-year-old Tamir Rice, who was shot by a police officer while playing with a toy gun, is a particularly tragic case in point, but a 2014 report published by the US Department of Education found that as early as preschool, black children are punished in school more often and more severely than their white classmates.

Another 2014 study found that black children are assumed to be older and "less innocent" than their white counterparts. In the study, college students and police officers were asked to look at photos of black and white children and assess their age and potential culpability; when shown photos of children and told that the children were felony suspects, the college students overestimated the age of both the white and black children, but they overestimated the black children's age by more than twice as much as they overestimated the age of white children. Shown the same photos, police officers *underestimated* the white children's age by nearly a year, but made the same age errors as college students when assessing photos of black children, believing them to be, on average, about 4.5 years older than they actually were.

When it comes to crime and punishment, the glaring racial disparities in both crime commission and crime victimization rates stem from poverty as well as from race. Across all races, the poor are more likely to be arrested, convicted, and incarcerated than the more affluent. (In part, this is simply because the crimes of the poor are easier to detect than those of the more affluent. In urban areas, the poor have little private space, and crimes are more likely to be committed within sight or hearing of others. White-collar crimes may be just as harmful, but are more easily concealed. When a wallet is stolen in an armed robbery, the crime is immediately apparent; when cyber fraud, identify theft, and insider trading occur, victims may not realize a crime has occurred for months or years.) Americans living in poverty were more than twice as likely to be victims of violent crimes as Americans living in high-income households.

But poverty and race are difficult to disentangle. In the United States, wealth inequalities are bound up with the legacy of racial discrimination in numerous and complex ways. Rates of violent victimization were similar for poor blacks and poor whites, for instance—but black American families are three times more likely than white families to live in poverty.

Ultimately, argues James Forman Jr., class matters as well as race, and while Michelle Alexander's Jim Crow analogy is powerful, it obscures class divisions within the black community. "Although mass incarceration harms black America as a whole, its most direct victims are the poorest, least educated blacks. While the lifetime rate of incarceration . . . for African American high school dropouts" has skyrocketed, Forman writes, it has "actually decreased slightly for black men with some college education," and these class dynamics affected the willingness of black leaders to promote tough-on-crime policies.

Similar class dynamics were often evident in the comments I heard from police officers. When my black colleague Auguste and his medic friend called 7D residents "animals" who should be "clipped" so they couldn't reproduce, their disdain had more to do with class than race. This is also why increasing the diversity of police departments is no panacea—implicit biases, class divisions, and powerful internal behavioral norms often combine to make minority police officers act in ways that are little different from those of their white peers. (Some studies suggest, for instance, that black and Hispanic police officers are slightly *more* likely to shoot people of color than white officers.)

Media attention tends to focus on "bad cops," those who deliberately harass black people; those who are trigger-happy with Tasers or guns; those who—like Derek Chauvin, the Minneapolis officer who killed George Floyd—sneer at the pain and misery they inflict on others. Those cops are out there—far too many of them. But the deeper problem is this: even normal, careful, lawful policing often ends up compounding devastating social inequalities. For police officers, the racism that has shaped the system for so long means that even the most thoughtful and fair-minded police officers—even those who see and decry the structural impact of racism— often face nothing but bad choices.

Say you're a street cop, and you apprehend a young black man who robbed an elderly black woman at gunpoint. If you arrest him and he's convicted of a felony, you're sending one more young black male into our country's overcrowded prison system, where he can't support his family, leaving any children or other dependents struggling in his absence, emo-tionally and financially. In prison he's unlikely to have access to education, job training, therapy, or anything else that might help him turn things around when he gets out, and even if he leaves prison with the best inten-tions, he's branded for life—job opportunities for former felons are few. In some states, he won't be able to vote, ever again.

But if you don't arrest him, what about the elderly lady he robbed? She's distraught; she wants justice; she wants you to get violent young men off the streets so she can walk to the corner store without fear. She knows that racism is real and virulent, and its legacy distorts the choices of many young men in her community. You can offer her a copy of *The New Jim Crow*, but she's probably not interested in theories of structural racism right now. Right now, she just wants to feel safe in her own neighborhood.

One Summer Day

MPD officers responded . . . for possible child abuse. . . . Upon arrival MPD officers made contact with Victim [age 12] who was conscious and breathing suffering from a laceration to the forehead. Victim states he was hit in the head by Suspect with listed item at listed location. Victim and Suspect were involved in a mutual fight which led to Suspect striking Victim in the head with a 5 lb weight. . . . Victim was transported to Childrens Hospital for medical treatment.

—MPD Joint Strategic and Tactical Analysis
Command Center, Daily Report

Make no mistake: although the flaws in the US criminal justice system are real and numerous, and racism and poverty play a major role in who ends up in prison and who does not, the existence of violent crime is not a right-wing myth dreamed up to justify the incarceration of minorities and the poor. Crime is real—and the misery, pain, and fear engendered by violent crime are visited most often on the very same demographic groups who are disproportionately likely to end up incarcerated.

It's easy to forget this, especially if you're white, affluent, and lucky enough to live in a neighborhood with very little crime. In some quarters of American society, including academia, critiques of the country's criminal justice system have become so pervasive that a casual listener might be excused for imagining that every arrestee is as worthy as Victor Hugo's Jean Valjean, imprisoned for stealing bread to feed his family in *Les Misérables*.

Some arrestees *are* like Jean Valjean. But many are not. Most criminals are neither martyrs nor sociopaths; they're just ordinary people who never had many good options, and who stumbled into the worst of them. But their actions hurt other people, often badly.

Sometimes, it reminded me of the Ugandan and Sierra Leonean child soldiers I had interviewed so many years earlier. Most had been forcibly conscripted and deliberately brutalized. There was no question in my mind that those child soldiers were victims: They hadn't asked to be press-ganged into rebel armies, and they hadn't asked to be born into societies riven with violent ethnic and political conflict. But those child soldiers were perpetrators as well as victims. Their actions had brought pain, death, and terror to other innocents. Some of those children wanted nothing more than to return to their peaceful former lives, but others did not—some, traumatized and brutalized for too long, could no longer imagine lives not dedicated to violence.

I felt much the same about the violent criminals caught up in DC's criminal justice system. Most had been born into a world where the cards were stacked against them. Discrimination, grinding intergenerational poverty, poor health care, addiction, dysfunctional families, haphazard schools, and little access to jobs left them vulnerable to the blandishments of crime. Many of the people who commit violent crimes have been crime victims themselves, growing up with parental neglect or abuse and the constant threat of robbery and assault. It's no great surprise that some of the poor and abused end up committing crimes themselves. Robbery and theft are one of the few ways for the very poor to access the toys so ubiquitous among the affluent: iPhones, cars, expensive clothes. For many young men, gangs and informal crews offer protection, a place to belong, and a substitute family to make up for absent or neglectful parents. But like the child soldiers I met in Uganda and Sierra Leone, America's violent criminals are undeniably perpetrators as well, and their actions cause untold misery to others in their communities.

Spend an hour skimming through the daily crime reports compiled by MPD and you'll sense the suffering. Despite the bureaucratic prose, the police jargon, and the omnipresent passive voice, you'll feel the sheer weight of human pain caused by crime.

Here's a list of the serious crimes (assaults, rapes, homicides, carjackings, robberies, burglaries, etc.) reported to the DC Metropolitan Police on a single, randomly chosen summer day in 2019:

- **Armed Kidnapping:** Complainant reports while walking in the listed location she was approached by an unknown [suspect]. The Suspect brandished a dark-colored handgun and ordered the Complainant to get into the vehicle. The Complainant jumped from the vehicle and was able to take a photo of the tag.

- **Assault with a Dangerous Weapon—Knife:** On the above listed date and time, Victim 1 reports that Suspect 1, her boyfriend, entered her residence at . . . and cut her with a foldable pocket knife above the left eye following a dispute over another woman. Witness 1 corroborated Victim 1's account, stating that Suspect 1 ran toward Victim 1 holding a pocket knife in between his fingers as he slashed at Victim 1's face. Suspect 1 was last seen fleeing the scene on foot.

- **Robbery:** Complainant 1 reports . . . she was approached by Suspect 1 and Suspect 2, who began to speak to her in English. Complainant 1 reported that she did not understand what Suspect 1 and Suspect 2 were stating because Complainant 1 does not speak English. . . . Complainant 1 reports that Suspect 1 pulled a black in color handgun and pointed it at her while Suspect 2 grabbed her left arm and then Suspect 2 grabbed her cell phone . . . and backpack out of her hand. Witness 1 reports that he observed Suspect 1 and Suspect 2 flee. . . .

- **Robbery/Armed Carjacking:** MPD responded . . . for an armed carjacking. Once on scene, Complainant 1 stated that he was with his mother, Reporting Party 1, when they parked the listed vehicle. . . . Complainant 1 stated that they parked the vehicle and started to walk. . . . Complainant 1 states that he forgot his phone in the vehicle and went to return to retrieve it. Complainant 1 states that he went to the passenger side of the vehicle and opened the door, leaned in, and retrieved his phone. Complainant 1 states that when he leaned back out of the car Suspect 1 was standing there with a black semiautomatic handgun pointed to his head. Suspect 1 stated "Get the fuck down on the ground." Complainant 1 stated that he told Suspect 1 that he did not have anything and tossed the listed property on the ground. Suspect 1 then picked up the listed items and fled in the listed vehicle.

- **Burglary:** Reporting Party states that an unknown Suspect 1 entered the apartment through the unlocked front door and took the listed items which were located in the common living area.

- **Burglary:** Victim 1 states that she was in the shower at the listed location when she heard Suspect yell "I'm here, where are you guys?" Victim 1 got out of the shower and didn't see anyone in the apartment. She locked the door and went back into the bathroom. Victim 1 heard someone tugging at the front door again so she went to look through the peephole. Victim 1 observes Suspect running away from the door. When Victim 2 arrived to the listed location, he discovered the listed property missing from his bag that was located inside the listed location sitting in a chair by the table.

- **Assault with a Dangerous Weapon:** Defendant was in a verbal altercation with Victim 1 and Victim 2. Defendant struck Victim 1 with his backpack three times. Defendant then struck Victim 2 with a large machete in the left arm area. Multiple citizens restrained Defendant 1 and subdued Defendant until MPD arrived on the scene to secure the area.

- **Robbery:** Complainant 1 reports that while returning to his vehicle he was struck in the back of his head by Suspect. Complainant reports that Suspect held him down, went through his pockets, and took his wallet. Complainant reports that Suspect then fled.

- **Assault with a Dangerous Weapon:** Victim reports on the listed date, time, and location he was standing at the corner . . . when he heard a popping noise. Victim then states that after hearing the popping noise he realized he was shot. Victim then states . . . he seen an unknown Suspect running in an unknown direction from the scene.

- **Assault with a Dangerous Weapon:** On the listed date and time officers were dispatched to the listed location for a stabbing. . . . Upon arrival officers met with Victim. Victim states he got into a verbal argument after himself and Suspect were drinking. Suspect presented a knife and stabbed Victim in the upper chest area (left side) once. Suspect begins chasing Victim.

- **Assault with a Dangerous Weapon:** Officers made contact with Victim, who stated that he was in a verbal altercation with Suspect over money. Victim stated Suspect broke a glass bottle and cut him in the left forearm, causing the listed injuries.

- **Robbery:** On the listed date and time, officers responded to the area for a robbery. . . . Victim was located in front of the listed address unconscious and bleeding from the back of his head. . . . Reporting Party advised that Suspect 1, Suspect 2, Suspect 3 assaulted Victim 1 and went through his pockets before fleeing on foot.

- **Homicide:** Officers received a ShotSpotter alert for sounds of gunshots. . . . Officers canvassed the area and found a [vehicle] with damage to the front end and what appeared to be a bullet hole in the top rear driver's side. While on scene Officers also located what appeared to be a pool of blood on the ground in front of the vehicle and several shell casings. . . . While on scene Officers were notified of a victim shot in the chest at [the hospital]. The Decedent was [subsequently] pronounced [dead].

- **Assault with a Dangerous Weapon:** Officers . . . were dispatched to the sound of gunshots. . . . Upon arrival Officers observed Victim with gunshot wounds to the leg. Officers administered the tourniquet to the left leg of Victim. Witness stated that Suspect was seen with a gun fleeing from the scene.

- **Robbery:** The listed victims report that they were working in a vacant residence located at the listed address, when they were approached by Suspect 1 and Suspect 2. Suspect 1 produced a handgun, pointed it each of the victims in turn, and demanded their property. Suspect 2 collected the listed property from each of the victims. Suspect 1 and Suspect 2 then fled on foot. . . .

- **Robbery:** On the listed date and time and in front of the listed location, Victim reports that as he was waiting for his Lyft passenger inside his vehicle, he was approached by Suspect, who was on a bicycle. Victim reports that suspect rode up alongside his driver's side window and asked if he was an Uber or Lyft. Victim reports that while talking on his cell phone, he rolled down his window to better understand Suspect. Victim reports that while his window was down, Suspect snatched the listed property out of Victim's hands. Victim reports that Suspect fled the scene.

- **Armed Carjacking:** Officers are dispatched to scene Armed Carjacking. Upon arrival officers make contact with Victim. After the investigation was conducted it was found that Suspect used a silver handgun to execute the carjacking of Victim. Suspect initially asked for Victim's wallet and after Victim denied having a wallet, Suspect told Victim to get out of the car.

- **Sexual Abuse:** Complainant disclosed [that] Suspect penetrated her vagina with his penis against her will and without her consent.

- **Assault with a Dangerous Weapon:** Victim advised he was sitting in front of the listed location when he got into a verbal altercation that turned physical with an unknown female. Victim advised [that] the unknown female then stabbed him in his legs.

- **Robbery:** Suspect approached Complainant and displayed a black firearm and told Complainant to give his shit up. Complainant reached in his pockets and gave listed items to Suspect.

- **Robbery:** On the listed date and time at the listed location Complainant got off the Metro bus and was followed by Suspect 1 and Suspect 2. When Complainant noticed Suspect 1 and Suspect 2 following him, he turned around and went the opposite direction. Suspect 1 and Suspect 2 then approached Complainant brandishing the handle of a knife demanding the listed property. Complainant gave Suspect 1 and Suspect 2 the listed property and fled.

- **Carjacking:** On the listed date and time at the listed location Complainant advised she was exiting the listed vehicle when Suspect 1 and Suspect 2 approached the vehicle and said "Get the fuck down!" Complainant then got on the ground and Suspect 1 and Suspect 2 got into the listed vehicle and fled in an unknown direction. . . .

- **Burglary:** Victim 1 and Victim 2 report that they were asleep at the listed residence when unknown suspect/s forced entry into their home between 0400 and 0600 hours through a locked back door by prying the door open with an unknown object. Once inside the location, the unknown suspect/s stole the listed items and exited through the front door.

Bad Choices

Injured Officer: Officer [redacted] injured his right shoulder and right knee while supporting the weight of a prisoner who attempted to hang himself in the cell block. The Officer was transported to the Police and Fire Clinic by MPD. 1130 hours.

—MPD Joint Strategic and Tactical Analysis
Command Center, Daily Report

For the most part, America's criminal justice system isn't deliberately cruel. It's just indifferent to the ways in which it breaks human beings. Few police officers want to contribute to mass incarceration or aid in the destruction of poor minority communities. But the absurdities and injustices are inherent in the system. Often, by the time the police get involved, the only available choices are bad ones.

One night in the spring of 2018, I was patrolling with Lowrey in the Fifth District. The evening had been a fairly peaceful one; we'd had a call reporting an unconscious man on the ground and had hung around while medics administered Narcan for an overdose; we'd mediated between an angry property owner and a woman who kept parking in his private parking lot without permission; we'd checked out a few burglar alarms. We were sitting in the car in a strip mall parking lot after one of the alarm calls, about to call it a night, when I noticed a struggle going on a few hundred feet away. Later, I wished I hadn't noticed, but by then it was too late.

I gave Lowrey's arm a quick nudge. "Hey, Lowrey, what's going on over there?" I pointed. "Looks like the Safeway security guard's fighting with someone."

We jumped out of the car and ran over. The uniformed security guard was struggling with a small woman holding a wheeled suitcase. She was trying to run away, and the guard was trying to hold her there. When the woman saw two MPD officers approaching, she gave up and just stood there waiting, shoulders sagging, head bowed. The guard seized her arm.

"What's going on?" I asked.

The guard pointed at the suitcase and opened the top compartment. "She stole this stuff from the Safeway."

I looked into the suitcase. It contained a large container of laundry detergent and a multipack of chicken thighs.

We all walked into the Safeway, and the guard cuffed the shoplifter, who started to cry.

"My grandbaby," she said. "We ain't got no food. I ain't eaten all day."

"What do you want to do?" I asked the guard. "She's stealing necessities. This doesn't seem like a situation where she needs to go to jail."

The guard, a dreadlocked young black guy, agreed. "She done this before, but yeah, I'm just gonna bar her."

"Barring" is essentially a formal notice prohibiting someone from entering private property. Once barred, the shoplifter would be subject to immediate arrest for trespassing if she returned, whether or not she stole anything again. It seemed like a reasonable solution, if you could call anything reasonable that was premised on tolerating a society in which some people were reduced to stealing laundry detergent and raw chicken.

It stank. I hadn't noticed when we were out in the parking lot, but somewhere along the line, the shoplifter had soiled herself. Maybe it was a side effect of whatever drugs she was on; her pupils were dilated and her voice was slurred. Or maybe it was just fear. Either way, she suddenly seemed to become aware of it as well.

"She needs to go to the restroom," the guard said.

Everyone looked at me. I was the only female officer. "Come on, ma'am, I'll take you."

We uncuffed her. I wasn't worried about her running off. She looked entirely defeated, and in any case, I didn't think she was going to be arrested, so I couldn't see any reason to make her use the restroom in handcuffs.

"I'm not . . . I'm not doin' anything else," she assured me. "It's just . . . we ain't had no food. We got nothing to eat today."

"Let's see if we can help you," I said as we walked toward the restroom in the back of the store. "I think he's gonna cut you a break. We don't like seeing people get arrested when they're hungry. It's a tough situation."

She stared at the ground. "What happened was, I did get caught. I'm not gonna lie. I was embarrassed. I got scared and I ran."

"It's a tough situation."

The women's room was occupied, so I commandeered the men's room for my prisoner. She washed out her pants in the sink, and it took a while. Finally she declared herself finished, though the room still stank. We walked back to Lowrey and the guard.

This wasn't going to end too badly, I thought. The shoplifter would get a barring notice, we'd try to steer her toward contacting social services, and I'd give her some cash before we let her go. We weren't going to solve the myriad problems she was clearly facing in her life, but at least we weren't going to be making things worse, and she'd be able to buy some food instead of stealing it.

But then things went wrong. While I was taking the shoplifter to the restroom, Lowrey checked to see if the woman had any outstanding warrants.

Procedurally, this was the right thing to do; she *had* committed a crime, even if we and the store guards were all willing to let her go with a barring notice. Checking for active warrants is considered good practice. It's not strictly required in such situations, but it's routinely done and strongly recommended; it would look bad for the department if officers had, say, a homicide suspect in their custody during a traffic stop and simply let him drive off because they didn't bother to check for warrants. So Lowrey, who was always conscientious, was doing the right thing by checking for warrants. For all we knew, our shoplifter was a serial killer, on the run from multiple murders.

Except she wasn't a serial killer, of course. In real life, there aren't many serial killers. There aren't even that many murderers, statistically speaking, and only a small percentage of violent crimes are committed by women. But our shoplifter did have an outstanding warrant. It wasn't for anything serious; it was a "failure to appear" warrant from another jurisdiction, which meant only that she had been charged with something in the past, been released pending further proceedings, and had neglected to show up at a scheduled court hearing. Odds were, the underlying offense was something as minor as tonight's theft of laundry detergent and chicken thighs.

But it was a warrant all the same, and once we knew about it, we no longer had any choice about whether or not to let her go. We had to arrest her.

"Shit," I said angrily. I was upset. Why had Lowrey checked for warrants? I knew it wasn't fair, but right then, I wished he hadn't been such a responsible officer. I didn't want to arrest this small, sad woman. Her ID said she was a decade younger than I was, but I'd have guessed she was two decades older. Poverty, misery, and drugs had launched her into premature old age.

When we broke the news, she was resigned. We let her call her family and make arrangements. She looked at me pleadingly. "I don't wanna go to jail in these filthy pants. Please."

Lowrey and I asked the Safeway guards if they sold sweatpants or any other clothes, but they only had a few souvenir sweatshirts. The best we could do was buy her a big packet of disinfectant wipes. We returned to the restroom and she did her best to clean her clothes more thoroughly. I was glad of this, since I knew I was the one who'd have to conduct a full search before she was transported to the station.

Lowrey and I were both embarrassed by the direction things had taken, and I could tell that Lowrey also wished he hadn't done a warrant check.

"I'm sorry this is turning out this way," I told the shoplifter. "I know you're having a bad day. Hopefully they'll make it quick. I hope tomorrow will be better."

"I am having a bad day," she agreed.

"Next time, if you run out of food," I said, "call the police station and ask them to help you find places that can provide emergency meals. There are places that do that, okay? We'll help if we can."

I hoped this wasn't a lie. I hoped that if she called the police station and asked for help, the phone would be answered by a decent officer willing to refer her to the right services, and not by some asshole who'd chew her out for wasting police time and then hang up.

I searched her and cuffed her again, and then I put her few personal possessions into a property bag. I turned her phone off so the battery wouldn't be dead when she got out of jail and tried to turn it on. When her back was turned, I took a twenty out of my wallet and tucked it into the bag containing her property, so she wouldn't be flat broke when she was released. I listed the twenty dollars on the property inventory as belonging to her.

"That's nice of you," the security guard said.

His comment just made me feel worse. I didn't feel like I was doing something nice. I still felt like I was doing something shitty, and twenty bucks didn't come close to making up for it.

Sometimes, having to arrest someone is a product of well-meaning reforms gone wrong. For instance, Washington, DC, has a mandatory arrest policy for domestic violence. If you have probable cause to believe an assault has taken place in the context of a domestic relationship, you have to arrest the perpetrator. You can't give a warning or refer the parties to counseling. The mandatory arrest law was initially passed to try to force police to take male-on-female intimate partner violence more seriously. Too often, officers responding to domestic violence calls would essentially turn a blind eye to abusive men, regarding domestic violence as a private matter, or as something too minor to merit an arrest, leaving women at the mercy of their abusive male partners.

But like all efforts to reduce biased decisions by reducing discretion, the mandatory arrest law had unintended consequences. Over time, domestic relationships were defined more and more broadly, to include all situations in which the parties were related by blood, adoption, or legal custody, as well as situations in which the parties had a child in common, had a former relationship, or shared or had ever shared a mutual residence. This brought physical fights between siblings, housemates, and even former housemates into the ambit of the mandatory arrest laws. Sometimes, physical fights involving siblings or former roommates can be severe and can involve the same dynamics of power and control often seen in intimate partner violence. But just as often, the rigid mandatory arrest requirement leads to outcomes that seem very punitive.

Once, for instance, we were dispatched to a domestic violence call and found that it involved an altercation between two adult sisters.

"I'm going downstairs to go put my clothes in the washing machine," explained the injured sister. "She got mad because I guess her clothes ain't got dry or whatever. She came to me and hit me in my face; I have this mark right here!"

She did have a bruise on her cheek, and her sister admitted hitting her. Under the law, it was a clear-cut case: the parties were in a domestic relationship, one assaulted the other, and that was that. Still, it didn't seem like the crime of the century. Both sisters agreed that violence between them was not the norm; this had never happened before. Things had just gotten unusually tense—the older sister was a nurse and was upset because her younger sister took her uniforms out of the laundry before they were dry, right when she was supposed to be heading off to work in a clean, dry uniform. Both sisters had young children and lived with their mother. Arresting the older sister would require her family to take care of her children and would prevent her from going to work.

"It's a shitty situation," my partner Jake told the older sister, who was by now resigned and apologetic. "But we don't have a choice. We gotta take you."

Like most arrestees, she was remarkably well-mannered about the whole thing. "I understand, officers, it ain't your fault. You mind if I call my boss and explain I ain't gonna get to work today, and just change my clothes before we go?"

That was no problem, we told her. We let her make calls, change clothes, and issue various instructions to the family members who looked on somberly. Finally, half an hour later, she was ready to go, and we searched and cuffed her. It was a fairly perfunctory search, since, at our suggestion, she was leaving all her personal possessions with her family to avoid the hassle of having to retrieve them from the station when she was released. We assured her that on a first offense, with something this minor, she'd be out again within a day or two. Shaking her head ruefully, she kissed her children good-bye and apologized again for losing her temper, and we loaded her into the car.

Was justice served by taking her off to jail for the night? I can't see how. But that was the law, and another person was sucked into the ravenous maw of the criminal justice system.

Another night, we were dispatched to take a report from a woman who said she had been raped. She was white, which was rare; in all the calls I went on during my time patrolling, I encountered white DC residents on only a handful of occasions.

Before we arrived, my partner Ben told me he had encountered this woman before, and locked her up for filing a false report. I was a little shocked—weren't we supposed to err on the side of believing women?

"Yeah, we are," Ben said, "but I know this lady. You'll see. She's pretty crazy."

"Well, she could be crazy and still get raped," I reminded him. "Crazy people get raped too."

"You'll see." The last two times he had responded to calls to her house, Ben said, she claimed to have been sexually assaulted by a black male, sending police on a wild goose chase in search of black males matching her extremely vague description. Each time, officers had stopped several men for questioning before concluding the crime had been fictitious.

The complainant was in her thirties or forties, leaning on a cane. Her name was Star, and her voice was girlish and vague, with occasional odd pauses between words. She had come out for a smoke, she said, and a man she didn't know had come up to her.

"He stuck his tongue . . . in my mouth." She offered a small, rather satisfied smile as she said this, as if she had just said something very clever.

What did he look like?

He was "tall, dark . . ."—she lingered over the word—"probably six-two, he was wearing a hoodie . . . black jeans and red shoes. But I think . . . that describes . . . a lot of people," Star said, with another strange little smile. "I was out gardening. He tried . . . to drag me into the alley. He thrust his *cock* in my mouth. I got away and I . . . ran in . . . the house and locked the doors. Yeah. I'm traumatized by it. I can't believe . . . there are guys who just *do* this to women." She sniffled a little and wiped her nose, then added primly, "I have not felt well since then."

On its face, it wasn't completely implausible. But after that, the story began to change. The incident had just taken place. It had taken place an hour ago. It had taken place two hours ago. He had hit her on the head. No, he had thrown her down on the ground and she hit her head when she fell.

There were no obvious marks or lumps on her head. I asked if her head hurt.

"No, it's just the . . . rest of my body . . . that's . . . tender."

He had "dragged" her. How had he dragged her, I asked? By the arm, by the leg?

"He grabbed me by my *boobs*." She let out a giggle when she said this.

Had anything like this ever happened to her before?

"Yes," she said, now tearful. "It happens to me *all the time* . . . I'm so *tired* of living in this neighborhood. I just want to go to the *hospital* and make sure that whatever he did to me, it doesn't give me a . . . *disease*."

"Ma'am," Ben finally said, "do you remember me? We had long conversation, about what was the truth, and not the truth?"

"Yes," Star agreed. She remembered that last time she called the police, Ben had been there. That time, her cell phone had been stolen, and it was *still missing*, she told Ben accusingly.

"The cell phone was returned to you," Ben corrected. "It was in a bar, and you left it there when you were intoxicated, but you reported that a black male had robbed it from you."

"I'm giving the truth," she insisted.

"All right," Ben said, giving me a resigned glance. "We're calling out our sexual assault unit."

He didn't look pleased about it, but agreed that notwithstanding Star's history of unsubstantiated victimization by vaguely described large black men, there needed to be an investigation.

Two detectives from the sexual assault unit came out. Star's story changed some more, and the investigators could find no evidence that she had been dragged around the side of the house, as she had claimed; the damp patch of earth where she said she had been dragged and assaulted appeared undisturbed. An ambulance came, but the medics found no signs of injury or assault. And, it turned out, there was an active warrant for her arrest; she had failed to appear at a previous court date.

In the end, we decided to arrest Star but have her taken to the city's emergency psychiatric clinic.

I climbed into the ambulance to break the bad news.

"I didn't fail to appear for anything," she moaned. "I'm a fucking . . . American . . . paying . . . *citizen*." Her voice was childlike and quavery. "My husband's a *veteran*. There are . . . fucking drug dealers on these streets, and you're going after . . . *me!*"

Her tremulousness disappeared, replaced by rage. "There's real drug dealers on the street. I haven't done *shit*! There's prostitutes everywhere, and black *rapists!*"

I was starting to run out of sympathy. But, I reminded myself, even crazy racists could still be sexually assaulted. Was it possible something truly had happened to her? I didn't want to think we were arresting someone who really had been victimized. On the other hand, arresting her might be the only way to get her into some kind of court-mandated treatment.

Star wasn't easy to like. When I put her ring into the property bag, she almost spat at me. "That's my *wedding* ring! It was given me by a . . . veteran. Who fucking . . . *died*! This is fucking *robbery*. If I don't get my ring back— that was from my husband, who fucking . . . died in Afghanistan, saving your *asses*—he died for *you* fucking people! And for me!" she shouted. "So go to hell!"

We closed the ambulance door, and she was taken away.

It Can Be Kind of Hard
to See Things Clearly

Prior to the end of their shift, members who are assigned [Body-worn cameras] shall: (1) Document activation of the BWC device at the beginning of their non-public narrative on Field Contact Reports, Incident and Offense Reports, Traffic Crash Reports, and Arrest Reports in the Records Management System (RMS), as well as on PD Forms 42 (Injury or Illness Report), PD Forms 43, PD Forms 61D (Violation Citations) and notices of infraction (NOIs). (a) . . . Document in the non-public narrative section of all related reports or their notebook any delay or failure to activate their BWC and any interruption of a BWC recording required by this order.

—MPD General Order 302.13,
Body-Worn Camera Program

The truth is, I wasn't an especially good cop, and I knew it.

I was slow, for one thing, and I tended to fumble. This was especially true in my first few months out of the academy. There were too many physical objects to keep track of: my notebook, my pen, my flashlight, my body-worn camera, my sunglasses, my two cell phones, my hat. I was always rushing, and in my first months on patrol, something was always falling or getting stuck or misplaced. I'd reach for my phone and my notebook would fall in the dirt; I'd pick up the notebook and my pen would fall. As soon as I grabbed the pen, my sunglasses would slide off. I'd open the patrol car door and try to jump out, but my holster or my ASP baton would get stuck on the seat belt and I'd have to pause to untangle myself. I hadn't felt this graceless in a long time. It reminded me of elementary school, when my lack of skill at kickball condemned me to be one of the kids chosen last whenever teams were picked. My klutziness filled me with mild panic, which only made things worse; the more determined I was to exit the patrol car gracefully and quickly, the more tangled up I got.

Also, there was so much to remember, and so much to keep track of. You had to monitor the radio at all times, for instance. This was a challenge. For one thing, some of the dispatchers had heavy accents, and especially in those early months after graduation, I often struggled to decode even the simplest statements. Added to that was the poor sound quality. You'd adjust the volume to hear the dispatcher, then another officer would come on the air almost inaudibly, so you'd turn up the volume, only to have your eardrums blasted when the dispatcher came back on. My arm kept brushing against the radio's volume knob too, and sometimes when the radio appeared blessedly quiet, I'd glance down to discover I had accidentally turned the volume nearly off.

Over the course of my first year on patrol, I tried various techniques to improve my ability to hear the radio. With no earpiece, the sound was fairly clear, but without an earpiece everyone around you could hear the radio too, which tended to distract interviewees, and was occasionally dangerous or a privacy issue—when you were talking to a suspect, he didn't need to know that other officers were around the corner in apartment 4B, searching unsuccessfully for shell casings. Many officers wore Secret Service–style earpieces, the kind with a clear coil and earpiece only in one ear. I tried this for a while, but found it unpleasant; the sound was tinny, and it was hard to hear external noises through the earpiece. When I wore it, I felt like I had a head cold and blocked sinuses on one side. Eventually I found an expensive brand of earpiece that was designed to allow external sound to filter through, and settled on this as the best compromise, but it was still awkward.

Even after a year of patrolling, I still sometimes struggled to respond to my own call sign. The trouble was, call signs changed day by day, and sometimes even during a single shift—if you were assigned to a foot beat halfway through your shift, for instance. Call signs were mostly numeric, and for me, at least, they tended to blend in with all the other numeric chatter on the radio. Dispatchers closed all radio interactions with the time; for instance: you'd say, "Copy," and the dispatcher would respond, "15:03," or "22:12" to mark the time. There were various numeric codes to contend with, as well. When you went into service you were 10-8, 10-4 (in service or back in service, with two officers in a vehicle), or 10-8, 10-99 (solo). When you wanted a warrant check, you asked for a 10-29. Your location was your 20 (short for 10-20, radio code for "What is your location?"). When you went out of service, you were 10-7. Between numeric codes, time checks, street addresses, and call signs, the radio traffic was a jumble of numbers.

"7041," the dispatcher would say.

"7041," the unit would acknowledge.

"7041, are you 10-8? I need a unit to at 1844 MLK, apartment 103 to assist 7032."

"No, ma'am, I'm still at 1722 Thirtieth Street with 7042, and I need numbers for simple assault."

"7041, your numbers are 17223976; I repeat, 17223976."

"I copy. And did you get a result for that 10-29?"

"Negative, 7041. No result."

"Copy."

"21:08."

"7051."

"7051."

"Ma'am, you can clear me from 2314 Twenty-second Street. I'm 10-8, 10-7."

"I copy, 7051. 21:09."

Especially early on, it was all an auditory blur. I preferred using the car's mobile data terminal when possible; I was more comfortable reading and writing than going over the air. But the MDT came with its own problems. Sometimes, for reasons of its own, it would reject the same password it had accepted during the previous shift, or decide to log you out just as you tried to check the address of a call. Other times it would freeze, or decide not to process whatever you had just typed in. The cables were always coming loose, and the Wi-Fi was unstable.

Also, it was locked into a stand between the driver's seat and passenger's seat, and though you could angle it toward either side of the car, there was no angle that allowed you to view it without straining your neck. Typing was also difficult, as the keyboard was also affixed to the center of the car, requiring you to contort your body to type. But you had to type reports on the MDT, because if you didn't you'd be stuck back at the station long after your shift was over, finishing reports you should have finished on the MDT, on calls you would by now have half forgotten and have to reconstruct from your notebook or by watching the body-worn camera videos.

The body-worn camera was equally difficult. In theory, we were supposed to start recording as soon as we were dispatched, or as soon as we began to "take police action" if we were flagged down or self-initiated a run (by stopping a car, for instance). In practice, almost no one did this, in part because it seemed silly to turn on the camera when all it would record for the next ten minutes was video footage of the steering wheel or the dashboard as you drove to the call. Often, you would forget to turn the camera on when you arrived, and halfway through the call you would remember with a jolt of alarm. Just as often, you'd remember to turn the camera on but would then forget to turn it off, only to realize while you were in the restroom of the 7-Eleven that your camera was still dutifully recording your every move.

Sometimes, the cameras turned themselves on. The department was undergoing a trial run with Tasers, and someone had decreed that whenever a Taser was turned on, even for testing purposes, all BWCs within a certain radius would turn on automatically. The idea, presumably, was to guard against the known tendency of officers to forget (or "forget") to turn on their cameras by taking the decision away from them, thus guaranteeing that all uses of the experimental Tasers would be recorded for departmental review. This had the effect, however, of greatly increasing the number of accidental toilet and locker room videos.

All BWC videos had to be labeled by the end of each shift, using our otherwise useless department-issued cell phones, "tagging" each video with the date, case number if there was one, address, and type of call. Officers spent a good deal of time debating how to label accidental toilet videos. Technically, there was a process for requesting that accidental videos be deleted, but everyone assumed that requesting deletion was a good way to guarantee that a video would be reviewed. It wasn't possible for the department to review all videos, however—there was simply too much footage. The prevailing theory was that accidental toilet videos were best labeled "BWC test," since test videos were less likely to be reviewed by a human.

For me, the BWC was just another piece of equipment to worry about. More than once, I realized only as a call was ending that I had forgotten to turn it on. No one ever gave me a hard time about it, but I fretted anyway. If you didn't turn your camera on, you could get in trouble. If nothing bad happened on the call, it wouldn't matter much, but if something went wrong and you hadn't activated your camera, who would believe the slip-up was inadvertent?

Of course, forgetting to turn the camera off could get you in trouble as well—not only because you might accidentally wander into the bathroom with the camera rolling, but because officers tended to reserve their franker assessments of suspects, victims, and the department itself for when they assumed the cameras were off. Accidentally keeping your camera on meant you'd get dirty looks from whichever colleague had just been waxing eloquent about what a fucking dirtbag the suspect on the last call had been, or wondering how a complete shitbird like Lieutenant Brown had managed to get promoted.

On top of everything else, I quickly discovered that I was probably the least observant cop in Washington, DC. I used up so much mental energy just trying to keep from dropping my notebook while listening to the radio and remembering to turn on my BWC that I didn't have many brain cells left over to process any of the other information coming my way. My partners were constantly alert, commenting on suspicious vehicles or people even as they chattered away or typed on the MDT. I rarely noticed the suspicious vehicles or people until they were pointed out to me. That car? The one missing the rear plates, oh, yeah. . . . That guy just tossed a baggie into the bushes, really? I didn't notice.

When I did notice things, I often noticed the wrong things. Dispatched to a call for "sounds of gunfire," my partner and I found eighteen bullet casings along the sidewalk and street, along with a car with its window shot out (and a very angry car owner). I didn't spot the bullet casings until I accidentally kicked one and almost tripped over another, but I did note several neat bullet holes drilled into a stop sign. I gestured to my partner and pointed at the sign, but he made an immediate and frantic shushing noise and shook his head violently. Seeing my bewilderment, he gestured for me to turn my camera off. Puzzled, I complied.

"This call is over. You did *not* see any bullet holes in that stop sign," he instructed once the camera was off.

"I didn't?"

"You didn't."

"Why not?"

"Because if you saw any bullet damage to that stop sign, we'd have to report it to the city office that deals with damaged DC property, and we'd have to fill out, like, a thousand forms, then we'd be stuck here all night waiting for someone to come inspect it."

In the end, I got stuck filling out forms for hours anyway. We put the bullet casings together in a single evidence bag and I filled out the appropriate forms describing our find as "eighteen shell casings," but the next day I received an email instructing me to return to the 7D property room to repackage the shell casings; the eighteen shell casings, I was informed, required eighteen separate evidence bags and eighteen separate forms.

One March night in 2017, when I was about six months out of the academy, we responded to a call for a drive-by shooting. A car window had been shot out this time as well, but on this occasion, the car had been occupied. Incredibly, no one was hurt, but the two women who'd been in the car were badly shaken. One of the women insisted that the shooter was the other woman's ex, and the two women started arguing about whether this was so, and whether the shooting was the result of her poor judgment in choosing her partners. The argument became so heated that the women started fighting physically, swatting at each other with their handbags, pulling hair, and scratching. We pulled them apart, positioned them on separate sides of the street, and urged them to refrain from further assaults on each other. By now several other officers had arrived and the detectives were on the way, so I went back to looking for potential evidence. A few minutes later, sweeping the street with my flashlight, I spotted something shiny in the gutter.

It was a ring. In fact, it looked like a wedding ring.

Aha, I thought. A *clue*.

Delighted with myself, I summoned my partner and pointed. "You think that could have something to do with this shooting?"

He gave the ring a jaundiced look. "Nah."

"But it sounds like this shooting was domestic—don't you think a discarded wedding ring in the gutter might be related?"

"I doubt it."

He was probably right, I knew.

"But—"

He interrupted. "You know what's going to happen if you touch that ring, even if it's totally unrelated to the shooting?"

"Um . . . I'd have to treat it as . . . lost property?"

"Mmm-hmm. And you know what that would mean?"

"I'd have to fill out a whole lot of forms and go back to the station?"

"You got it. So, you see a ring on the street?" He looked at me meaningfully.

"Ah. No. I . . . *thought* I saw a ring, but . . . now that I'm looking more closely, I think it was maybe just . . . some kind of reflection off a puddle, or something."

He nodded approvingly. "Yeah, it's pretty dark out here. It can be kind of hard to see things clearly, you know?"

As a reserve officer, I was a sort of permanent rookie. While my full-time colleagues worked forty hours a week, I typically worked less than a quarter of that time. Cop skills are perishable; they improve with constant practice, and deteriorate rapidly when not in use. So even after more than a year on patrol, I was always starting over, trying to remember whether my username for the MDT was rosabrooks, rosa.brooks, rbrooks, or brooksr.

Or maybe it was just age. Most of my partners were young enough to be my children, if I had started having kids at twenty or twenty-one. They were millennials, used to shifting between cell phones and video game consoles. Maybe their brains were just more elastic than mine.

Either way, it was humbling. Here I was, with two advanced degrees and years of professional success under my belt. But in my role as part-time cop, I was . . . adequate. On a good day.

It was an uncomfortable realization. By the time I hit forty, I had grown accustomed to being good at what I did and being recognized for it. In other parts of my life, I was an expert. Reporters called and asked me for quotes on the news of the day; students sent me emails soliciting my advice on their careers; strangers paid me to speak at their conferences. Being merely adequate was a jarring experience.

The only thing that consoled me was my growing awareness that being a good cop was hard. In fact, it was nearly impossible. There was just too much to keep track of. Many officers were better at it than I was, but no one consistently did it well, because no one *could* always do it well.

On top of the radio, the cameras, and all the rest of the gear, there was the actual policing to be done. You had to know the law: Was this shoplifting or theft? Burglary 1 or Burglary 2? You had to stay calm in chaotic and sometimes frightening situations, and stay polite even when people were screaming at you. You had to notice the right things, ask the right questions, write down the right information, fill out the right forms in the right manner, and notify the right officials. Some calls required you to notify your sergeant; others required you to notify the command information center or the teletype office, or detectives, or Child and Family Services, or the watch commander, or all of the above. Certain incidents and all offenses required you to request a "central complaint number," or CCN, from the dispatcher; tow trucks—"tow cranes"—required TCNs, or towing control numbers. If you needed an ambulance you asked the dispatcher to notify "the board," and you had to record the engine number and medic number of the responding fire trucks and medics.

Then there were all the officer safety lessons drilled into us at the academy, which were impractical and often impossible in the chaos of real scenes. You could hardly avoid interviewing people in their kitchens, for instance, and unless you were willing to summon enough backup to put everyone preventively in cuffs, a tactic unlikely to produce cooperative witnesses, you couldn't really prevent half the people present at a domestic violence call from wandering around and reaching into pockets, drawers, closets, and bags at will. In 7D, even the tiniest apartments were often bursting with people. Grandma was napping on the sofa; adult siblings sat at the table and offered commentary on the protagonists' character flaws; small children ran about underfoot; dogs barked; and neighbors barged in to complain about the noise or offer corroborating or contradictory information. Half the time, scenes were out of control when you arrived and they simply stayed that way, no matter how many cops showed up and stood around looking stern.

And most officers spent a lot of time being anxious. You had to worry about your physical safety, to start—would that crowd on the corner turn nasty? Would the suspect you were interviewing in the kitchen, against your better judgment, prove the officer safety videos right by suddenly grabbing a knife?

But mostly, officers worried about being second-guessed. The thicket of rules and regulations was impenetrable. MPD general orders were constantly being revised, and every day, new teletypes arrived outlining new requirements or modifying previous procedures. Making things worse, when teletypes landed in your inbox, they often had subject headings like "TT-05-031-20: ADDENDUM TO TELETYPE #03-064-20," and the body of the email contained no information beyond "see attachment," forcing you to download and open an attachment before you could even determine whether the teletype contained vitally important information or merely corrected a typographical error in a previous announcement.

Even if you didn't screw up in some major, obvious way—getting mad and cursing at a witness, or losing vital evidence, or, God forbid, shooting an unarmed citizen—you were sure to screw up in a multitude of minor ways. You would forget to turn your camera on or off, or fail to notify the right official, or fill out the wrong form, or fill out the right form the wrong way, or write the report the wrong way, or piss off the sergeant or the lieutenant. Citizens could complain about you. The crazy lady you lost your temper at could turn out to be the mayor's best friend from elementary school, and she'd have it all recorded on her cell phone. And you were tired, so tired from working ten-hour shifts and still having to show up for court in the morning. So you were going to make mistakes.

All this meant that if some desk jockey in the department wanted to fuck you over, they could always find a reason. Screwing up was preordained; it was the nature of policing. It was just a question of whether the department wanted to go after you. There were always rumors swirling around about cops getting jammed up for silly things. Every officer I knew, including the best ones, was absolutely convinced that they were one trivial mistake away from being scolded, suspended, or fired.

There is an irony here. Structurally, cops are in precisely the same position as drivers. There are so many traffic rules, some of them so trivial and ambiguous, that any cop worth his salt can easily find a reason to pull over almost any car. No driver, no matter how careful, will manage to abide by every single traffic rule 100 percent of the time, because there are just too many rules, and no one can remember them all. This makes all drivers vulnerable. A racist cop can always find reasons to stop a black driver; a sadistic cop can always find reasons to hand out multiple costly tickets.

Similarly, cops are always vulnerable to the bureaucracies that send them out on the streets. If the bureaucracy chooses to skewer one of its own, it can do so for a good reason, a bad reason, or no reason at all. There are too many rules, and too many contradictory imperatives. Every police officer, no matter how conscientious, has done *something* wrong. And most of those mistakes are on video.

Add one more source of pressure and stress, the toll taken by each day's dose of misery and pain.

Police officers see a lot of bad things. A 2015 study of officers in small and midsize police departments found that on average, officers had experienced 189 "critical incidents" in their careers. Critical incidents were defined as the type of experience that frequently leads to trauma, such as dealing with dead bodies, neglected or abused children, or sexual abuse; making death notifications; being held hostage; experiencing or being threatened with serious injury; dealing with threats to harm family members; seeing another person killed or seriously injured; and the like. Cops don't talk about this much; police culture, like military culture, has historically favored stiff upper lips.

Looking at the list of critical incidents identified by researchers as likely to trigger trauma, I added up my own exposure as I worked on this book. In the period between graduating from the police academy in October 2016 and finishing my field training in May 2018—a bit more than 480 hours of patrolling, spread over eighteen months—I had experienced eight different types of critical incidents myself, several of them more than once.

I was fortunate—my life gave me all the ingredients needed to process difficult situations without much lasting trauma. I was older; I had worked in many other difficult situations and had, perhaps, more sense of perspective than many young officers; I was female, and women face less stigma than men when openly discussing difficult experiences; I was well informed about the ways in which trauma can manifest itself; and I had friends and family I could talk to (including my father, a psychologist who provides consulting services on trauma to international human rights and humanitarian organizations).

Most of all, I was just a part-timer. Whereas full-time career officers spent forty or more hours immersed in other people's misery each week, I only had to spend twenty-four hours on patrol each month. I was a volunteer—if I didn't like the roll call sergeant on Saturday evening duty, I could choose a different shift, or even patrol in a different district. And I didn't need the job. It's easy to be resilient when you can just walk away. It's a lot harder when you're trapped.

And traumatic experiences add up. Officers who have experienced more critical incidents are more likely to have substance abuse problems or show signs of PTSD. Police officers experience PTSD at roughly five times the rate of the general population, and most years, suicide kills far more police officers than on-duty incidents. The trauma of policing hurts communities too: PTSD can interfere with judgment and risk perception, making officers with unaddressed symptoms more likely to use force or respond angrily instead of defusing tense situations.

In impoverished high-crime communities, like 7D, the estimated incidence of untreated PTSD is also sky-high; virtually every resident has family members and friends who've been robbed, beaten, stabbed, shot, or taken to prison. Trauma affects both how community members respond to one another and how they respond when approached by police. And when traumatized citizens interact with traumatized cops, a lot can go wrong.

You'll Get Yours

Injured Officer: Officer [redacted] was bitten on his right arm while breaking up a large group fight. The Officer will report to the Police and Fire Clinic in the morning.

—*MPD Joint Strategic and Tactical Analysis Command Center, Daily Report*

During my time as a patrol officer, I helped break up several fights, was dispatched to numerous "sound of gunshots" calls, and responded to countless calls involving assaults in progress. Sometimes, people shouted insults and epithets as I walked by ("Fuck the police" and "Fucking white pig bitch!" were the most common, though "I smell bacon!" remained a runner-up). Once, a drunk and combative suspect had to be held down by other officers while I cuffed him. We were arresting him for punching his girlfriend in the face, and when we tried to get him into the wagon, he went into a rage, twisting and writhing and shouting threats over his shoulder: "You'll get yours! I'm coming to get you! Until the day I die, I promise, you'll get yours—I'm *coming* for you, motherfuckers!"

Despite all this, I never seriously worried about my safety. In part, this is because I was so preoccupied by my fear of making embarrassing mistakes that I had no time left to worry about being injured or hurt. But mostly, I wasn't frightened because the existence of serious threats to my safety seemed largely fanciful. Despite all the officer safety videos we had watched in the academy, I wasn't persuaded that policing in Washington, DC, was particularly dangerous. Certainly, it wasn't more dangerous than traveling as an unarmed civilian in Afghanistan, Iraq, Kosovo, Uganda, Sierra Leone, Palestine, or many of the other places work had previously brought me.

It's almost heretical to say this; the belief that police face constant mortal danger is a central part of most officers' sense of professional identity. Statistically, however, being a police officer is less dangerous than most people think. According to the Bureau of Labor Statistics, the most dangerous jobs in America are logging, fishing, being a pilot or flight engineer, roofing, refuse collection, structural iron- and steelwork, truck driving, farming and ranching, construction supervision and first-line extraction, and ground maintenance. Police work doesn't even make it into the top ten. As dangerous jobs go, being a cop ranks just below construction labor and just above electrical power line installation and repair.

Granted, police officers face a higher risk of death due to intentional harm than those in most other lines of work. While roofers and farmers have high fatal injury rates, they rarely die in workplace homicides. But taxi and limousine drivers are twice as likely to be murdered on the job than cops. (Oddly, food service workers have the third highest homicide victimization rate.) When cops die on the job, it's usually the result of illness or accident. In 2018, for instance, just thirty-nine police officers were "feloniously killed," according to FBI statistics; another thirty-one died in accidents (almost all of which involved vehicle-to-vehicle or vehicle-to-pedestrian collisions).

Washington, DC, is a particularly safe place to be a police officer. The Officer Down Memorial Page lists 122 line-of-duty deaths since MPD was founded in 1861. Of those listed, sixty-nine were intentionally shot, stabbed, or deliberately run over by vehicles, while the rest died in accidents—mostly vehicle crashes—or from illnesses. Of the seven MPD officer deaths in the past twenty years, three were due to accidents and three were due to illness.

The only MPD officer to die in a homicide in the past twenty years was Sergeant Clifton Rife, and there's no reason to believe he was killed because of his occupation—Rife was off duty and outside Washington, DC, when he was shot during an attempted robbery. (Although Rife is listed as an officer killed in the line of duty on MPD's website, the District of Columbia Court of Appeals found that the DC Police and Firefighters' Retirement and Relief Board was justified in refusing to pay an annuity to his widow, since Rife "died while off-duty in the State of Maryland from a fatal gunshot as a victim of an attempted robbery, and not in the performance of duty.")

Cops do have difficult, dangerous jobs. The fatal injury rate for police officers is roughly four times higher than that of the average American worker, and police officers really do run toward the sound of gunfire while everyone else is running away. People call the police only when something goes wrong, and officers willingly walk into potentially volatile situations a dozen times each day. They deal with all the problems too dangerous, dirty, or dull for anyone else: shootings, stabbings, assaults, robberies, rapes, traffic crashes, overdose deaths.

It's just that being a cop isn't nearly as dangerous as cops think it is. This matters, because an exaggerated sense of risk drives how officers respond to the unexpected. When you start with the belief that you're in constant danger, you're more likely to perceive situations as threatening. You'll shout and jump at a girl for reaching into her handbag in her own living room. You'll stop and frisk people who look at you funny and put their hands in their pockets. And maybe, eventually, you'll shoot and kill a driver who's reaching for his wallet, or a child playing with a toy gun.

In the early to late 1980s and early '90s—during the height of the crack epidemic—Washington, DC, was the homicide capital of the United States, with 479 homicides in 1991. By the late 1990s, DC police officers had one of the highest rates of officer-involved shootings in the nation—MPD officers reportedly fired at suspects more than twice as often as officers in other major US police departments. MPD invited the Justice Department to evaluate its practices, and the results of the investigation led MPD to enter into a memorandum of agreement with the Justice Department, promising an overhaul of use-of-force policies, training, and investigations. The reforms made a substantial difference: When an independent review team examined MPD's use-of-force practices in 2016, the audit concluded that MPD had "plainly" become "a very different, and much better, law enforcement agency" than it was in 1999, when the Justice Department investigation began. While the review team identified some ongoing issues, it found that MPD no longer had a problem with using excessive force.

This was consistent with my experience in MPD. While I saw much that troubled me when I patrolled, I never saw an officer use what looked like unnecessary force, and with only a handful of exceptions, the officers I worked with showed courtesy, professionalism, and restraint, even in situations where things could easily have gone wrong, such as with angry, aggressive suspects, or when the unexpected suddenly occurred. The man who started to struggle and shout threats when arrested for assaulting his girlfriend, for instance, was hustled into the wagon by officers holding each of his arms, but they still took the time to warn him to duck his head so he wouldn't hit it on the top of the doorframe. Responding to a call reporting a man with a gun inside a supermarket (perhaps a common phenomenon in some states, but alarming and rare in DC, which has some of the nation's most stringent gun control laws), officers approached the suspect calmly and courteously, with their own weapons still holstered.

Early in my field training, my partner and I were dispatched to an apartment to investigate a possible burglary: the burglar alarm had sounded. The dispatcher told us that the tenant was out of town and the apartment was supposed to be unoccupied. But when we arrived, we found the outer door open a crack. No light or sound came through. My partner Jake was a former marine. He looked at the darkness behind the door and looked at me, then unholstered his weapon and held it down at his side. I followed suit, and we tiptoed into the apartment.

The living room was empty, and we were about to move toward the inner hall when there was a sudden burst of light in the hall, and a silhouetted head and torso popped into our line of vision. Jake and I both startled, and the figure at the end of the hall gave a yelp and vanished again.

In the simulations we went through during firearms training and our twice-a-year re-qualification courses, this was the kind of situation in which bullets immediately started to fly, and I remember thinking: Oh shit. This could end badly. I wasn't planning to shoot anyone, but I had no idea how Jake would react to having someone suddenly jump out from the blackness in an apartment undergoing a possible burglary.

But after his first slight twitch of surprise, Jake stayed calm and kept his weapon at his side, pointed down. "Hi there," he said, his voice slow and relaxed. "MPD. Sorry to startle you. We got called over here because the alarm went off. Do me a favor, would you, and step out here so we can see you?"

"I, uh, can't," said a voice. The voice was male, nervous, and young.

"Why not?"

"I got no clothes on."

Jake and I looked at each other.

"You live here?" Jake asked.

"Uh, no, it's my dad's place. I live with my mom. I just came over to do my laundry and take a shower. So all my clothes are in the wash and I just got out of the shower."

"Well, could you maybe put something on real quick, like a towel?" Jake suggested.

"Um, yeah, okay, yeah, I could do that." There was a pause, then a boy stepped out, eyes wide as saucers, torso still naked and dripping, clutching a towel to his waist. He looked to be fifteen or sixteen. Jake and I holstered our weapons.

"Okay, thanks," Jake said. "Your dad know you're here?"

"Uh, I dunno."

"See some ID?" The kid retreated back into what I assumed was the bathroom—clouds of steam were billowing out—then reappeared, holding out a wallet. I glanced at his school ID, then we radioed in and asked the dispatcher for the tenant's phone number. A few minutes later, we had the tenant on the line. He confirmed that he had a son by that name, and asked to speak to him. I handed the kid my phone, and after a short conversation (annoyed voice on the other end of the line, embarrassed voice on the kid's side), he handed it back to me.

I put the phone to my ear. "Everything good, sir?" I asked.

"Yeah, everything good, I just told him he needs to remember the damn alarm code, and close the door next time."

It was a short encounter, and from the perspective of the official record, it was a nonevent—since there was no burglary, no report was required; we cleared the call and went off to the next assignment. But I've often thought about that night, and how easy it would have been for things to end differently. What if a different officer had been my partner? What if it had been Reid, the officer who nearly drew his weapon on a girl reaching into her purse in her own living room? It wasn't hard to imagine someone jumpier than Jake shooting first and asking questions later.

In fact, it wasn't even hard to imagine an officer like Reid telling us that our slowness to point our weapons had placed us in serious danger, and our survival was pure dumb luck. I could hear his voice in my head: "You just walked right in! You should have called for backup the second you saw that open door. Then you should have made a tactical entry like you were taught in the training center, with one of you sweeping left with your weapon, one sweeping right, then clearing each room in turn. Your weapons should have been up and ready. Sure, it turned out to be just an unarmed kid, but you didn't know that. What if you had interrupted an armed burglar and he had come out pointing his gun at you? What if there were other armed guys back there too? Or what if the kid went back inside and got a gun when you let him out of your sight to go get his ID? In any of those situations, you'd have been sitting ducks. How would your kids feel if you didn't come home because you took a stupid risk?"

If Reid had been there to say all that, he wouldn't have been entirely wrong. We *had* taken some risks. We could have called for backup. We could have done a tactical room-clearing. We could have kept our guns at the ready position, our fingers on the triggers. We could have shouted at the kid to get down on the floor, cuffed him, and kept him cuffed until we were sure there were no weapons or other potential assailants present. If we had encountered someone armed and violent, having our own guns ready would have lessened the odds of one of us getting killed. And yes, I would hate to look down from the afterlife and see that my children were motherless because I had been too trusting and slow.

But I'd do the same thing again, and I hope my partner would too. Perhaps we had risked our own safety by not having our guns up—but keeping our guns down had decreased the risk to someone else. All in all, I'd rather my children lose their mother than make another mother lose her child. If my gun had been up and ready when that figure popped out from the dark hallway, I might have pulled the trigger out of pure reflex—at the range, when a target faces, you fire—and then there would have been a dead kid.

It wouldn't have been too hard to justify such a shooting, at least as far as the law is concerned. By now, I could easily compose the bureaucratic prose in my head:

On the above-listed date and time, officers were dispatched to investigate a report of a possible burglary at the listed location. After ascertaining that the authorized resident was out of town and being informed by the dispatcher that the apartment should have been unoccupied, we arrived on scene and noted that the front door of the residence was partially open, indicating, based on my knowledge and experience, that a burglar might have effected an entry and remained on the premises. Being aware that the neighborhood in which we were located had experienced a high rate of violent crime, including multiple recent homicides and several recent burglaries in which a firearm had been used by the perpetrator, I drew my service weapon and entered the apartment while holding my weapon at the ready position as I had been instructed to do during my training. The apartment was dark, and without warning, a male figure appeared from behind a closed door and appeared to lunge in my direction. I had only a split second to make a decision. I believed that my life was in imminent danger, so I fired three shots: two to the body, one to the head, as instructed during my training.

While it later transpired that the suspect had not been armed, this could not have been determined for certain at the time due to the speed at which events unfolded and to the poor lighting conditions, which made it impossible to determine detail. Given the totality of the circumstances, I reasonably believed that my life, the life of my partner, and potentially the lives of other innocent people in the building were in imminent danger and that the use of lethal force was therefore justified.

There would have been street protests, of course, and the chief of police would have issued a statement calling the shooting a tragedy, and the department might have rapped me on the knuckles for tactical failures, such as neglecting to call for backup. But I wouldn't have gone to jail. Even today, after the mass protests of 2020 and the outpouring of public pain over police killings and racial injustices, prosecutors rarely pursue criminal charges in such circumstances, and when they do, juries rarely convict. It was a dangerous neighborhood. Violent crimes and armed burglaries were all too common. The apartment was supposed to be unoccupied. The burglar alarm had gone off. The front door was partially open. The apartment was dark. Someone jumped out at us without warning.

This is why police in America end up killing so many people. It's not that they're sadists, or that they don't care about the lives of black Americans (this may be true of a few, but not of most). It's just that everything in police training and culture tells them to expect danger from every quarter. Officers are trained to be hypervigilant and respond to potential threats instantly. They're told they have "a right to go home safe." Too often, they forget that other people have a right to go home safe too.

In some ways, it's a surprising aspect of police culture. No one tells soldiers that they have "a right" to go home safe. On the contrary, when you sign up for military service, you're agreeing that your right to preserve your own life is secondary to the nation's needs. Soldiers are trained to take reasonable precautions, but ultimately, they accept that accomplishing their mission is more important than staying alive.

Police too should be trained to view their first mission as preserving the lives of members of the public. That doesn't mean they shouldn't defend themselves—but it does mean that officers should be encouraged to think in a different way about risk, and about who should bear the cost of mistakes.

This is what it comes down to. Police training tends to focus on risks to officers and the potential costs—to officers—of taking risks and making mistakes. This is why trained police officers are often so sympathetic to cops who end up killing people. When you're trained to believe that potential threats can come from anywhere, you start seeing threats everywhere. Nine hundred and ninety-nine times out of a thousand, a person reaching into a pocket during an encounter with police is doing so for innocent reasons—but police training tends to encourage a fixation on the one time in a thousand that someone is reaching for a weapon, making cops prone to overreact whenever anyone reaches into a pocket (or a glove compartment, or a purse), and inevitably making some cops decide that it's safer to just pull the trigger.

Most encounters between police officers and members of the public contain a degree of uncertainty and ambiguity, and it's not difficult for an officer to make a mistake when assessing the degree of threat. But at the moment, both police culture and the law push the costs of mistakes onto members of the public. If a police officer misreads an ambiguous situation as a threat and shoots someone, the law generally excuses the shooting as long as the officer's mistake was "reasonable."

That's not a high standard, and it's inherently subjective. The Supreme Court has held that while an officer's use of force must be "objectively reasonable" to pass constitutional muster, "the 'reasonableness' of a particular use of force must be judged from the perspective of *a reasonable officer on the scene*, rather than with the 20/20 vision of hindsight." Is it "reasonable" for an officer to fear that a suspect who reaches without warning into a hidden compartment could be reaching for a weapon, or that a suspect who suddenly raises a hand containing a dark object is raising a gun? Under the Supreme Court's standard, the answer is nearly always yes. The officer may be mistaken and may end up killing an innocent person armed only with a wallet or cell phone, but the mistake, in this view, is reasonable.

Imagine changing how we think about who bears the costs of mistakes. What if instead of telling officers they have a right to go home safe, police training focused on reminding officers that members of the *public* have a right to go home safe? What if we reminded officers that they are voluntarily taking a risky job, and that if someone dies because of a mistake, it's better that it be a police officer who is trained and paid to take risks than a member of the public?

No question, more police officers might get killed if police training shifted to emphasize acceptance of risk and protection of the public. And I'm okay with that. Police officers *are* trained and paid. When Jake and I walked into that dark apartment, we could have had our guns up. That might have protected us if there had indeed been an armed assailant on the premises, but it would also have increased the risk that one of us would end up mistakenly shooting someone who posed no threat. In the end, to me it came down to the odds. What were the odds of encountering an armed and violent assailant? And what were the odds of mistakenly shooting someone harmless? I knew the statistics: the likelihood that Jake or I would be killed was statistically low—much lower than the risk that we'd shoot someone ourselves.

Most important, it was our job to accept some risks. We knew when we signed up that being a police officer meant accepting some danger. But the kid taking a shower in his dad's empty apartment hadn't signed up to take risks. He was just a kid.

10-99

It is during the field training period that probationary officers form the critical behavior patterns and work habits that will provide the foundation for their law enforcement career.

—*MPD General Order 201.33, Field Training Program*

Full-time MPD officers usually finish their field training in twelve to sixteen weeks, but since I only worked part-time, it took me nearly a year and a half to complete the 480 hours of patrol duty required for certification. All told, I had put in almost nine hundred hours of MPD volunteer time in the eighteen months after graduating from the academy, but roughly half of those hours were spent on non-patrol activities such as training workshops and special event details, which didn't count toward patrol certification. When I graduated from the academy I was considered a level two reserve officer, meaning I was permitted to carry a firearm, patrol, and make arrests while in 10-4 status—that is, accompanied by a more senior officer, as uncertified officers are not allowed to patrol alone. After certification, I would become a level one reserve officer, able to patrol alone, in a 10-99 capacity, and entitled to wear my service weapon even while off duty. (I never saw the appeal of walking around with a gun, but in a city with some of the nation's most restrictive gun control laws, this was a perk many reserve officers valued.)

The certification process involved several steps. First, I had to assemble a field training binder containing photocopies of all the incident, offense, and arrest reports I had produced during my 480 patrol hours, together with copies of traffic tickets, run sheets, and field training forms signed by my shift partners, who were considered my de facto field training instructors for reserve corps certification purposes. After each tour of duty, field training officers were supposed to provide written feedback and numerical ratings of their trainee's "professional demeanor," "knowledge," "field performance," "radio usage," "safety," "court procedures," "use of force," and "guiding principles." In typical MPD fashion, most of my partners declined to do more than sign their names at the bottom of the forms, leaving the page reserved for remarks blank and instructing me to give myself whatever numerical ratings I considered appropriate.

At the beginning, I modestly gave myself a lot of 2 ratings: "average" (though I couldn't resist immodestly declaring myself a 4, "outstanding," when it came to "Reports: spelling and grammar"). My "personal appearance/uniform" could hardly be viewed as other than "average," since I was constitutionally averse to ironing boards and never polished my boots or belt buckles; and my radio usage, I thought, was only so-so. On the other hand, I thought I was pretty good at "accepts criticism" and "customer service." I gave myself a 3 on those.

My partners were appalled by my low self-ratings, however. "You got to rate yourself higher," Jake ordered. "Otherwise people will think I'm an asshole."

"Well, you do the ratings, then," I retorted. "So you can prove you're not an asshole."

"No way. Boring. You do it. Just give yourself a mix of threes and fours. Make it all fours and people will think I'm soft, but don't put down anything lower than three, or people will wonder why I'm not teaching you anything."

Only Reid, the officer who proudly declared himself a Second Amendment single-issue voter, took the time to offer extensive comments on my training forms.

> Officer Brooks and I operated Unit 7043 in a 10-4 capacity. The main focus of our time together was situation awareness, tactical mindset and officer safety. Officer Brooks began the tour well. She was properly dressed in full MPD Class B uniform and she arrived on time. We began our tour by performing mock traffic stops. We discussed the "A" and "B" pillar concepts, approaches, keeping her eye on the threat and how to position the scout car. . . . Further officer safety lessons included being sure not to stop next to the window of a neighboring vehicle and being sure to leave enough room for evasive maneuvers. . . . While responding to calls for service, Officer Brooks learned about fatal funnels . . . and about watching subjects' hands. . . . We visited various hot spots to walk through specific high stress situations (i.e., sounds of gunshots), including a discussion of cover versus concealment.

After putting together my field training binder, I was required to meet with the reserve corps' field training coordinator. He flipped through my binder, counting arrests and traffic tickets, then grilling me on procedures. "So you get to a domestic violence call. What do you do?" "You're dispatched to a suspected child abuse situation. How do you proceed?" When he finally declared himself satisfied, I was allowed to move on to the next phase of the certification process, the "cert ride."

Cert rides had to be arranged with district training sergeants. Essentially, you spent a shift driving around with a sergeant rather than another officer. After observing you for a few hours, the training sergeant would either recommend certification or order you to complete additional supervised patrol hours, focusing on your areas of weakness, before you were permitted to try again.

Cert ride horror stories abounded. Some sergeants, I had heard, grilled certification candidates relentlessly on geography, MPD general orders, or the arcana of district procedures ("When filling out a property form, are days of the week spelled out in full, or given using two-letter abbreviations?"). My weakest area was geography—unlike much of Washington, most streets in 7D follow neither a grid pattern nor an alphabetical principle, so there were no shortcuts to learning your way around. Before my cert ride, I spent several days driving around 7D and poring over maps, trying to memorize the district's many geographical quirks (both Second Street and Sixth Street SE somehow merge with Fourth Street, for instance, and Savannah Street, Savannah Place, and Savannah Terrace are all in different places). I read through all the recruit instructional materials and my class notes from the academy, memorized lists of required notifications, and practiced spelling out names using MPD's idiosyncratic phonetic alphabet ("Brooks": Brown, Robert, Ocean, Ocean, King, Sam).

My cert ride itself was an anticlimax. On a sunny early May afternoon in 2018, I was assigned to spend a shift with Sergeant Matthews, one of 7D's rare female sergeants. I liked Sergeant Matthews; she was smart, with a wry sense of humor. We drove around for a bit, and checked out a complaint about some men conducting a car repair business on the street. I managed to drive to the appropriate address without consulting my GPS. Then we were dispatched to take a robbery report. The victim, a young white guy who was new to DC, had put his iPhone up for sale using the Letgo app. He had been contacted by a potential buyer, who proposed meeting in 7D. When the victim arrived he was met by three young teenage boys claiming to be potential buyers. They asked to look at the phone before making a decision, then ran off with it into an alley. The victim was able to give a detailed description of the boy who had taken his phone, however, so we left him with another officer and drove around the neighborhood. Within minutes we spotted the young thief, who hadn't even bothered to remove his distinctive sweatshirt. The victim confirmed the thief's identity, and we arrested him.

Just then, something urgent came over the radio. Sergeant Matthews told me she needed to get back, and asked the other officer to give me a ride to the Juvenile Processing Center to get the kid booked in.

"My cert ride's over?" I asked.

She gave me a half smile. "Yeah. Just handle the arrest, and you're good."

I spent the next few hours dealing with the paperwork for our fifteen-year-old thief. Because he was only fifteen and had no prior record, he was eligible for a new pilot youth diversion program, but no one seemed to know how the process worked. After a good deal of back-and-forth discussion between the officers assigned to the Juvenile Processing Center, I was instructed to fill out the arrest forms in longhand or as PDFs instead of entering the information into the online reporting system, so the station would have a record of what had happened but the arrest would not appear in electronic searches. The boy's mother was called to pick him up. She berated him ("I told you not to be spending time with those boys! I knew they'd talk you into some kind of trouble! You are grounded!") and took him home. I hitched a ride back to 7D with another officer.

Later that day, I was cc'd on an email from Sergeant Matthews:

MEMORANDUM

TO: Commander, Seventh District

RE: Patrol Certification of Reserve Officer Rosa Brooks

Officer Rosa Brooks was appointed to the Metropolitan Police Department on April 12, 2016. Upon graduation from the Maurice T. Turner Institute of Police Science, Officer Brooks was assigned to the Seventh District. During her training period, I assisted with the monitoring of her training.

Officer Brooks successfully completed all tasks and assignments required of her during her training period. She has demonstrated a working knowledge of the laws and regulations of the District of Columbia as well as a substantial working knowledge of laws of arrest, search and seizure. Officer Brooks has also demonstrated knowledge of General Order 901.1.

On May 5th, 2018, I rode with Officer Brooks in order to ascertain her readiness to ride in a 10-99 capacity. During the (6) six-hour evaluation period, Officer Brooks demonstrated an ability to respond to various locations within the Seventh District without assistance. She responded to various radio assignments and handled each in a professional manner.

At the conclusion of the certification ride, I reviewed her training progress and it is my opinion that Officer Rosa Brooks has acquired the necessary skills to carry out the duties of a Metropolitan Police Officer and it is recommended that she be certified to patrol in a 10-99 status.

. . .

I t was a milestone, and I wasn't quite sure how to feel about it.

Whatever it was I wanted to prove had been proven, I supposed. I was one of just a few women in the MPD Reserve Corps, and when I finished my field training, I became the only woman serving as a certified level one reserve officer. I had weathered my family's skepticism and survived the academy; I had done more push-ups than I ever imagined I could do, and learned how to fight, shoot a gun, and administer emergency medical care. As a patrol officer, I had handled hundreds of calls in Washington's most difficult and violent neighborhoods, and for the most part, I felt like I had handled them reasonably well. If I never entirely mastered the skill of managing my countless pieces of equipment or remembering to fill out the correct forms in the correct manner, I felt good about my ability to calm tense situations and treat both victims and perpetrators with respect.

I mostly felt good about my fellow MPD officers, too. Each year, nearly a thousand people are killed by police in the United States, a level of violent death so high that policing can reasonably be compared to war, and critics of policing are justified in viewing both the stunningly high number of police killings and the racial inequities marring our criminal justice system as tragic and inexcusable. But policing is not a malevolent conspiracy; most police officers take seriously their role as public servants. The widely publicized incidents of police violence and abuse often lead us to forget that the vast majority of police officers spend the vast majority of their time helping people who ask for their help. Americans call 911 both in genuine emergencies and for trivial reasons, and police officers don't get to choose whether to respond.

Often, police officers help people in concrete and direct ways. They give CPR and Narcan to addicts lying unconscious on the street; they check for intruders when residents are too frightened to enter their homes; they wade into the middle of fights and put their own bodies between the combatants. They help victims of domestic violence apply for restraining orders against their abusers, try to persuade the mentally ill to seek care, drive homeless people to shelters, comfort victims of robbery and assault, and mediate disputes between family members and neighbors. During my time as a patrol officer I did all these things, and if much of what I saw made me sad, I went home after most shifts feeling that my colleagues and I had helped a few people, or at least prevented some bad situations from getting worse.

I felt less good about many of the arrests I made. They were all lawful arrests—"good" arrests, from MPD's perspective. But I doubt most of those arrests made the community safer or more prosperous.

It's hard to say for sure, but I know that of the twenty or so arrests I made or helped make during my field training period, almost all involved minor, nonviolent offenses: driving without a permit, destruction of property, unlawful entry, failure to appear at a court hearing, and the like. Even the arrests I made for violent offenses mostly involved misdemeanor-level assaults.

In the majority of those cases, arresting the perpetrators accomplished nothing of value. By the time we arrived on the scene, their brief burst of violence was usually over. After a night in jail, the perpetrators were released back into the same unhappy situations that had led them to break the law: too little money, too little education, too few decent jobs, too much family conflict, too few conflict resolution skills. Getting arrested didn't help the people driving without permits get properly licensed, and it didn't help the people who lashed out at friends or family members learn to control their tempers.

Mostly, those arrests just made bad situations worse. The people I arrested ended up with longer criminal records and a reduced ability to get or keep a job. If they went to prison, their families lost caregivers and income; their communities gained more children with absent parents, more children being brought up by distant relatives or strangers, and more children in desperate and painful situations.

Those arrests weren't costless for "the system," either. Even arrests for minor offenses take officers off the street for several hours, and the city bears the expense of feeding, housing, and guarding prisoners awaiting their first appearance, as well as the expense of all the work prosecutors must put in to review arrest paperwork. All told, the average arrest costs the city several thousand dollars—even when arrestees are ultimately released without formal charges.

Nearly a third of all DC arrests are "no-papered," meaning they don't lead to formal charges because prosecutors decide not to move forward with the case. Sometimes, this is because the underlying police work was poor quality—the police reports don't establish probable cause, or police errors in handling suspects or evidence make a successful prosecution unlikely. But much of the time, cases are no-papered because prosecutors deem the offenses too minor to merit formal charges. Prosecutors have heavy workloads, and very few want to spend hours pursuing cases against people who steal cans of soda or hit someone with a broom. When police make arrests that are subsequently no-papered, thousands of dollars of taxpayer money— money that might have been spent on education, job training, and mental health care—is essentially wasted on cases too trivial or weak to merit prosecution.

As an uncertified officer, I'd been required to patrol at least twenty-four hours each month or risk being dropped from the reserve corps, and while there was no formal arrest quota, the reserve corps training coordinator instructed uncertified officers to aim for at least eight to fifteen arrests during the field training period. Since everyone wanted to get certified, officers had a strong incentive to make the requisite number of arrests during field training. I was no exception. I didn't go looking for reasons to arrest people, but when I found them, I was pleased to have more arrest reports to add to my field training binder.

After certification, reserve officers are free to spend their MPD volunteer time as they wish. They can teach reserve recruit classes at the academy, participate in optional training workshops, or sign up to help in specialized units or at headquarters. Once I was certified, I cut down my patrol time to a shift every month or so and found other ways to fulfill my volunteer obligations. I didn't want to lose all the skills I had so painfully acquired— but I didn't want to keep arresting poor people for trivial offenses, either.

There are people who need to be arrested and imprisoned. I lost no sleep over arresting the man who beat his girlfriend and spat out angry threats as we wrestled him into the wagon, for instance. His girlfriend's battered face and his enraged cries—"I'm *coming* for you, motherfuckers!"— were enough to make me glad he'd been caught and cuffed. But most of the people I arrested didn't need to be in jail. They were poor and sad; sometimes they were addicts, or mentally ill. And I didn't want to keep locking them up.

Epilogue

It is better to know some of the questions than all of the answers.

—*James Thurber*

At the police academy, I was bothered both by the contradictory messages we received and by our instructors' near-complete silence on so many of the most difficult issues facing modern policing. Shortly before graduation, I had written up my proposal for the fellowship program designed to encourage young officers to confront what I thought of as "the hard questions": What's policing *for*? Do we know what "good policing" looks like? Can we measure it? How should we foster it? How should modern police grapple with the painful legacy of past police abuses, and the ways in which the legacy of racial discrimination still distorts our criminal justice system?

What I wanted, I suppose, was a way to build a bridge between my own two parallel lives: my life as a part-time police officer and my other life, my "real" life as a law professor, a writer, and someone committed to making the world a little bit more just.

Ben Haiman, the MPD official to whom I originally handed the proposal (and my occasional reserve corps patrol partner), was initially cautious about trying to move forward. MPD was between chiefs at the time, and it

wasn't the right moment, Ben thought, to float something new and potentially risky. But in early 2017, shortly after Peter Newsham was confirmed
as MPD's new chief, I got a call from Ben. MPD, he told me, had sent him
to a course on public management offered by George Washington University. All the students in the program worked for the DC government, and
they had been divided into small teams and instructed to come up with a
project that could be sponsored by one or more city agencies and implemented, or at least launched, by the end of the spring semester. "I've been
thinking," he said. "You know that fellowship proposal you wrote? No prom-
ises, but I think the chief might have some interest in getting behind an
effort like that. How would you feel if my team in the DC public management program adopted your proposal as our course project, and worked
with you to make it happen? If you're okay with that idea, I think we might
be able to do something real with this."

We did something real.
    Throughout the spring of 2017, I worked with Ben and the rest
of his team to flesh out the project, which we dubbed the Police for Tomorrow initiative. We would invite applications from officers and MPD civilian
employees with less than a year on the job, we decided. Those selected as
fellows would participate in intensive monthly workshops on topics such as
race and policing, implicit bias, poverty and crime, DC's changing demographics and the impact of gentrification on policing, mental illness, adolescent brain development, police use of force, and innovative approaches
to reducing violence, over-criminalization, and mass incarceration. At the
end of the workshop phase of the fellowship, each would develop a capstone
community project related to one of these issues.

    With some trepidation, I suggested that we invite a few of my George-
town Law colleagues to help design the workshops. As a rule, cops are wary

of both lawyers and professors, and I wasn't sure MPD would be open to working with strangers who combined both of these suspect professions. But Ben liked the idea, and the higher-ups gave it the thumbs-up as well, seeing a collaboration with Georgetown as a way to give academic credibility to the Police for Tomorrow program.

I was also worried about the reaction of my law school colleagues. At Georgetown, I was part of a student-faculty working group on racial justice established by the dean and chaired by my colleague Paul Butler, who had written extensively about race and policing. As I had feared, some members of the group were vehemently opposed to anything that looked like helping the cops. But others were intrigued by the idea of opening up a dialogue with the Metropolitan Police Department.

And just like that, the Police for Tomorrow program was up and running. The dean of the law school offered to provide start-up funding, and I pulled together four of my colleagues to run things on the Georgetown end.

They were a diverse and talented group. There was Paul Butler, who spent his early career as a prosecutor in DC before coming to the conclusion that he was no longer willing to be a black man who spent his days sending a parade of other black men to jail. He became a law professor instead, and a powerful chronicler of how racism continues to shape the American criminal justice system. There was Christy Lopez, who had spent much of her career at the Justice Department investigating police abuses before coming to Georgetown; Christy had been the primary author of the Justice Department's report on discriminatory and abusive practices by the police department in Ferguson, Missouri. Then there was Kristin Henning, a former public defender, the head of Georgetown Law's Juvenile Justice Clinic, and a major national voice on race and juvenile justice. Finally, there was Shon Hopwood, one of Georgetown's newest faculty hires. Shon had spent twelve years in federal prison after a failed bank robbery committed in his early twenties. In prison, he became a "jailhouse lawyer," writing briefs so powerful they caught the attention of Supreme Court justices and the Solicitor General. After his release, Shon went to law school, becoming a prominent prison reform advocate.

And, of course, there was me—a writer, a law professor, and an ambivalent, part-time police officer.

At times, our meetings reminded me of those old jokes: "A cop, a robber, a prosecutor, and a defense lawyer walk into a bar . . ." In many ways, we could hardly have been more different. But although we each saw different pieces of the elephant that is the American criminal justice system, we shared a common belief in the magic that can occur when people are willing to ask each other hard questions.

We dubbed ourselves the Innovative Policing Program, an entity we invented solely for the purpose of sponsoring the Police for Tomorrow Fellowship. Before long, we had hashed out a memorandum of understanding between Georgetown Law and MPD. Georgetown's Innovative Policing Program would plan and host the Police for Tomorrow fellows' workshops, providing the physical space, arranging guest speakers and readings, and managing the discussions. MPD would provide each Police for Tomorrow fellow with a handpicked senior "mentor" in the department, someone who could help our young fellows navigate the bureaucracy as they launched their careers. We would jointly interview applicants and select the fellows. At the end of the program, after a year of workshops and a successful capstone project, the Police for Tomorrow fellows would receive certificates signed by both the dean of the law school and the chief of police.

In June 2017, we formally launched the program. Brenda Richardson, a community activist who lived in the Seventh District, hosted the launch at her nonprofit's headquarters, and Chief Peter Newsham, the law school's vice dean, and a host of other Georgetown faculty and MPD officials welcomed nineteen new Police for Tomorrow fellows into the program.

It was an experiment, and like most experiments, it was not initially clear whether it would succeed or implode. But in this case, it didn't take long for us to see that the experiment was working. The young officers who joined the first cohort of Police for Tomorrow fellows were an extraordinary group.

There was Cody, a young officer from Massachusetts who arrived at his Police for Tomorrow selection interview fresh from his first shooting scene. He was so upset that he was still shaking. "I knew this kind of thing would happen," he told us. "But seeing someone just bleeding on the street like that—it shocked me." He apologized for being so rattled. He was embarrassed by his own distress, but at the same time, he told us, he was frightened of losing the part of himself that could be shocked and saddened by someone else's tragedy. "I'm worried about getting cynical," he said. "I don't want to turn into the kind of cop who just shrugs when someone gets shot."

There was Akintayo, who had emigrated to the United States from Nigeria. He was short, skinny, and earnest. He wanted to help people, he said, and believed that arresting people was rarely good for anyone; he wanted to know how to persuade his fellow officers that there were better ways to respond to most calls.

There was Ricardo, who had emigrated from Nicaragua as a boy, went to art school before becoming a cop, and was thinking about becoming a social worker; and Salah, who was half-Palestinian and half-Hungarian, had lived and worked in Chile, Israel, and Jordan, and had founded his own international nonprofit. There was Emma, who wanted to work on anti-human-trafficking initiatives, and Qasim, who hoped to join MPD's Emergency Response Team.

There was Ashley, a victim support specialist, and Assante, who spent a year at a sub sandwich shop after college and swore he'd never work in fast food again, and Gentry and Daniel, who were crime analysts at headquarters. There was Shayne, who wanted to be a detective, and Renae, who worked as an investigator in MPD's equal opportunity office, and Sean, who said he hoped to be chief of police someday. There was Shania, and Zack, and Tatiana, and Paris. Our final fellow was the reserve corps sergeant who had been my physical training and defensive tactics instructor at the police academy. We debated whether to accept him as a fellow—our focus was on new MPD employees, and he satisfied the eligibility criteria only in a technical sense, since he had been a reserve officer for years but had just recently taken a full-time civilian job at MPD. In the end, we decided that his role teaching scores of recruits each year made him a valuable participant; he understood both officer culture and recruit culture, and he had the ability to influence far more people in his role as an instructor than we could hope to reach in the Police for Tomorrow program's first year.

The Police for Tomorrow program exceeded all our expectations. (Interested readers can learn more about it in Appendix B.) Our fellows were eager—sometimes even desperate—to have a forum in which they could talk about their own hopes and frustrations with policing, and the group soon grew close. After they visited a nearby homeless shelter and spent an hour with a formerly homeless man who spoke about how terrifying his first nights on the streets had been, almost everyone ended up in tears. We brought in innovative police chiefs from other cities to speak to our fellows. We took our fellows to the Anacostia Community Museum for an exhibit on the impact of gentrification on DC's minority communities, and to the U Street corridor for a walking tour of DC's old "black Broadway." We met with scholars, activists, and DC high school kids. We talked about alternative ways to handle minor crimes without arresting people, and about the best way to intervene when a partner was doing something risky or inappropriate. We discussed the value of slowing down and focusing on prevention and de-escalation, instead of rushing heedlessly into fraught situations. We talked about how even the most junior officers could become effective change advocates within MPD.

Chief Newsham met with the fellows, listened to their stories and proposals, and told them to keep asking questions. "If each of you talks about this kind of thing with ten other officers, our department will be a hundred times better," he said. When we celebrated the first cohort of fellows' "graduation" from the program in October 2018, almost the whole MPD command staff came to the ceremony at the law school. "I want you to be an infection," Newsham told the fellows. "An infection that spreads through this department from the bottom to the top." It wasn't the metaphor I would have chosen, but it worked well enough.

I invited my mother to one of the Police for Tomorrow workshops. She sat through it quietly and left a few minutes before the session ended, before I had a chance to ask her what she thought. But she called me the next day.

"That was wonderful. Thank you for inviting me to sit in. You know, when you started this police thing, I was very concerned about it. I just didn't understand it at all."

"Really?" I asked dryly. "I'd never have guessed."

"But you did something good with it. I shouldn't have doubted you."

I had doubted myself much of the time, so I couldn't entirely blame her.

The next year, we expanded the program at MPD's request, launching a second cohort of fellows and bringing a series of guest lecturers to the police academy to speak to all the recruits. Christy Lopez and I developed and co-taught a practicum course on innovative policing at the law school, and we trained our law students to serve as discussion facilitators at the police academy. MPD asked us to help rethink the entire academy curriculum, and a team of law students worked with academy staff to develop proposals for change. We put other student teams to work helping MPD

rethink its performance evaluation system, develop new approaches to recruiting, and analyze the data on police stops to identify and address racial
disparities. We expanded beyond MPD as well, helping a community activist in New Orleans launch a Police for Tomorrow–like program with the
New Orleans Police Department and working with other innovative departments on similar programs. We applied for grants, and hired a program
director to help us manage the growing range of activities.

In the spring of 2019, Scott Ginsburg, a Georgetown Law graduate, made
a large gift to the law school. The gift included funding for several en-
dowed professorships, including my own, and as part of the deal, the dean
asked me to give a formal lecture on a topic of my choosing. At first, I wasn't
sure what to talk about—my 2016 book on war and the military? My earlier
work on law and violence? In the end, I decided it was finally time to talk
to my colleagues and students about some of the issues swirling around in
my mind after my time as a police officer.

In keeping with university tradition, everyone on the faculty wore their
academic robes to my lecture, and we filed into the law school auditorium
to the strains of classical music played by a chamber ensemble. The atmo-
sphere was as unlike that of the 7D station as possible.

Walking to the podium, I looked out at the audience. Paul Butler, Kris
Henning, Shon Hopwood, and Christy Lopez, my Innovative Policing Program partners, were there, along with dozens of my faculty colleagues.
Some of the students from my criminal justice class and the Innovative
Policing Practicum I taught with Christy were there as well. And to my
amazement and delight, many of our Police for Tomorrow fellows were in
the audience too, some sitting stiff and uncomfortable in their patrol uniforms, but smiling back at me. Ben Haiman was there, sitting next to Commander Ralph Ennis, the head of the police academy. Friends and colleagues

from around Washington were in the audience too, and in the front row, my husband and children sat with my brother, my sister-in-law, my mother-in-law, and my mother.

I told the audience about my lifelong preoccupation with the complex and paradoxical relationship between violence and law, and how it had led me to human rights work, to studying the military, and eventually to becoming a reserve police officer. I talked about my previous writing on war and the military, and the ways in which our tendency to view more and more global threats through the lens of war had undermined the rule of law even as it expanded the role of the military. When it came to domestic, US issues, I said, we were seeing a strikingly similar phenomenon: we were categorizing more and more behaviors as crimes, with devastating consequences for the most vulnerable Americans, and we were steadily expanding the role of police.

In recent decades, I told my audience, we've seen an explosion of over-criminalization, at both the state and the federal levels. Minor civil infractions have been legislatively redefined as criminal misdemeanors, offenses once considered misdemeanors have been redefined as felonies, and violations of complex regulatory codes have increasingly been criminalized, often creating brand-new and obscure crimes that lack a mens rea (criminal intent) requirement.

These shifts in how we think about crime have contributed to mass incarceration—and our proliferating criminal laws have mainly been enforced against people of color and the poor. At the same time, over-criminalization has expanded the role of the police. When you have more crimes, you need more cops—and when you have more cops, you find more ways to use them. (In the US, for instance, we consider it normal to have armed police officers enforce compliance with traffic regulations, even though most traffic violations don't constitute criminal offenses. It's the equivalent of routinely sending armed police to enforce IRS regulations or municipal building code regulations. It makes little sense, and increases the number of police-citizen encounters with the potential to go badly wrong.)

As a reserve police officer in Washington, DC, I said, I had seen first-hand the pressure on police officers to be all things to all people, playing multiple and often contradictory roles. American society asks police officers to use violence when needed to enforce the law, but we also ask them to serve as mediators, protectors, social workers, mentors, and medics. But it's very difficult to play any *one* of these roles well—and it's almost impossible to be good at them all.

We're caught in a vicious spiral: as American cities and states slash funds for education, health care, rehabilitation programs, and other social services, the resulting poverty and hopelessness fuel more crime and dysfunction, which leads to calls for more police and higher law enforcement budgets—but the more we spend on enforcement, the less we have available to spend on the vital social services that, in the long run, help reduce crime. The budget disparities are striking. In 2017, for instance, the city of Oakland, California, spent 41 percent of the city's general fund on policing—and for every dollar spent on policing, human services received less than 30 cents. The city of Baltimore spent $480 million each year on a police department with about 3,300 officers, and only $265 million on a school system with more than 80,000 students.

In a world that is increasingly obsessed with security issues, both international and domestic, we can expect the push toward more enforcement to increase, despite intermittent calls to "defund" or even abolish the police. I had written a book called *How Everything Became War and the Military Became Everything*; now, it seemed to me, we might also say that everything was becoming a crime, and the police were becoming everything.

The connections between these two stories—one about war and the military, the other about crime and policing—go even deeper, I told the audience. One aspect of the blurring and expansion of our concept of war is that war and war fighting increasingly blur into criminal law enforcement and policing. Everyone has seen the disturbing images of police in American cities riding in tanks and Humvees, wearing military-style uniforms and armed with military-grade assault weapons. The blurring is more subtle too: we're increasingly seeing the importation of practices associated with national security threats—such as nonpublic proceedings and invocation of the "state secrets" doctrine—into court proceedings related to violations of domestic criminal law, for instance. I think of it as "trickle-down war," and perhaps it's inevitable—terrorism and cyberattacks, to give two examples, are seen as both war and crime, so it's no surprise that our legal and institutional responses have begun increasingly to converge.

The "militarization" of police is a by-product of this convergence. In a nation in which both "homegrown" and foreign-originating terrorism are serious threats—in which sophisticated global drug cartels and organized criminal gangs often make use of military weapons and tactics, and in which mass shootings such as those in Newtown, Orlando, Las Vegas, and Parkland have become dismayingly routine—police officers are increasingly trained to respond to threats that resemble war as much as they resemble crime, which has fueled increased police use of military weapons and tactics, as well as high-tech surveillance and analysis tools. Around the nation, police departments are struggling to adapt to the growing sophistication and lethality of many criminal actors, even as they face a crisis of legitimacy relating to the use of force and racially biased enforcement.

My time as a police officer didn't leave me with any easy answers, but I ended the lecture with a warning, and a challenge.

"Here's the warning," I told the audience. "We live in a world in which everything has become war and the military has become everything, everything is becoming crime and the police are becoming everything, and war and policing are becoming ever more intertwined, both on the level of law and the level of institutions. These trends remain invisible to most Americans—but they are having a devastating effect on human rights, democratic accountability, and the rule of law, and are likely to continue to do so.

"And here's the challenge: It's up to us—and particularly, up to those of you who are young—to find a better way forward. We need to acknowledge the very real threats we face, but at the same time, we need to develop new legal and institutional safeguards to keep America from becoming a society that's obsessed with security at the expense of both liberty and justice. I have a few ideas about how to do this—but I know that *you* will have better ones."

As I stepped away from the podium, relieved to be done, I looked out at my audience—at the faculty members in their academic robes, the students in their T-shirts and jeans, the police officers in their uniforms, and my family, dressed with uncharacteristic formality for the occasion. My daughters were wearing skirts, and even my mother had dressed up. Everyone was beaming up at me, and I felt a sudden surge of joyous vertigo: all my worlds, finally converging.

·

ACKNOWLEDGMENTS

I still find it strange that the DC Metropolitan Police Department was willing to give a badge and a gun to a writer (aren't pens and keyboards dangerous enough?). But I'm grateful. MPD isn't perfect, but it's a police department that tries hard to do the right thing, and I'm proud to have been part of it.

Special thanks also goes to the instructors at the Metropolitan Police Academy and to my many field training officers and partners in the MPD Reserve Corps and the 7th District: they put up with my questions and helped me when I struggled. My classmates in Reserve Recruit Class 16-01 kindly pretended not to laugh at my snail-like pace on the 1.5 mile run, didn't complain when my practice handcuffing left bruises on their wrists, and were right there beside me when we all got a face full of OC spray.

Thanks, especially, to Ben Haiman, whose integrity, intelligence, and common sense constantly impress me, and to Ken Mabry, Ralph Ennis, Salah Czapary, Raul Mendez, Booker Griffin, James Meagher, Jessica Bress, Paula Gormley, Matt Bromeland, Gary Miller, Ivan Lawit, Garth Robins, Graham Campbell, Leo Pinson, Dan Billingsley, Nik Isoldi, Chris Dietz, Brian Coleman, Gerard Barretto, Esteban Beamon, Matt Malacaria, Anita Ravishankar, Cody Robinson, Ron Koch, Ryan Sullivan, Jonathan Rosnick, Antoinette Martin, Vimary Serrano, Elijah Lamar, Brad Bennett, Christina Laurie, Elisee Chery, Travis Reed, Linda Daniels, Sylvester

Garvin, and James Vandermeer. If I have inadvertently omitted any names, I apologize.

I'm also grateful to MPD Chief Peter Newsham, who took a risk on the Police for Tomorrow program and has continued to support it through thick and thin, and to Cohorts 1 and 2 of the Police for Tomorrow Fellowship Program, who give me hope that the future of American policing will be brighter than its past: Akintayo Akintunde, Tatiana Benard, Sean Bickersteth, Salah Czapary, Tom Flaherty, Emma Hicks, Paris Hughes, Shania Hughes, Renae Lee, Ricardo Perez, Ashley McHenry, Cody Robinson, Gentry Schaffer, Dan Sebastian, Qasim Sheroz, Zach Speck, Assante Thomas, Shayne Wallace, Eric Abreu, Carimaxy Benitez-Garcia, Stephen Benson, Jeremy Brady, Tipi Brookins, Mike Brumbaugh, Lisa Burton, Evan Douglas, Jose Guzman, Dan Kornfield, Anam Mumtaz, Cory Novick, Chris Paige, Tim Parrish, Dillon Savage, Corbin Seward, Tamicka Smithson, John Sullivan, and Harry Weiss.

Nicole Boykin, Bobby Gboyor, Carlos Johnston, and Milena Yordanova adopted the Police for Tomorrow program as their project in 2017: without their work and faith (as well as the work of Ben Haiman and the support of Chief Robert Contee), it would never have gotten off the ground. My Georgetown colleagues Kris Henning, Paul Butler, Shon Hopwood, and, especially, Christy Lopez poured their time and energy into building what is now a national model, and their friendship and thoughts have immeasurably enriched my understanding of what changes are needed to make policing more just. Georgetown Law Dean Bill Treanor and former Vice Dean Jane Aiken gave the Innovative Policing Program and the Police for Tomorrow Fellowship vital moral and financial support as the project was getting off the ground.

Georgetown Law students in my Criminal Justice class and the Innovative Police Practicum were a crucial sounding board and source of ideas and insights for this book, and Jenny Gilbert, Nick Joynson, and

ACKNOWLEDGMENTS

Johanna Moody provided invaluable research assistance. Thanks also goes to Brent Godfrey, Brandon del Pozo, Sue Rahr, Scott Thomson, Chuck Wexler, Kevin Hay, Fred Rogers, Chris Magnus, Ron Davis, Talhia Tuck, Tanya Weinberg, Mimi Koumanelis, Monica Stearns, Chris Hammer, Ben Purse, Melanie Hudgens, Jaclyn Diaz, Gene Finn, Tom Clark, Jonny Reck, Brianna Walden, Lionel Beehner, Peter Bergen, Dan Rothenberg, Pete Singer, Anne Marie Slaughter, and the fellows and staff at New America, West Point's Modern War Institute and the Charles Koch Foundation, all of whom provided ideas, inspiration or support at critical moments.

My agent, Kris Dahl, believed in this book well before I did. At Penguin, Ann Godoff and Casey Dennis helped it take shape and were patient with my occasional fits of ambivalence. My parents, John Ehrenreich, Sharon McQuaide, and Barbara Ehrenreich read early drafts and offered comments and love, as did Deirdre English, my "goddess mother." John McGough provided the renovated one-room Wyoming schoolhouse in which I wrote most of this book. My husband, Joe, and my two beloved children, Anna and Clara, tolerated my strange new policing hobby and provided me with hugs and humor when I needed it most. Scout the dog won't be able to read this, but my long walks with her in Wyoming helped me keep things in perspective.

I'm also grateful to the hundreds of Washington, DC, residents whose lives I glimpsed as a patrol officer. Most of them were struggling, in one way or another, but almost without exception, they offered my MPD colleagues and me their trust and cooperation. Often, their kindness and courage were humbling.

Finally, I'm grateful to the hundreds of thousands of Americans who took to the streets to call for more just and responsive forms of policing— and to the many police officers, in Washington, DC, and around the nation, who are trying their best to transform policing from within.

APPENDIX A:

WHAT HAPPENED NEXT?

In spring 2020, two things happened that have the potential to forever change American policing: the COVID-19 epidemic and the mass protests that followed the killing of George Floyd by Minneapolis police officers. First, the COVID-19 pandemic brought an abrupt end to business as usual for people all over the world. Police departments also faced urgent new challenges: when routine police practices such as stops, searches, and arrests risk exposing officers and suspects alike to a potentially deadly illness, everything's up for grabs. Policing is "a contact sport," as one of my academy instructors put it, and there's no way to completely eliminate the risk of infection to police or community members. But, like many law enforcement agencies, the Washington, DC, Metropolitan Police moved quickly to reduce custodial arrests for minor crimes and change other high-risk practices. Among other things, the department ended in-person papering and trained dispatchers to screen calls and direct callers, when possible, to more appropriate city services, dispatching patrol officers only to those calls clearly requiring a police response. It's too soon to say how many of these changes will endure once the pandemic ends, but it's clear that the crisis has shaken up settled assumptions in ways that may have far-reaching consequences for the future of policing. Second, the death of George Floyd sparked a nationwide outpouring of anger and grief over police brutality and racial injustice. Diverse crowds gathered in every US state, and political leaders at every level pledged to work for change. Although calls to "defund" or abolish the police are supported (as of July 2020) by only about a quarter of Americans, these demands have triggered an important conversation about the role of police and the allocation of resources between police and social services. As with the COVID epidemic, it's difficult to know whether the protests following George Floyd's death will lead to genuine and sustainable changes—but as I write this in July 2020, changes that once seemed impossible are beginning to seem both necessary and possible.

Even before the pandemic and the protests, MPD had begun to make significant changes. Partly as a result of feedback from the Police for Tomorrow fellows, the police academy's curriculum and requirements are being overhauled. Achieving a particular cut-off score on the PT test is no longer a graduation requirement; instead, the test is used as a self-assessment tool and to evaluate recruits' effort and improvement. In 2019 MPD and Georgetown's Innovative Policing Program convened the first national police academy directors' symposium, bringing together academy directors from departments around the country to discuss new approaches to police training and education.

MPD has made other important changes as well, overhauling the department's performance evaluation system, reexamining the recruiting system, changing the district assignment system, revamping policies for dealing with young offenders, and changing the way data is collected on police stops and frisks, among other things.

Chief Peter Newsham continues to be a strong supporter of the Police for Tomorrow Fellowship, and Ben Haiman, the reserve officer and MPD civilian who helped create the program, was promoted to serve as head of MPD's Professional Development Bureau, a position equivalent to that of assistant chief of police.

Of the sixteen people who started in Reserve Recruit Class 2016-01, only six remain with MPD. The first to leave was Gregson, who quit abruptly after just a few months. Several of my classmates left when they moved to different cities or deployed. Smith transferred to the FBI, and Ramos switched to become a full-time MPD officer. Lowrey, the rocket scientist, stuck with the reserve corps and became one of the most dedicated and thoughtful reservists I know. The Metropolitan Police Reserve Corps now has more than a hundred officers, but still includes only half a dozen women.

Auguste returned to the Boston area as soon as he was able to get a job with a local police department, but Murphy, Jeremiah, Reid, Jake, and Yusef still work in 7D. Sergeant Flanagan graduated from the Police for Tomorrow program and still works full-time at the police academy, training recruits in defensive tactics and reminding them to behave with decency and common sense.

Patrol officers rarely learn what happens next to the people they encounter while patrolling, but here's what I was able to find out about some of the people I met when responding to calls:

- Prosecutors decided not to move forward with the assault charges against Imani. She went back to living with her grandmother, but her relationship with both her grandmother and her mother remained contentious. Police responded to her grandmother's house on at least one other occasion following reports of a fight between Imani and her grandmother, and on another occasion, they responded to another report of a fight between Imani and her mother. No arrests were made on either occasion. Imani's mother also continued to have a contentious relationship with her other children—police were called on several occasions—and with her boyfriend (the one from whom Imani had requested money, setting off the events that led to her arrest on charges of assaulting her mother). The boyfriend was arrested on multiple occasions for assaulting Imani's mother; on one occasion he was arrested for setting fire to her house. Imani's mother was arrested on at least one occasion for assaulting her boyfriend. Both the mother and her boyfriend were also arrested on multiple occasions for other crimes, ranging from burglary and drug possession to armed robbery.

- Prosecutors also decided not to move forward with assault charges against the young man who said he threw up because his girlfriend was pregnant. A few months later, he was questioned by the police about an alleged sexual assault on his younger stepbrother, but no charges were filed.

- Prosecutors did not proceed with charges against the nurse who hit her sister during a fight over laundry. Her record was otherwise clean.

- The man who threatened us after we arrested him for assaulting his girlfriend eventually pled guilty to assault. He had been on probation for a previous offense and his probation was revoked; he was sentenced to 180 days in jail. His arrest for assault was part of a long string of arrests for a range of offenses, many of them involving assaults and threats.

- The shoplifter with a failure-to-appear warrant continued to move in and out of the criminal justice system. Before we encountered her, she had been arrested on several previous occasions for shoplifting as well, on one occasion making off with $396 worth of merchandise from Walmart and on another occasion with $222.71 worth of groceries from another Safeway. On other occasions, she was arrested for drug possession, failure to pay Metro fare, and driving on a suspended license. She was also a victim of domestic violence at the hands of a boyfriend.

- Star, the woman who claimed to have been raped by a mysterious black man, continued to have problems. Within the next few months, she called 911 again on several occasions, claiming that her parked car had been damaged, a fan had been stolen, a window had been smashed, and a brick had been thrown through her bedroom window. On each occasion, she said, the suspects fled before police could arrive. On three other occasions, third parties called police after finding Star apparently drunk and unconscious. On one of those occasions she told police that an unknown person had come up behind her and pushed her to the ground. A few months later, Star called 911 to report that on the previous day, another unknown black male, armed with a handgun, had tried to kidnap, rape, and kill her. She told police that she had called 911 at the time and been taken to the hospital for treatment of injuries incurred during her abduction. A subsequent investigation found no record of related 911 calls or hospitalization, and the friends and neighbors Star said had witnessed some of these events denied that they had occurred. Star agreed to voluntarily admit herself to the hospital for psychiatric treatment.

- The boy I arrested for robbery during my certification ride was eligible for diversion release, since he was a minor with no prior record. A month later, however, he was involved in a fight along with a number of other teens and ended up stabbing a young woman in the face with a knife. She was able to identify him and directed police to his house. His mother opened the door willingly to the police and pointed them to her son's bedroom, where police arrested him. While searching him, they found a knife in his waistband and a bloodstained T-shirt on his bed.

- Zari and Darius continued to try to take care of their mother, who was also constantly in and out of the criminal justice system. She had a long string of arrests and police involvement in her life, for issues ranging from drug possession to vehicular offenses, assaults, and family disturbances.

APPENDIX B:
POLICE FOR TOMORROW

If you'd like to learn more about Georgetown's Innovative Policing Program and the Georgetown/MPD Police for Tomorrow Fellowship, you might be interested in some of the media coverage about the program:

- "Police for Tomorrow," *Georgetown Law*, Spring/Summer 2019, www.pageturnpro.com/Georgetown-Law/90551-Georgetown-Law-Magazine--SpringSummer-2019/flex.html.

- Angela Morris, "Law School Tackles Police Reform," *American Bar Association Journal*, January 1, 2019, www.abajournal.com/Magazine/Article/Law_School_Tackles_Police_Reform.

- Theresa Vargas, "A Roomful of Cops Asked if It's Better to 'Do Nothing' Sometimes. Why That's a Good Thing," *Washington Post*, December 15, 2018, www.washingtonpost.com/local/a-roomful-of-cops-asked-if-its-better-to-do-nothing-sometimes-why-thats-a-good-thing/2018/12/14/3b8bd058-ffe9-11e8-862a-b6a6f3ce8199_story.html.

APPENDIX B

- Karen Sloan, "Can Law Schools Reform Policing? Georgetown Is Trying," *National Law Journal*, October 23, 2018, www.law.com /nationallawjournal/2018/10/23/can-law-schools-reform -policing-georgetown-is-trying/.

- "Our Fresh Takes on Policing This Week," *USA Today*, December 17, 2018, www.usatoday.com/story/opinion/policing/2018/12/ 17/policing-usa-newsletter-white-clergy-black-lives-matter-first -step-act-d-c-police/2334444002/.

- "Georgetown Program Fosters Police Tactics of the Future," *NBC4* video, 91 seconds, October 24, 2018, www.nbcwashington .com/news/local/georgetown-program-fosters-police -tactics-of-the-future_washington-dc/169746/.

- "Policing for Tomorrow," April 11, 2018, in *The Podcast @ DC*, podcast, 38 minutes, soundcloud.com/user-768286365/policing-for -tomorrow.

- Cameron Luttrell, "Georgetown Law Launches Police Fellowship Program," *Patch*, June 6, 2017, patch.com/district-columbia/george town/georgetown-law-launches-police-fellowship-program.

- Peter Hermann, "Georgetown Law Program Offers Fellowship for Young D.C. Police Officers," *Washington Post*, June 5, 2017, www.washingtonpost.com/local/public-safety/georgetown -law-program-offers-fellowship-for-young-dc-police-officers /2017/06/05/b21ec920-4a17-11e7-a186-60c031eab644_story.html.

- Mikaela Lefrak, "D.C. Police Team Up with Georgetown to Train and Retain Young Officers," June 7, 2017, WAMU 88.5 radio broadcast, wamu.org/story/17/06/07/d-c-police-team-georgetown -train-retain-young-officers/.

NOTES

13 **"We are looking for dedicated"**: "Metropolitan Police Department," Reserve Police Officer (Volunteer), Government of the District of Columbia, https://joinmpd.dc.gov/career-position -2020/reserve-police-officer.

15 **American police killed**: Swaine, Jon, and Ciara McCarthy, "Young Black Men Again Faced Highest Rate of US Police Killings in 2016," *Guardian*, January 8, 2017, www.theguardian .com/us-news/2017/jan/08/the-counted-police-killings-2016-young-black-men.

ANIMALS

20 **"Shee-*it*." He closed**: Later, as I became more experienced, I found that mention of Donald Trump's presidency offered a fairly reliable test of mental alertness. Otherwise-stuporous people could be jolted quickly back to consciousness—often irate consciousness—by mention of Trump's name, and the test worked even if you didn't name names.

One night, responding to another "man down" call, we found a woman slumped against the curb, unconscious. After some gentle shaking, poking, and cajoling, she revived a bit, and by the time the ambulance arrived, she could raise her head and was able to give her name, the correct date, and our location in a quavering voice, though she still seemed half-dazed.

"Great, you're doing great. Just one more question," the medic told her. "You know who the president is?"

For a moment, her eyes fogged over, but then they snapped back into focus and she jerked herself upright. "That . . . white . . . mother*fucker*!"

"Yeah, she's good," said the medic, jotting a note on his tablet. "Fully oriented to time, place, and person."

26 **The acronyms were**: In April 2018, MPD eliminated the old abbreviations and issued a list containing more than two hundred new ones, most just as opaque. (ACCUNK stands for "Accident with Unknown Injuries," for instance, while THRTPER stands for "Threat—In Person" and BERGMACHRPT stands for "Burglary of Machine, More than 30 Minutes Ago.")

THE ABYSS

38 **during the first:** Lartey, Jamiles, "By the Numbers: US Police Kill More in Days Than Other Countries Do in Years," *Guardian*, June 9, 2015, www.theguardian.com/us-news /2015/jun/09/the-counted-police-killings-us-vs-other-countries.

38 **For America's first:** Alexander, Michelle, *The New Jim Crow: Mass Incarceration in the Age of Colorblindness* (New York: New Press, 2010).

39 **America charges:** In 2014, US residents committed more than 14,000 murders, along with over 1.2 million other violent crimes. Some 68 percent of US homicides involved firearms, which isn't too surprising, since there are an estimated 270 million to 357 million firearms sloshing around the United States. If you're wondering if that's a big number, it is: some studies suggest that between 35 and 50 percent of all civilian-owned guns in the world are in the United States.

Compare these figures to rates of gun ownership and violent crime in other countries and the scale of America's violence problem becomes clear. In Britain, there are only 6.6 guns per 100 people; in Germany and France, there are roughly 30 guns per 100 people. In the United States, there are somewhere between 88 and 112 guns per 100 people. The per capita US homicide rate also far outpaces other developed countries: it's roughly three times higher than in France, four times higher than in Britain, five times higher than in Germany, and 13 times higher than in Japan.

The United States' violence problem has obvious implications for American police officers and how they think about their on-the-job encounters. British cops can safely assume that most of the people they see around them aren't armed. In the United States, police officers often assume the opposite, and given the astounding number of guns around, they're often right to do so. In 7D, finding a gun is easy. It's finding a way out that's hard. See "Crime in the United States 2014: Murder," FBI, ucr.fbi.gov/crime-in-the-u.s/2014 /crime-in-the-u.s.-2014/offenses-known-to-law-enforcement/murder; "FBI Releases 2014 Crime Statistics," FBI, September 28, 2015, www.fbi.gov/news/pressrel/press-releases/fbi-releases-2014-crime-statistics; "Crime in the United States 2014: Murder, Types of Weapons Used," FBI, ucr.fbi.gov/crime-in-the-u.s/2014/crime-in-the-u.s.-2014/tables/expanded-homicide-data /expanded_homicide_data_table_7_murder_types_of_weapons_used_percent_distribution _by_region_2014.xls; Ingraham, Christopher, "There Are Now More Guns Than People in the United States," *Washington Post*, October 5, 2015; Karp, Aaron, "Completing the Count: Civilian Firearms," in *Small Arms Survey* (Cambridge, UK: Cambridge University Press, 2007), 39–71; Karp, Aaron, "Completing the Count: Civilian Firearms, Annexe 4," in *Small Arms Survey*; Morris, Hugh, "Mapped: The Countries with the Most Guns (No Prizes for Guessing #1)," *Telegraph*, October 22, 2016; and "Global Study on Homicide," United Nations, https://www.unodc.org/unodc/en/data-and-analysis/global-study-on-homicide.html.

39 **But as the legal scholar:** Cover, Robert M., "Violence and the Word," *Yale Law Journal* 95, no. 8 (1986): 1601–29.

40 **In his 1992 book:** Browning, Christopher R., *Ordinary Men: Reserve Police Battalion 101 and the Final Solution in Poland* (New York: Harper Perennial, 2017).

MODEL RECRUIT

65 **Moral: people have had:** Law is old, and crime and punishment are old, but no one really knows when the first police force came into being. The Bible tells us that Cain slew his brother Abel, and God punished Cain by sending him off to be "a restless wanderer . . . on the earth," but as far as we know, God did his own detective work, and Cain accepted his punishment without need of police officers to drag him off in cuffs.

NOTES

Most historians assume that early policing was essentially viewed as a collective responsibility; communities might punish those who violated significant norms, but there were no "professional" police. When force was required to stop or punish wrongdoing, the affected citizenry and their families or friends did what they considered necessary. As societies grew more complex and specialized, in many states professional soldiers occasionally performed what today we might think of as "law enforcement" functions, at the behest of the governing authorities. Similarly, private citizens and groups (merchants, priests, artisans) often paid others to serve as guards and gatekeepers, keeping watch over temples, storerooms, and marketplaces. In the United States, what we would today recognize as "police departments" emerged only in the midnineteenth century.

66 **Later, the emperor Justinian:** Like their modern counterparts, police in the ancient world were often accused of brutality and corruption. A papyrus from around 1000 BC advises Egyptian citizens to do whatever was needed to keep the cops on their side:

> Befriend the herald [policeman] of your quarter,
> Do not make him angry with you.
> Give him food from your house,
> Do not slight his requests;
> Say to him: "Welcome, welcome here."
> No blame accrues to him who does it.

In ancient China, specialized criminal justice officers (distinct from the military) seem to have emerged by the time of the Shang dynasty (1783 to 1134 BC). By the Han dynasty period, cities and prefectures had police chiefs and officers—who were sometimes unwilling conscripts—and the behavior of Han dynasty officers seems frequently to have dismayed the populace. The *Book of Han*, written in the first century AD, tells approvingly of a provincial governor who solved the problem of police corruption and abuse by raising police salaries: after getting a substantial raise, the police finally "considered themselves important and did not care to violate the law or unauthorizedly arrest and detain people."

The first known police officers in ancient Greece were enslaved foreigners. (This will perhaps not surprise today's patrol officers, who may be inclined to feel that their own lot—at the mercy of an unfeeling bureaucracy, ordered around by hostile sergeants—has much in common with that of a slave.) Writing in the second century AD, Julius Pollux described the "Scythian archers" active in Athens in the fifth century BC. These were "public slaves," with the task of "restraining those who behaved inappropriately and those who said what should not be said."

In his comic plays, the Greek playwright Aristophanes paints an unflattering portrait of their capabilities: in *Lysistrata*, for instance, the Scythians, sent by a magistrate to arrest Lysistrata, prove no match for the band of angry women she summons to her aid: "Come out . . . you market women who sell grain and eggs, garlic and vegetables, and those who run our bakeries and taverns, to the attack! Hit them, stomp on them, scratch their eyeballs, smother them with your abuse! Don't hold back!" The Scythian guards are quickly routed by the mob of women, and Lysistrata has to order her makeshift army not to add insult to injury by stripping the police of their weapons. In another Aristophanes play, a Scythian police guard watching a prisoner is easily persuaded to abandon his duties by the prospect of sex with an attractive dancing girl.

All this suggests, however, that one of the central paradoxes of policing has been with us for millennia: police function as enforcers for the establishment, but are locked out of the establishment themselves. From the earliest times, police have been charged with protecting the powerful from the hungry and powerless, but police themselves have no independent wealth or power; historically, they have been foreigners, slaves, and hired hands, creating a recipe for corruption and resentment all around. Only relatively recently did police come to view themselves as protectors of ordinary people and defenders of the rule of law, rather than merely as servants of those with power. (See: Dollinger, André, "Egyptian Merchants in the Old Kingdom," Introduction to the History and Culture of Pharaonic Egypt, 2001, www.reshafim.org.il/ad/egypt/trade/market_scene.htm; "Tombs of Ancient Egypt: The Mastaba of Niankhkhnum and Khnumhotep," Osirisnet, www.osirisnet .net/mastabas/niankhkhnoum_khnoumhotep/e_niankhkhnum_khnumhotep_02.htm; Dollinger, "The Police in Ancient Egypt," Introduction to the History and Culture of Pharaonic Egypt, www.reshafim.org.il/ad/egypt/law_and_order/police.htm; Kemp, Barry J., *Ancient Egypt: Anatomy of a Civilization* (Abingdon, UK: Routledge, 1992), www.amazon .com/Ancient-Egypt-Civilization-Barry-Kemp/dp/0415063469; Davies, Norman de Garis, *The Rock Tombs of El Amarna* (London: Gilbert and Rivington, 1900), archive.org/details /rocktombsofelama14davi; Mark, Joshua L., "Police in Ancient Egypt," Ancient History Encyclopedia, July 21, 2017, www.ancient.eu/article/1104/police-in-ancient-egypt/; Wong, Kam C., *Chinese Policing: History and Reform* (New York: Peter Lang, 2009), books.google .com/books?id=jjBTi-GEZe4C&pg=PA39&lpg=PA39&dq=the+%22book+of+han%22 +police&source=bl&ots=P_rc_2_C6r&sig=LmrLKmK6kcR4d2gUwiuWZbfNd3Q&hl =en&sa=X&ved=2ahUKEwiXxJLf5IHdAhXNbZoKHcwEAhYQ6AEwE3oECAMQAQ#v =onepage&q=prefect&f=false; "Alphabetical Glossary." In Ku, Pan. Homer H. Dubs, trans-lator. *The History of the Former Han Dynasty*, *v*ol. 1. (Baltimore: Waverly, 1938), web.archive .org/web/20130117062103/http://library.uoregon.edu/ec/e-asia/read/Chp1-5FINAL_D.pdf; library.uoregon.edu/ec/e-asia/reada/crowell-chp8.pdf; Benn, Charles, *China's Golden Age* (Oxford, UK: Oxford University Press, 2002), books.google.com/books?hl=en&lr=&id =ile3jSveb4sC&oi=fnd&pg=PR9&dq=%22Gold+Bird+Guards#v=onepage&q =%22Gold%20Bird%20Guards%22&f=false, Aristophanes, *Lysistrata*, trans. Ian Johnson, Vancouver Island University, uofi.app.box.com/s/48etuhz2thdbzroq7sx1hp8fimokurjn, p. 30; "Aristophanes, *Thesmophoriazusae*," Perseus Digital Library, Tufts University, www .perseus.tufts.edu/hopper/text?doc=Perseus:abo:tlg,0019,008:1222&lang=original.)

66 **The colonies imported:** In early colonial America, policing initially reflected the settlers' English heritage. Appointed sheriffs were responsible for tax collection, the enforcement of court judgments, and a range of administrative tasks, and the detention of criminals was a relatively minor part of their job. In some cities and towns, sheriffs were supplemented by paid constables; in others, a town "watch" was formed, consisting of volunteers or townsmen more or less conscripted into serving. Town watchmen also responded to fires and external attacks, and often the watchmen and the local militia were one and the same.

On the whole, the evidence suggests that preventing and responding to violent crime was not a major preoccupation in colonial America, in part because towns were small enough and conditions beyond them frightening enough to the early settlers that commu-nities had strong incentives to self-police. Early settlers depended heavily on one another, and exile was akin to a death sentence. Thus, the policing function was not viewed as separate from other colonial institutions designed to maintain order, and public safety was viewed as a communal responsibility.

Only as English-speaking settlements spread and inequalities in wealth grew did both property crime and violent crime become more common. Demands for policing increased accordingly. In the north, greater demand for policing was linked to rising inequality and, later, to industrialization, immigration, and the growth of cities; as communities became more populous and urbanized, the relatively informal mechanisms of social control that had prevailed in the early colonies began to be perceived by elites as inadequate.

NOTES

In the South, the institution of slavery shaped the evolution of policing. By the early 1700s, several southern colonies created formal "slave patrols" charged with capturing runaways and putting down slave revolts. They were brutal enforcers of a brutal institution. As one patroller put it, their job was to "apprehend any negro whom we found from his home, and if he made any resistance, or ran from us, fire upon him immediately." (See: Olson-Raymer, Gayle, "The Evolving Colonial Criminal Justice System," History 110, Humboldt State University, gorhistory.com/hist110/unit1/criminaljustice.html; Williams, Kristian, "Foreword: Police and Power in America," in *Our Enemies in Blue* [New York: Soft Skull Press, 2004], www.google.com/books/edition/Our_Enemies_in_Blue/QWNhCgAAQBAJ?hl=en&gbpv=1&bsq=foreword.)

67   **Thus the first:** See Brooke, John L., *Columbia Rising: Civil Life on the Upper Hudson from the Revolution to the Age of Jackson* (Chapel Hill: University of North Carolina Press, 2013); Ellis, Franklin, *History of Columbia County, New York. With Illustrations and Biographical Sketches of Some of Its Prominent Men and Pioneers* (Philadelphia: Everts & Ensign, 1878).

67   **Instead, Reserve Recruit:** The British statesman Sir Robert Peel is usually credited with ushering in the era of "modern" policing, in which police officers are full-time, salaried employees of the state, working within a formal, centralized municipal or regional police organization, and charged specifically and solely with law enforcement duties. In 1829, at Peel's urging, Parliament passed legislation creating the London Metropolitan Police force.

Peel's vision of policing was in many ways a radical one. The police, he believed, should serve the people and not merely the powerful. The general orders given by Peel to all London Metropolitan Police officers contain nine principles of policing, which are still taught in police academies today. The purpose of the police, according to his nine principles, was:

1. To prevent crime and disorder, as an alternative to their repression by military force and severity of legal punishment.

2. To recognise always that the power of the police to fulfil their functions and duties is dependent on public approval of their existence, actions and behaviour, and on their ability to secure and maintain public respect.

3. To recognise always that to secure and maintain the respect and approval of the public means also the securing of the willing co-operation of the public in the task of securing observance of laws.

4. To recognise always that the extent to which the co-operation of the public can be secured diminishes proportionately the necessity of the use of physical force and compulsion for achieving police objectives.

5. To seek and preserve public favour, not by pandering to public opinion, but by constantly demonstrating absolutely impartial service to law, in complete independence of policy, and without regard to the justice or injustice of the substance of individual laws, by ready offering of individual service and friendship to all members of the public without regard to their wealth or social standing, by ready exercise of courtesy and friendly good humour, and by ready offering of individual sacrifice in protecting and preserving life.

6. To use physical force only when the exercise of persuasion, advice and warning is found to be insufficient to obtain public co-operation to an extent necessary to secure observance of law or to restore order, and to use only the minimum degree of physical force which is necessary on any particular occasion for achieving a police objective.

7. To maintain at all times a relationship with the public that gives reality to the historic tradition that the police are the public and that the public are the police, the police

being only members of the public who are paid to give full-time attention to duties which are incumbent on every citizen in the interests of community welfare and existence.

8. To recognise always the need for strict adherence to police-executive functions, and to refrain from even seeming to usurp the powers of the judiciary, of avenging individuals or the State, and of authoritatively judging guilt and punishing the guilty.

9. To recognise always that the test of police efficiency is the absence of crime and disorder, and not the visible evidence of police action in dealing with them.

67 **and thence to:** In the United States, the London Metropolitan Police became a model for the creation of new urban police departments, beginning with the Boston Police Department in 1838. New York created its first police department in 1845, and Washington, DC, followed suit in 1861 with the creation of the Metropolitan Police Department. But despite Peel's idealistic principles, America's early police forces were rife with corruption and brutality. In New York, Chicago, and other northern and midwestern cities, police departments quickly became tools of machine politics; in the cities of the South, police departments inherited many of the structures, attitudes, and even personnel of the pre–Civil War slave patrols.

67–68 **The Justice Department:** In the more than century and a half since the first US police organizations were formed, American police departments have expanded and professionalized— but the contradictions that have characterized policing throughout history remain visible today. Police are deployed by those with power to protect the existing social order, but officers rarely possess social or economic power themselves. They are both needed and despised by the populace; they enforce laws they do not make, and protect elites they are rarely able to join. At the same time, most modern police departments genuinely struggle to make good on the promise of Peel's nine principles: to be protectors of the poor and vulnerable rather than predators against the weak, to prevent crime rather than simply react to it, to work in partnership with rather than in opposition to communities.

70 **We could all talk:** Even today, most of what I know about my mother's emotional state at that time comes from her published writing, not from anything she has told me directly. She has written about this period in a memoir, *Living with a Wild God*. Even today, it pains me to read that book and think of all the missed opportunities for connection, both on her side and on my own.

YOU LIVE WITH THAT FOREVER

123 **Officially, we also:** Government of the District of Columbia, *Metropolitan Police Department Annual Report, 2016*, mpdc.dc.gov/sites/default/files/dc/sites/mpdc/publication/attachments /MPD%20Annual%20Report%202016_lowres.pdf.

123 **We didn't talk:** Government of the District of Columbia, *Annual Report 2016*; "QuickFacts: District of Columbia," US Census Bureau, www.census.gov/quickfacts/fact/table/DC/RHI 225218; Washington Lawyers' Committee for Civil Rights and Urban Affairs, *Racial Disparities in Arrests in the District of Columbia, 2009–2011* (2013), www.washlaw.org/pdf /wlc_report_racial_disparities.pdf.

124 **At the federal level:** Copland, James R., and Rafael A. Mangual, *Overcriminalizing America: An Overview and Model Legislation for States* (New York: Manhattan Institute, 2018), media4.manhattan-institute.org/sites/default/files/R-JC-0818.pdf.

124 **But we didn't:** "Rising Incarceration Rates," in *The Growth of Incarceration in the United States: Exploring Causes and Consequences*, ed. Jeremy Travis and Bruce Western (Washington, DC: National Academies Press, 2014), 33–69.

124 **We didn't talk:** "District of Columbia Profile," Prison Policy Initiative, www.prisonpolicy .org/profiles/DC.html; "New Prison and Jail Population Figures Released by U.S. Depart-

ment of Justice," The Sentencing Project, April 25, 2019, www.sentencingproject.org/news
/new-prison-jail-population-figures-released-u-s-department-justice/.

125 **The worst of it:** Mock, Brentin, "What New Research Says About Race and Police Shootings,"
CityLab, August 6, 2019, www.citylab.com/equity/2019/08/police-officer-shootings-gun-vio
lence-racial-bias-crime-data/595528/; Jacobs, Tom, "Black Cops Are Just as Likely as White
Cops to Kill Black Suspects," *Pacific Standard*, August 9, 2018, psmag.com/social-justice
/black-cops-are-just-as-likely-as-whites-to-kill-black-suspects.

WAS THAT WHO I WAS?

133 **"Hmm," I said neutrally:** It was.

133 **Statistically, I knew:** Most police officers never fire their weapons outside the range. The
majority of those who do fire their weapons fire at dogs, not at humans (Morin, Rich, and
Andrew Mercer, "A Closer Look at Police Officers Who Have Fired Their Weapon on
Duty," Pew Research Center, February 8, 2017, www.pewresearch.org/fact-tank/2017/02/08
/a-closer-look-at-police-officers-who-have-fired-their-weapon-on-duty/).

136 **With no sergeants:** Once certified, we would also be permitted to carry our MPD-issued
firearms even while off duty. For many of my classmates, this prerogative was highly
motivating. DC has some of the nation's strictest gun control laws, so being permitted to
carry a weapon marked one out as special—not just an ordinary citizen, but someone supe-
rior and trusted.

NO PLOT

177 **I liked patrolling:** In Washington, DC, full-time career officers rarely move once they're
assigned to a district. Moving is difficult unless you're promoted, and many officers spend
their entire careers in the same district. The advantage of this system is that experienced
officers can come to know their corner of the city extraordinarily well. The disadvantage
is that distinct subcultures form in different districts. Common practices in the Second
District are virtually unheard of in 7D, and vice versa.

181 **Like most poor:** A recently published study found that killings by police officers are highest
in neighborhoods with the greatest concentrations of low-income residents. Feldman, Justin
M. et al., "Police-Related Deaths and Neighborhood Economic and Racial/Ethnic Polariza-
tion, United States, 2015–2016," *American Journal of Public Health* 109, no. 3 (2019): 458–64,
ajph.aphapublications.org/doi/10.2105/AJPH.2018.304851.

181 **But over-policing:** The public, writ large, chooses when and how to deploy police. We
could, for instance, order police to conduct traffic stops only where there is an urgent and
immediate threat to public safety or when they have probable cause to believe a vehicle or
its occupant is involved in a serious crime, and create a cadre of civilian officials akin to
parking or code enforcement officials, who would handle all citations for broken headlights
and minor moving violations. We don't ask sworn, armed law enforcement officers to investigate minor building code violations—why do we have police enforcing similar traffic
regulations? Civilianizing most traffic regulation enforcement might greatly reduce arrests
for minor issues and reduce friction between police and communities—yet we continue to
ask police to serve as traffic law enforcers.

181 **In recent years:** Farzan, Antonia Noori, "BBQ Becky, Permit Patty and Cornerstore Caroline:
Too 'Cutesy' for Those White Women Calling Police on Black People?" *Washington Post*,
October 19, 2018, www.washingtonpost.com/news/morning-mix/wp/2018/10/19/bbq-becky
-permit-patty-and-cornerstore-caroline-too-cutesy-for-those-white-women-calling
-cops-on-blacks/; Hutchinson, Bill, "From 'BBQ Becky' to 'Golfcart Gail,' List of

Unnecessary 911 Calls Made on Blacks Continues to Grow," *ABC News*, October 19, 2018, https://abcnews.go.com/US/bbq-becky-golfcart-gail-list-unnecessary-911-calls/story?id= 58584961.

MOTHERS AND DAUGHTERS

195 **She did go:** DC has a mandatory arrest law for domestic violence (16 D.C. Code § 16-1031[a]), a legacy of early efforts to prevent officers from walking away from abusive men with a nod and a wink. But officers fearful of getting in trouble for failing to make an arrest when required tended to interpret the statute rigidly. To me, Imani's fight with her mother suggested a family in desperate need of help, but I wouldn't have categorized it as domestic violence, just as the lashing out of a hurt child.

OFFICER FRIENDLY

205 **The Supreme Court:** "Confidence in Institutions," Gallup, https://news.gallup.com /poll/1597/confidence-institutions.aspx.

205 **Republicans are more:** Fingerhut, Hannah, "Deep Racial, Partisan Divisions in Americans' Views of Police Officers," Pew Research Center, September 15, 2017, www.pewresearch .org/fact-tank/2017/09/15/deep-racial-partisan-divisions-in-americans-views-of -police-officers/.

PORTRAYING A PERSON

225 **According to official:** "District of Columbia," Treatment Advocacy Center, 2018, www .treatmentadvocacycenter.org/browse-by-state/district-of-columbia.

225 **Within the city's homeless:** "District of Columbia CoC FY2018 Point in Time Fact Sheet," Community Partnership for the Prevention of Homelessness, 2018.

PARALLEL WORLDS

239 **In the academic world:** The right-wing caricature of students as precious little snowflakes is unfair—most students are reasonable young adults—but carries a grain of truth, as most professors will admit. At a workshop I attended in 2019 for criminal law and procedure professors, for instance, virtually every professor present had a horror story about student hypersensitivity. In particular, classroom discussions of race and sexual assault could be minefields: in every class, there was a student or two ready to declare themselves offended or traumatized by someone else's comments, and further traumatized if their feelings were not instantly acknowledged as worthy of collective respect. Most professors take the easy way out and try to avoid uncomfortable topics, which is a shame, because discomfort can be a powerful learning tool. In 7D's more rough-and-tumble culture, feelings were often bruised, but perhaps the conversations were more honest.

LIKE A SPARROW

244 **Many lay responders:** American Red Cross, *First Aid/CPR/AED: Participant's Manual* (Stamford, CT: StayWell, 2016), https://www.amerimedcpr.com/wp-content/uploads /American-Red-Cross-CPR-First-Aid-Manual.pdf.

252 **In Washington, DC:** "State and Territorial Data," Centers for Disease Control and Prevention, www.cdc.gov/nchs/fastats/state-and-territorial-data.htm.

252 **In 2018, there were:** "District Crime Data at a Glance," Metropolitan Police Department, 2019, mpdc.dc.gov/page/district-crime-data-glance.

252 **Ninety-two DC pedestrians:** Lazo, Luz, "Pedestrians Continue to Be at High Risk on Washington Region's Roads, Data Show," *Washington Post*, February 9, 2019, www.washingtonpost.com/local/trafficandcommuting/pedestrians-continue-to-be-at-high-risk-on-washington-regions-roads-data-show/2019/02/09/e6a4e7a8-1f52-11e9-8b59-0a28f2191131_story.html.

252 **36 vehicle occupants:** "Traffic Fatalities," Metropolitan Police Department, 2019, mpdc.dc.gov/page/traffic-fatalities.

THE SECRET CITY

256–57 **But about a third:** Schmitt, Angie, "Death Toll Keeps Rising from Police Chases," *Streetsblog USA*, October 19, 2018, usa.streetsblog.org/2018/10/19/death-toll-keeps-rising-from-police-chases/.

CAGES

265 **What research exists:** Foley, Pamela F., Mary Kelly, and Cristina Guarneri, "Reasons for Choosing a Police Career: Changes over Two Decades," *International Journal of Police Science and Management* 10, no. 1 (2008): 2–8.

265 **In 2017, 3,837 sworn:** Government of the District of Columbia, *Metropolitan Police Department 2017 Annual Report*, https://mpdc.dc.gov/sites/default/files/dc/sites/mpdc/publication/attachments/MPD%20Annual%20Report%202017_lowres.pdf.

268 **In this sense:** Marimow, Ann E., "When It Comes to Pretrial Release, Few Other Jurisdictions Do It D.C.'s Way," *Washington Post*, July 4, 2016, www.washingtonpost.com/local/public-safety/when-it-comes-to-pretrial-release-few-other-jurisdictions-do-it-dcs-way/2016/07/04/8eb52134-e7d3-11e5-b0fd-073d5930a7b7_story.html; Pretrial Services Agency for the District of Columbia, "FY 2017 Release Rates for Pretrial Defendants within Washington, DC," https://www.psa.gov/sites/default/files/2017%20Release%20Rates%20for%20DC%20Pretrial%20Defendants.pdf.

268 **If you have children:** Martin, Eric, "Hidden Consequences: The Impact of Incarceration on Dependent Children," National Institute of Justice, March 1, 2017, nij.ojp.gov/topics/articles/hidden-consequences-impact-incarceration-dependent-children.

269 **And if their behavior:** Sweeney, Chris, "Juvenile Detention Drives Up Adult Incarceration Rates, MIT Study Finds," *Boston Magazine*, June 11, 2015, www.bostonmagazine.com/news/2015/06/11/juvenile-detention-mit-study/.

269 **A recent Justice Department:** Alper, Mariel, Matthew R. Durose, and Joshua Markman, "2018 Update on Prisoner Recidivism: A 9-Year Follow-up Period (2005–2014)," Bureau of Justice Statistics, May 23, 2018, www.bjs.gov/index.cfm?ty=pbdetail&iid=6266.

269 **Maybe your difficulties:** Harding, David J. et al., "Short- and Long-Term Effects of Imprisonment on Future Felony Convictions and Prison Admissions," *Proceedings of the National Academy of Sciences* 114, no. 42 (2017): 11103–8.

BAKED INTO THE SYSTEM

270 **In contrast, New York:** "Police Employment, Officers Per Capita Rates for U.S. Cities," Governing, www.governing.com/gov-data/safety-justice/police-officers-per-capita-rates-employment-for-city-departments.html.

271 **There are Metro Transit police:** "Law Enforcement Agencies in DC," Washington Peace Center, washingtonpeacecenter.org/dccops.

271 **In 2017, 31,560 adults:** Government of the District of Columbia, *Metropolitan Police Department 2017 Annual Report*.

271 **In New York:** "Adult Arrests: 2009–2018," New York State Division of Criminal Justice Services, www.criminaljustice.ny.gov/crimnet/ojsa/arrests/nyc.pdf.

271 **The high DC arrest rate:** "Appendix: States of Incarceration: The Global Context 2018," Prison Policy Initiative, www.prisonpolicy.org/global/appendix_2018.html; Austermuhle, Martin, "District of Corrections: Does D.C. Really Have the Highest Incarceration Rate in the Country?" WAMU 88.5, September 10, 2019, wamu.org/story/19/09/10/district-of -corrections-does-d-c-really-have-the-highest-incarceration-rate-in-the-country/.

271 **in a country with:** The United States locks up a higher percentage of its population than any other country in the world. If you look at local, state, and federal prison and jail populations, this country currently incarcerates more than 2.4 million people, a figure that constitutes roughly 25 percent of the total incarcerated population of the entire world. If the incarcerated population of the United States were a country, it would have a larger population than about fifty other countries, including Namibia, Qatar, Gambia, Slovenia, Bahrain, and Iceland. And the long-term trend is toward increased growth; over the past thirty years, the incarcerated population of the United States has gone up by a factor of four. Wagner, Peter, and Wendy Sawyer, "States of Incarceration: The Global Context 2018," Prison Policy Initiative, June 2018, www.prisonpolicy.org/global/2018.html; "Criminal Justice Facts," The Sentencing Project, www.sentencingproject.org/criminal-justice -facts/.

271 **A 2019 ACLU report:** "Racial Disparities in D.C. Policing: Descriptive Evidence from 2013–2017," ACLU District of Columbia, www.acludc.org/en/racial-disparities-dc-policing -descriptive-evidence-2013-2017.

271 **Overall, black men:** Gramlich, John, "The Gap Between the Number of Blacks and Whites in Prison Is Shrinking," Pew Research Center, April 30, 2019, www.pewresearch.org/fact -tank/2019/04/30/shrinking-gap-between-number-of-blacks-and-whites-in-prison/.

273 **But although the:** Forman, James Jr., *Locking Up Our Own: Crime and Punishment in Black America* (New York: Farrar, Straus & Giroux, 2017).

274 **In recent decades:** Friedman, Lauren F., and Katie Jennings, "The US Has a Staggering Gap Between Black and White Life Expectancy," *Business Insider*, August 21, 2014, www .businessinsider.com/huge-black-white-gap-in-life-expectancy-in-us-2014-8.

274 **They're more likely:** Williams, Jhacova, and Valerie Wilson, "Labor Day 2019: Black Workers Endure Persistent Racial Disparities in Employment Outcomes," Economic Policy Institute, www.epi.org/publication/labor-day-2019-racial-disparities-in-employment/; Bridges, Brian, "African Americans and College Education by the Numbers," UNCF, August 27, 2019, www .uncf.org/the-latest/african-americans-and-college-education-by-the-numbers; Sauter, Michael B., "Faces of Poverty: What Racial, Social Groups Are More Likely to Experience It?" *USA Today*, October 10, 2018, www.usatoday.com/story/money/economy/2018/10/10/faces -poverty-social-racial-factors/37977173/; "Criminal Justice Fact Sheet," NAACP, www.naacp .org/criminal-justice-fact-sheet/.

274 **Black Americans are:** Langley, Marty, and Josh Sugarmann, *Black Homicide Victimization in the United States: An Analysis of 2011 Homicide Data* (Washington, DC: Violence Policy Center, 2014), www.vpc.org/studies/blackhomicide14.pdf.

274 **antiblack hate crimes:** Levin, Brian, Kevin Grisham, and Lisa Nakashima, *Report to the Nation: 2019: Factbook on Hate and Extremism in the U.S. & Internationally* (San Bernardino, CA: Center for the Study of Hate and Extremism, 2019), csbs.csusb.edu/sites /csusb_csbs/files/CSHE%202019%20Report%20to%20the%20Nation%20FINAL %207.29.19%2011%20PM.pdf; Edwards, Griffin Sims, and Stephen Rushin, "The Effect of President Trump's Election on Hate Crimes," SSRN, January 18, 2018, papers.ssrn.com/sol3 /papers.cfm?abstract_id=3102652.

274 **much of it comes:** Mooney, Chris, "Across America, Whites Are Biased and They Don't Even Know It," *Washington Post*, December 8, 2014, www.washingtonpost.com/news/wonk /wp/2014/12/08/across-america-whites-are-biased-and-they-dont-even-know-it/.

275 **Similarly, studies have found:** Bertrand, Marianne, and Sendhil Mullainathan, "Are Emily and Greg More Employable Than Lakisha and Jamal? A Field Experiment on Labor Market Discrimination" (working paper, National Bureau of Economic Research, Cambridge, MA, 2003), www.nber.org/papers/w9873.pdf.

275 **a 2014 report:** "2013–2014 Civil Rights Data Collection: A First Look," US Department of Education, www2.ed.gov/about/offices/list/ocr/docs/2013-14-first-look.pdf.

275 **Another 2014 study:** Goff, Phillip Atiba et al., "The Essence of Innocence: Consequences of Dehumanizing Black Children," *Journal of Personality and Social Psychology* 106, no. 4 (2014): 526–45, www.apa.org/pubs/journals/releases/psp-a0035663.pdf.

276 **When a wallet is stolen:** Looney, Adam, and Nicholas Turner, *Work and Opportunity Before and After Incarceration* (Washington, DC: Brookings Institution, 2018), www.brookings.edu /wp-content/uploads/2018/03/es_20180314_looneyincarceration_final.pdf.

276 **Americans living in poverty:** Carson, E. Ann, "Prisoners in 2014," Bureau of Justice Statistics, September 17, 2015, www.bjs.gov/index.cfm?ty=pbdetail&iid=5387.

276 **Rates of violent victimization:** None of this is coincidental. Black Americans inherit an economic and social landscape marred by the poisonous legacy of slavery and segregation, from discriminatory mortgage lending to discrimination in zoning practices and employment decisions.

276 **This is also why:** Carbado, Devon W., and L. Song Richardson, "The Black Police: Policing Our Own," *Harvard Law Review*, May 10, 2018.

277 **Some studies suggest:** Mock, "What New Research Says About Race and Police Shootings"; Jacobs, "Black Cops Are Just as Likely as White Cops to Kill Black Suspects."

277 **In some states:** "State Felon Voting Laws," ProCon.org, felonvoting.procon.org/view.re source.php?resourceID=000286.

277 **Right now:** See Forman, *Locking Up Our Own*.

ONE SUMMER DAY

278 **Crime is real:** My colleague Paul Butler writes about this in his book *Chokehold: Policing Black Men*. He notes that few African American activists and criminal justice activists want to grapple openly with the reality that black men "are disproportionately at risk for violence, as victims and harm doers," for fear of undermining the impetus for criminal justice reform. As Butler notes, "black men are about 6.5% of the population but they are responsible for approximately half of all murders in the United States," as well as 54 percent of robberies, 39 percent of assaults, and 41 percent of all violent felonies. "Because violent crime is mainly intra-racial, Black men are also about 50% of murder victims" in the United States. Butler, Paul, *Chokehold: Policing Black Men* (New York: New Press, 2018).

IT CAN BE KIND OF HARD TO SEE THINGS CLEARLY

308 **Critical incidents were defined:** Green, Douglas William, "Traumatic Stress, World Assumptions, and Law Enforcement Officers," (PhD thesis, City University of New York, 2016), academicworks.cuny.edu/cgi/viewcontent.cgi?article=2402&context=gc_etds.

309 **Police officers experience:** Hartley, Tara A. et al., "PTSD Symptoms Among Police Officers: Associations with Frequency, Recency, and Types Of Traumatic Events," *International Journal of Emergency Mental Health and Human Resilience* (2013): 241–53; Southall, Ashley, "4 Officer Suicides in 3 Weeks: N.Y.P.D. Struggles to Dispel Mental Health Stigma," *New York Times*, June 27, 2019, www.nytimes.com/2019/06/27/nyregion/nypd-suicides.html.

NOTES

YOU'LL GET YOURS

311 **As dangerous jobs go:** Kiersz, Andy, "The 34 Most Dangerous Jobs in America," *Business Insider India*, July 20, 2018, www.businessinsider.in/the-34-most-dangerous-jobs-in-america /articleshow/65061755.cms.

311 **But taxi and limousine drivers:** Hannagan, Charley, "By the Numbers: Taxi Driver Is the Job with the No. 1 Murder Rate," *Syracuse*, January 29, 2015, www.syracuse.com/opinion /2015/01/by_the_numbers_job_with_the_number_1_murder_rate_taxi_drivers.html.

311 **In 2018, for instance:** "2018 Crime in the United States," FBI, ucr.fbi.gov/crime-in-the-u.s /2018/crime-in-the-u.s.-2018.

311 **Of the seven MPD officer:** "District of Columbia Line of Duty Deaths," Officer Down Memorial Page, www.odmp.org/search/browse?state=DC.

312 **Although Rife is listed:** "Sergeant Clifton Rife, II," Officer Down Memorial Page, www .odmp.org/officer/17341-sergeant-clifton-rife-ii; Rife v. District of Columbia, 940 A.2d 964, 965 (2007).

312 **The fatal injury rate:** Sauter, Michael B., and Charles Stockdale, "The Most Dangerous Jobs in the US Include Electricians, Firefighters and Police Officers," *USA Today*, January 8, 2019, www.usatoday.com/story/money/2019/01/08/most-dangerous-jobs-us-where-fatal -injuries-happen-most-often/38832907/.

312 **In the early to late:** Escobar, Gabriel, "Washington Area's 703 Homicides in 1990 Set a Record," *Washington Post*, January 2, 1991, www.washingtonpost.com/archive/politics/1991 /01/02/washington-areas-703-homicides-in-1990-set-a-record/ee71dd1f-59c8-4f03 -af62-05b0a6134365/.

312 **By the late 1990s:** Bromwich Group, *The Durability of Police Reform: The Metropolitan Police Department and Use of Force: 2008–2015* (Washington, DC: Office of the District of Columbia Auditor, 2016), zd4l62ki6k620lqb52h9ldm1.wpengine.netdna-cdn.com/wp-content /uploads/2018/07/Full-Report_2.pdf.

313 **MPD invited the:** *Memorandum of Agreement, United States Department of Justice and the District of Columbia and the D.C. Metropolitan Police Department*, United States Department of Justice, June 13, 2001, www.justice.gov/crt/memorandum-agreement-united -states-department-justice-and-district-columbia-and-dc-metropolitan.

313 **While the review:** Bromwich Group, *The Durability of Police Reform*.

319 **That's not a high standard:** Graham v. Connor, 490 U.S. 386 (1989), emphasis added.

320 **I knew the statistics:** A recent study published by the *Proceedings of the National Academy of Sciences* found that among men of all races, ages twenty-five to twenty-nine, police killings are the sixth leading cause of death. Ingraham, Christopher, "Police Shootings Are a Leading Cause of Death for Young American Men, New Research Shows," *Washington Post*, August 8, 2019, www.washingtonpost.com/business/2019/08/08/police-shootings-are -leading-cause-death-young-american-men-new-research-shows/.

10-99

327 **I was one:** Since June 2018, several other women have successfully become certified.

327 **Each year, nearly:** "Police Shootings Database, *The Washington Post*, https://www.washingtonpost .com/graphics/investigations/police-shootings-database/.

327 **But policing is not:** And most police departments try, genuinely (if not always effectively or appropriately), to improve public safety.

329 **All told, the average:** Downey, P. Mitchell, John Roman, and Akiva Liberman, *Adult Criminal Justice Case Processing in Washington, DC* (Washington, DC: District of Columbia Crime Policy Institute, 2012), www.urban.org/sites/default/files/publication/25371/412562 -adult-criminal-justice-case-processing-in-washington-dc.pdf.

While the economic costs of arrests can be estimated, the cost in community trust and goodwill is harder to quantify. When police are perceived as too quick to arrest people for trivial and nonviolent offenses (disorderly conduct, driving on a suspended license, etc.), communities can come to view policy with fear rather than trust, which in turn affects their willingness to share information with police and help reduce more serious crime.

329 **Nearly a third:** Austermuhle, Martin, "Those with a Criminal Record in D.C. May Soon Find It Easier to Bounce Back," WAMU 88.5, September 14, 2017, wamu.org/story/17/09 /14/criminal-record-d-c-may-soon-find-easier-bounce-back/.

329 **When police make arrests:** Since officers rarely get any feedback on why their cases were no-papered, they don't change their behavior in response. This is one of the reasons law is often an ineffective means of driving change in police behavior. If police officers are unaware that their reports contain legally insufficient statements of probable cause, for instance, they'll continue to make arrests that don't pass constitutional muster, but they may never know it. Even if they do learn that their cases were no-papered for lack of probable cause, they may not care. If the institutional incentives in their department favor making arrests as the when-in-doubt default response, subsequent prosecutorial dismissals may be irrelevant to street-level officers.

EPILOGUE

339 **Minor civil infractions:** We also direct police officers to enforce traffic laws, vendor laws, taxi regulations, and a range of other laws that could be enforced instead by unarmed civilian officials (just as parking enforcement and building code enforcement are largely relegated to civilians). A high percentage of arrests and use-of-force incidents arise out of traffic stops, many of which need not have been made at all.

340 **The city of Baltimore:** Hamaji, Kate et al., *Freedom to Thrive: Reimagining Safety & Security in Our Communities* (Brooklyn, NY: Center for Popular Democracy, 2017), popular democracy.org/sites/default/files/Freedom%20To%20Thrive%2C%20Higher%20Res% 20Version.pdf.